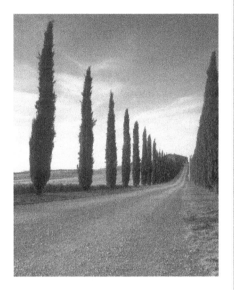

THE APOCRYPHA

BOOKS

14 Biblical books you may not know exits

APOCRYPHA
14 Biblical books you may not know about are in this volume. These books may not be in the Bible you grew up with.

Larry A. Jaggard
www.lajaggard.com

Content

The First Book of Esdras..........................2
The Second Book of Esdras...................67
The First Book of the Maccabees............184
The Second Book of the Maccabees.......316
The Book of Baruch................................404
The Book of Bel and the Dragon.............424
Ecclesiastes or the Preacher..................431
The Book of Esther................................452
The Book of Judith.................................473
The Prayer of Manasseh........................529
The Song of Solomon.............................531
The History of Susanna..........................541
The Book of Tobit...................................550
The Book of Wisdom..............................586

The First Book of Esdras

{1:1} And Josias held the feast of the Passover in Jerusalem unto his Lord, and offered the Passover the fourteenth day of the first month;

{1:2} Having set the priests according to their daily courses, being arrayed in long garments, in the temple of the Lord.

{1:3} And he spake unto the Levites, the holy ministers of Israel, that they should hallow themselves unto the Lord, to set the holy ark of the Lord in the house that king Solomon the son of David had built:

{1:4} And said, Ye shall no more bear the ark upon your shoulders: now therefore serve the Lord your God, and minister unto his people Israel, and prepare you after your families and kindreds,

{1:5} According as David the king of Israel prescribed, and according to the magnificence of Solomon his son: and standing in the temple according to the several dignities of the families of you the Levites, who minister in the presence of your brethren the children of Israel,

{1:6} Offer the Passover in order, and make ready the sacrifices for your brethren, and keep the Passover according to the commandment of the Lord, which was given unto Moses.

{1:7} And unto the people that was found there Josias gave thirty thousand lambs and kids, and three thousand calves: these things were given of the king's allowance, according as he promised, to the people, to the priests, and to the Levites.

{1:8} And Helkias, Zacharias, and Syelus, the governors of the temple, gave to the priests for the passover two thousand and six hundred sheep, and three hundred calves.

{1:9} And Jeconias, and Samaias, and Nathanael his brother, and Assabias, and Ochiel, and Joram, captains over thousands, gave to the Levites for the Passover five thousand sheep, and seven hundred calves.

{1:10} And when these things were done, the priests and Levites, having the unleavened bread, stood in very comely order according to the kindreds,

{1:11} And according to the several dignities of the fathers, before the people, to offer to the Lord, as it is written in the book of Moses: and thus did they in the morning.

{1:12} And they roasted the Passover with fire, as appertaineth: as for the sacrifices, they sod them in brass pots and pans with a good savour,

{1:13} And set them before all the people: and afterward they prepared for themselves, and for the priests their brethren, the sons of Aaron.

{1:14} For the priests offered the fat until night: and the Levites prepared for themselves, and the priests their brethren, the sons of Aaron.

{1:15} The holy singers also, the sons of Asaph, were in their order, according to the appointment of David, to wit, Asaph, Zacharias, and Jeduthun, who was of the king's retinue.

{1:16} Moreover the porters were at every gate; it was not lawful for any to go from his ordinary service: for their brethren the Levites prepared for them.

{1:17} Thus were the things that belonged to the sacrifices of the Lord accomplished in that day, that they might hold the Passover,

{1:18} And offer sacrifices upon the altar of the Lord, according to the commandment of king Josias.

{1:19} So the children of Israel which were present held the

Passover at that time, and the feast of sweet bread seven days.

{1:20} And such a Passover was not kept in Israel since the time of the prophet Samuel.

{1:21} Yea, all the kings of Israel held not such a Passover as Josias, and the priests, and the Levites, and the Jews, held with all Israel that were found dwelling at Jerusalem.

{1:22} In the eighteenth year of the reign of Josias was this Passover kept.

{1:23} And the works or Josias were upright before his Lord with an heart full of godliness.

{1:24} As for the things that came to pass in his time, they were written in former times, concerning those that sinned, and did wickedly against the Lord above all people and kingdoms, and how they grieved him exceedingly, so that the words of the Lord rose up against Israel.

{1:25} Now after all these acts of Josias it came to pass, that Pharaoh the king of Egypt came to raise war at Carchemish upon Euphrates: and Josias went out against him.

{1:26} But the king of Egypt sent to him, saying, what have I to do with thee, O king of Judea?

{1:27} I am not sent out from the Lord God against thee; for my war is upon Euphrates: and now the Lord is with me, yea, the Lord is with me hasting me forward: depart from me, and be not against the Lord.

{1:28} Howbeit Josias did not turn back his chariot from him, but undertook to fight with him, not regarding the words of the prophet Jeremy spoken by the mouth of the Lord:

{1:29} But joined battle with him in the plain of Megiddo, and the princes came against king Josias.

{1:30} Then said the king unto his servants, Carry me away out of the battle; for I am very weak. And immediately his servants took him away out of the battle.

{1:31} Then gat he up upon his second chariot; and being brought back to Jerusalem died, and was buried in his father's sepulchre.

{1:32} And in all Jewry, they mourned for Josias, yea, Jeremy the prophet lamented for Josias, and the chief men with the women made lamentation for him unto this day: and this was given out for an ordinance to be done continually in all the nation of Israel.

{1:33} These things are written in the book of the stories of the kings of Judah, and every one of the acts that Josias did, and his glory, and his understanding in the law of the Lord, and the things that he had done before, and the things now recited, are reported in the book of the kings of Israel and Judea.

{1:34} And the people took Joachaz the son of Josias, and made him king instead of Josias his father, when he was twenty and three years old.

{1:35} And he reigned in Judea and in Jerusalem three months: and then the king of Egypt deposed him from reigning in Jerusalem.

{1:36} And he set a tax upon the land of a hundred talents of silver and one talent of gold.

{1:37} The king of Egypt also made king Joachim his brother king of Judea and Jerusalem.

{1:38} And he bound Joacim and the nobles: but Zaraces his brother he apprehended, and brought him out of Egypt.

{1:39} Five and twenty years old was Joacim when he was made king in the land of Judea and Jerusalem; and he did evil before the Lord.

{1:40} Wherefore against him Nabuchodonosor the king of Babylon came up, and bound him with a chain of brass, and carried him into Babylon.

{1:41} Nabuchodonosor also took of the holy vessels of the Lord, and carried them away, and set them in his own temple at Babylon.

{1:42} But those things that are recorded of him, and of his uncleaness and impiety, are written in the chronicles of the kings.

{1:43} And Joacim his son reigned in his stead: he was made king being eighteen years old;

{1:44} And reigned but three months and ten days in Jerusalem; and did evil before the Lord.

{1:45} So after a year Nabuchodonosor sent and caused him to be brought into Babylon with the holy vessels of the Lord;

{1:46} And made Zedechias king of Judea and Jerusalem, when he was one and twenty years old; and he reigned eleven years:

{1:47} And he did evil also in the sight of the Lord, and cared not for the words that were spoken unto him by the prophet Jeremy from the mouth of the Lord.

{1:48} And after that king Nabuchodonosor had made him to swear by the name of the Lord, he forswore himself, and rebelled; and hardening his neck, his heart, he transgressed the laws of the Lord God of Israel.

{1:49} The governors also of the people and of the priests did many things against the laws, and passed all the pollutions of all nations, and defiled the temple of the Lord, which was sanctified in Jerusalem.

{1:50} Nevertheless the God of their fathers sent by his messenger to call them back, because he spared them and his tabernacle also.

{1:51} But they had his messengers in derision; and, look, when the Lord spake unto them, they made a sport of his prophets:

{1:52} So far forth, that he, being wroth with his people for their great ungodliness, commanded the kings of the Chaldees to come up against them;

{1:53} Who slew their young men with the sword, yea, even within the compass of their holy temple, and spared neither young man nor maid, old man nor child, among them; for he delivered all into their hands.

{1:54} And they took all the holy vessels of the Lord, both great and small, with the vessels of the ark of God, and the king's treasures, and carried them away into Babylon.

{1:55} As for the house of the Lord, they burnt it, and brake down the walls of Jerusalem, and set fire upon her towers:

{1:56} And as for her glorious things, they never ceased till they had consumed and brought them all to nought: and the people that were not slain with the sword he carried unto Babylon:

{1:57} Who became servants to him and his children, till the Persians reigned, to fulfil the word of the Lord spoken by the mouth of Jeremy:

{1:58} Until the land had enjoyed her sabbaths, the whole time of her desolation shall she rest, until the full term of seventy years.

{2:1} In the first year of Cyrus king of the Persians, that the word of the Lord might be accomplished, that he had promised by the mouth of Jeremy;

{2:2} The Lord raised up the spirit of Cyrus the king of the Persians, and he made proclamation through all his kingdom, and also by writing,

{2:3} Saying, Thus saith Cyrus king of the Persians; The Lord of Israel, the most high Lord, hath made me king of the whole world,

{2:4} And commanded me to build him a house at Jerusalem in Jewry.

{2:5} If therefore there be any of you that are of his people, let the Lord, even his Lord, be with him, and let him go up to Jerusalem that is in Judea, and build the house of the Lord of Israel: for he is the Lord that dwelleth in Jerusalem.

{2:6} Whosoever then dwell in the places about, let them help him, those, I say, that are his neighbours, with gold, and with silver,

{2:7} With gifts, with horses, and with cattle, and other things, which have been set forth by vow, for the temple of the Lord at Jerusalem.

{2:8} Then the chief of the families of Judea and of the tribe of Benjamin stood up; the priests also, and the Levites, and all they whose mind the Lord had moved to go up, and to build an house for the Lord at Jerusalem,

{2:9} And they that dwelt round about them, and helped them in all things with silver and gold, with horses and cattle, and with very many free gifts of a great number whose minds were stirred up thereto.

{2:10} King Cyrus also brought forth the holy vessels, which

Nabuchodonosor had carried away from Jerusalem, and had set up in his temple of idols.

{2:11} Now when Cyrus king of the Persians had brought them forth, he delivered them to Mithridates his treasurer:

{2:12} And by him they were delivered to Sanabassar the governor of Judea.

{2:13} And this was the number of them; A thousand golden cups, and a thousand of silver, censers of silver twenty-nine, vials of gold thirty, and of silver two thousand four hundred and ten, and a thousand other vessels.

{2:14} So all the vessels of gold and of silver, which were carried away, were five thousand four hundred threescore and nine.

{2:15} These were brought back by Sanabassar, together with them of the captivity, from Babylon to Jerusalem.

{2:16} But in the time of Artexerxes king of the Persians Belemus, and Mithridates, and Tabellius, and Rathumus, and Beeltethmus, and Semellius the secretary, with others that were in commission with them, dwelling in Samaria and other places, wrote unto him against them that dwelt in Judea and Jerusalem these letters following;

{2:17} To king Artexerxes our lord, Thy servants, Rathumus the storywriter, and Semellius the scribe, and the rest of their council, and the judges that are in Celosyria and Phenice.

{2:18} Be it now known to the lord king, that the Jews that are up from you to us, being come into Jerusalem, that rebellious and wicked city, do build the marketplaces, and repair the walls of it and do lay the foundation of the temple.

{2:19} Now if this city and the walls thereof be made up again, they will not only refuse to give tribute, but also rebel against kings.

{2:20} And forasmuch as the things pertaining to the temple are now in hand, we think it meet not to neglect such a matter,

{2:21} But to speak unto our lord the king, to the intent that, if it be thy pleasure it may be sought out in the books of thy fathers:

{2:22} And thou shalt find in the chronicles what is written concerning these things, and shalt understand that that city was rebellious, troubling both kings and cities:

{2:23} And that the Jews were rebellious, and raised always wars therein; for the which cause even this city was made desolate.

{2:24} Wherefore now we do declare unto thee, O lord the king, that if this city be built again, and the walls thereof set up anew, thou shalt from henceforth have no passage into Celosyria and Phenice.

{2:25} Then the king wrote back again to Rathumus the storywriter, to Beeltethmus, to Semellius the scribe, and to the rest that were in commission, and dwellers in Samaria and Syria and Phenice, after this manner;

{2:26} I have read the epistle which ye have sent unto me: therefore I commanded to make diligent search, and it hath been found that that city was from the beginning practicing against kings;

{2:27} And the men therein were given to rebellion and war: and that mighty kings and fierce were in Jerusalem, who reigned and exacted tributes in Celosyria and Phenice.

{2:28} Now therefore I have commanded to hinder those men from building the city, and heed to be taken that there be no more done in it;

{2:29} And that those wicked workers proceed no further to the annoyance of kings,

{2:30} Then king Artexerxes his letters being read, Rathumus, and Semellius the scribe, and the rest that were in commission with them, removing in haste toward Jerusalem with a troop of horsemen and a multitude of people in battle array, began to hinder the builders; and the building of the temple in Jerusalem ceased until the second year of the reign of Darius king of the Persians.

{3:1} Now when Darius reigned, he made a great feast unto all his subjects, and unto all his household, and unto all the princes of Media and Persia,

{3:2} And to all the governors and captains and lieutenants that were under him, from India unto Ethiopia, of a hundred twenty and seven provinces.

{3:3} And when they had eaten and drunken, and being satisfied were gone home, then Darius the king went into his bedchamber, and slept, and soon after awaked.

{3:4} Then three young men, that were of the guard that kept the king's body, spake one to another;

{3:5} Let every one of us speak a sentence: he that shall overcome, and whose sentence shall seem wiser than the others, unto him shall the king Darius give great gifts, and great things in token of victory:

{3:6} As, to be clothed in purple, to drink in gold, and to sleep upon gold, and a chariot with bridles of gold, and an headtire of fine linen, and a chain about his neck:

{3:7} And he shall sit next to Darius because of his wisdom, and shall be called Darius his cousin.

{3:8} And then everyone wrote his sentence, sealed it, and laid it under king Darius his pillow;

{3:9} And said that, when the king is risen, some will give him the writings; and of whose side the king and the three princes of Persia shall judge that his sentence is the wisest, to him shall the victory be given, as was appointed.

{3:10} The first wrote, Wine is the strongest.

{3:11} The second wrote, the king is strongest.

{3:12} The third wrote, Women are strongest: but above all things Truth beareth away the victory.

{3:13} Now when the king was risen up, they took their writings, and delivered them unto him, and so he read them:

{3:14} And sending forth he called all the princes of Persia and Media, and the governors, and the captains, and the lieutenants, and the chief officers;

{3:15} And sat him down in the royal seat of judgment; and the writings were read before them.

{3:16} And he said, Call the young men, and they shall declare their own sentences. So they were called, and came in.

{3:17} And he said unto them, declare unto us your mind concerning the writings. Then began the first, who had spoken of the strength of wine;

{3:18} And he said thus, O ye men, how exceeding strong is wine! it causeth all men to err that drink it:

{3:19} It maketh the mind of the king and of the fatherless child to be all one; of the bondman and of the freeman, of the poor man and of the rich:

{3:20} It turneth also every thought into jollity and mirth, so that a man remembereth neither sorrow nor debt:

{3:21} And it maketh every heart rich, so that a man remembereth neither king nor governor; and it maketh to speak all things by talents:

{3:22} And when they are in their cups, they forget their love both to friends and brethren, and a little after draw out swords:

{3:23} But when they are from the wine, they remember not what they have done.

{3:24} O ye men, is not wine the strongest, that enforceth to do thus? And when he had so spoken, he held his peace.

{4:1} Then the second, that had spoken of the strength of the king, began to say,

{4:2} O ye men, do not men excel in strength that bear rule over sea and land and all things in them?

{4:3} But yet the king is mightier: for he is lord of all these things, and hath dominion over them; and whatsoever he commandeth them they do.

{4:4} If he bid them make war the one against the other, they do it: if he sends them out against the enemies, they go, and break down mountains walls and towers.

{4:5} They slay and are slain, and transgress not the king's commandment: if they get the victory, they bring all to the king, as well the spoil, as all things else.

{4:6} Likewise for those that are no soldiers, and have not to do with wars, but use husbandry, when they have reaped again that which they had sown, they bring it to the king, and compel one another to pay tribute unto the king.

{4:7} And yet he is but one man: if he commands to kill, they kill; if he commands to spare, they spare;

{4:8} If he commands to smite, they smite; if he command to make desolate, they make desolate; if he commands to build, they build;

{4:9} If he commands to cut down, they cut down; if he command to plant, they plant.

{4:10} So all his people and his armies obey him: furthermore he lieth down, he eateth and drinketh, and taketh his rest:

{4:11} And these keep watch round about him, neither may any one depart, and do his own business, neither disobey they him in anything.

{4:12} O ye men, how should not the king be mightiest, when in such sort he is obeyed? And he held his tongue.

{4:13} Then the third, who had spoken of women, and of the truth, (this was Zorobabel) began to speak.

{4:14} O ye men, it is not the great king, nor the multitude of men, neither is it wine, that excelleth; who is it then that ruleth them, or hath the lordship over them? are they not women?

{4:15} Women have borne the king and all the people that bear rule by sea and land.

{4:16} Even of them came they: and they nourished them up that planted the vineyards, from whence the wine cometh.

{4:17} These also make garments for men; these bring glory unto men; and without women cannot men be.

{4:18} Yea, and if men have gathered together gold and silver, or any other goodly thing, do they not love a woman which is comely in favor and beauty?

{4:19} And letting all those things go, do they not gape, and even with open mouth fix their eyes fast on her; and have not all men more desire unto her than unto silver or gold, or any goodly thing whatsoever?

{4:20} A man leaveth his own father that brought him up, and his own country, and cleaveth unto his wife.

{4:21} He sticketh not to spend his life with his wife. and remembereth neither father, nor mother, nor country.

{4:22} By this also ye must know that women have dominion over you: do ye not labour and toil, and give and bring all to the woman?

{4:23} Yea, a man taketh his sword, and goeth his way to rob and to steal, to sail upon the sea and upon rivers;

{4:24} And looketh upon a lion, and goeth in the darkness; and when he hath stolen, spoiled, and robbed, he bringeth it to his love.

{4:25} Wherefore a man loveth his wife better than father or mother.

{4:26} Yea, many there be that have run out of their wits for women, and become servants for their sakes.

{4:27} Many also have perished, have erred, and sinned, for women.

{4:28} And now do ye not believe me? is not the king great in his power? do not all regions fear to touch him?

{4:29} Yet did I see him and Apame the king's concubine, the daughter of the admirable Bartacus, sitting at the right hand of the king,

{4:30} And taking the crown from the king's head, and setting it upon her own head; she also struck the king with her left hand.

{4:31} And yet for all this the king gaped and gazed upon her with open mouth: if she laughed upon him, he laughed also: but if she took any displeasure at him, the king was fain to flatter, that she might be reconciled to him again.

{4:32} O ye men, how can it be but women should be strong, seeing they do thus?

{4:33} Then the king and the princes looked one upon another: so he began to speak of the truth.

{4:34} O ye men, are not women strong? great is the earth, high is the heaven, swift is the sun in his course, for he compasseth the heavens round about, and fetcheth his course again to his own place in one day.

{4:35} Is he not great that maketh these things? therefore great is the truth, and stronger than all things.

{4:36} All the earth crieth upon the truth, and the heaven blesseth it: all works shake and tremble at it, and with it is no unrighteous thing.

{4:37} Wine is wicked, the king is wicked, women are wicked, all the children of men are wicked, and such are all their wicked works; and there is no truth in them; in their unrighteousness also they shall perish.

{4:38} As for the truth, it endureth, and is always strong; it liveth and conquereth for evermore.

{4:39} With her there is no accepting of persons or rewards; but she doeth the things that are just, and refraineth from all unjust and wicked things; and all men do well like of her works.

{4:40} Neither in her judgment is any unrighteousness; and she is the strength, kingdom, power, and majesty, of all ages. Blessed be the God of truth.

{4:41} And with that he held his peace. And all the people then shouted, and said, Great is Truth, and mighty above all things.

{4:42} Then said the king unto him, ask what thou wilt more than is appointed in the writing, and we will give it thee, because thou art found wisest; and thou shalt sit next me, and shalt be called my cousin.

{4:43} Then said he unto the king, Remember thy vow, which thou hast vowed to build Jerusalem, in the day when thou camest to thy kingdom,

{4:44} And to send away all the vessels that were taken away out of Jerusalem, which Cyrus set apart, when he vowed to destroy Babylon, and to send them again thither.

{4:45} Thou also hast vowed to build up the temple, which the Edomites burned when Judea was made desolate by the Chaldees.

{4:46} And now, O lord the king, this is that which I require, and which I desire of thee, and this is the princely liberality proceeding from thyself: I desire therefore that thou make good the vow, the performance whereof with thine own mouth thou hast vowed to the King of heaven.

{4:47} Then Darius the king stood up, and kissed him, and wrote letters for him unto all the treasurers and lieutenants and captains and governors, that they should safely convey on their way both him, and all those that go up with him to build Jerusalem.

{4:48} He wrote letters also unto the lieutenants that were in Celosyria and Phenice, and unto them in Libanus, that they should bring cedar wood from Libanus unto Jerusalem, and that they should build the city with him.

{4:49} Moreover he wrote for all the Jews that went out of his realm up into Jewry, concerning their freedom, that no officer, no ruler, no lieutenant, nor treasurer, should forcibly enter into their doors;

{4:50} And that all the country which they hold should be free without tribute; and that the Edomites should give over the villages of the Jews which then they held:

{4:51} Yea, that there should be yearly given twenty talents to the building of the temple, until the time that it were built;

{4:52} And other ten talents yearly, to maintain the burnt offerings upon the altar every day, as they had a commandment to offer seventeen:

{4:53} And that all they that went from Babylon to build the city should have free liberty, as well they as their posterity, and all the priests that went away.

{4:54} He wrote also concerning. the charges, and the priests' vestments wherein they minister;

{4:55} And likewise for the charges of the Levites, to be given them until the day that the house was finished, and Jerusalem builded up.

{4:56} And he commanded to give to all that kept the city pensions and wages.

{4:57} He sent away also all the vessels from Babylon, that Cyrus had set apart; and all that Cyrus had given in commandment, the same charged he also to be done, and sent unto Jerusalem.

{4:58} Now when this young man was gone forth, he lifted up his face to heaven toward Jerusalem, and praised the King of heaven,

{4:59} And said, From thee cometh victory, from thee cometh wisdom, and thine is the glory, and I am thy servant.

{4:60} Blessed art thou, who hast given me wisdom: for to thee I give thanks, O Lord of our fathers.

{4:61} And so he took the letters, and went out, and came unto Babylon, and told it all his brethren.

{4:62} And they praised the God of their fathers, because he had given them freedom and liberty

{4:63} To go up, and to build Jerusalem, and the temple which is called by his name: and they feasted with instruments of music and gladness seven days.

{5:1} After this were the principal men of the families chosen according to their tribes, to go up with their wives and sons and daughters, with their menservants and maidservants, and their cattle.

{5:2} And Darius sent with them a thousand horsemen, till they had brought them back to Jerusalem safely, and with musical [instruments] tabrets and flutes.

{5:3} And all their brethren played, and he made them go up together with them.

{5:4} And these are the names of the men which went up, according to their families among their tribes, after their several heads.

{5:5} The priests, the sons of Phinees the son of Aaron: Jesus the son of Josedec, the son of Saraias, and Joacim the son of Zorobabel, the son of Salathiel, of the house of David, out of the kindred of Phares, of the tribe of Judah;

{5:6} Who spake wise sentences before Darius the king of Persia in the second year of his reign, in the month Nisan, which is the first month.

{5:7} And these are they of Jewry that came up from the captivity, where they dwelt as strangers, whom Nabuchodonosor the king of Babylon had carried away unto Babylon.

{5:8} And they returned unto Jerusalem, and to the other parts of Jewry, every man to his own city, who came with Zorobabel, with Jesus, Nehemias, and Zacharias, and Reesaias, Enenius, Mardocheus. Beelsarus,
Aspharasus, Reelius, Roimus, and Baana, their guides.

{5:9} The number of them of the nation, and their governors, sons of Phoros, two thousand an hundred seventy and two; the sons of Saphat, four hundred seventy and two:

{5:10} The sons of Ares, seven hundred fifty and six:

{5:11} The sons of Phaath Moab, two thousand eight hundred and twelve:

{5:12} The sons of Elam, a thousand two hundred fifty and four: the sons of Zathul, nine hundred forty and five: the sons of Corbe, seven hundred and five: the sons of Bani, six hundred forty and eight:

{5:13} The sons of Bebai, six hundred twenty and three: the sons of Sadas, three thousand two hundred twenty and two:

{5:14} The sons of Adonikam, six hundred sixty and seven: the sons of Bagoi, two thousand sixty and six: the sons of Adin, four hundred fifty and four:

{5:15} The sons of Aterezias, ninety and two: the sons of Ceilan and Azetas threescore and seven: the sons of Azuran, four hundred thirty and two:

{5:16} The sons of Ananias, an hundred and one: the sons of Arom, thirty-two: and the sons of Bassa, three hundred twenty and three: the sons of Azephurith, an hundred and two:

{5:17} The sons of Meterus, three thousand and five: the sons of Bethlomon, an hundred twenty and three:

{5:18} They of Netophah, fifty and five: they of Anathoth, an hundred fifty and eight: they of Bethsamos, forty and two:

{5:19} They of Kiriathiarius, twenty and five: they of Caphira and Beroth, seven hundred forty and three: they of Pira, seven hundred:

{5:20} They of Chadias and Ammidoi, four hundred twenty and two: they of Cirama and Gabdes, six hundred twenty and one:

{5:21} They of Macalon, an hundred twenty and two: they of Betolius, fifty and two: the sons of Nephis, an hundred fifty and six:

{5:22} The sons of Calamolalus and Onus, seven hundred twenty and five: the sons of Jerechus, two hundred forty and five:

{5:23} The sons of Annas, three thousand three hundred and thirty.

{5:24} The priests: the sons of Jeddu, the son of Jesus among the sons of Sanasib, nine hundred seventy and two: the sons of Meruth, a thousand fifty and two:

{5:25} The sons of Phassaron, a thousand forty and seven: the sons of Carme, a thousand and seventeen.

{5:26} The Levites: the sons of Jessue, and Cadmiel, and Banuas, and Sudias, seventy and four.

{5:27} The holy singers: the sons of Asaph, an hundred twenty and eight.

{5:28} The porters: the sons of Salum, the sons of Jatal, the sons of Talmon, the sons of Dacobi, the sons of Teta, the sons of Sami, in all an hundred thirty and nine.

{5:29} The servants of the temple: the sons of Esau, the sons of Asipha, the sons of Tabaoth, the sons of Ceras, the sons of Sud, the sons of Phaleas, the sons of Labana, the sons of Graba,

{5:30} The sons of Acua, the sons of Uta, the sons of Cetab, the sons of Agaba, the sons of Subai, the sons of Anan, the sons of Cathua, the sons of Geddur,

{5:31} The sons of Airus, the sons of Daisan, the sons of Noeba, the sons of Chaseba, the sons of Gazera, the sons of Azia, the sons of Phinees, the sons of Azare, the sons of Bastai, the sons of Asana, the sons of Meani, the sons of Naphisi, the sons of Acub, the sons of Acipha, the sons of Assur, the sons of Pharacim, the sons of Basaloth,

{5:32} The sons of Meeda, the sons of Coutha, the sons of Charea, the sons of Charcus, the sons of Aserer, the sons of Thomoi, the sons of Nasith, the sons of Atipha.

{5:33} The sons of the servants of Solomon: the sons of Azaphion, the sons of Pharira, the sons of Jeeli, the sons of Lozon, the sons of Israel, the sons of Sapheth,

{5:34} The sons of Hagia, the sons of Pharacareth, the sons of Sabi, the sons of Sarothie, the sons of Masias, the sons of Gar, the sons of Addus, the sons of Suba, the sons of Apherra, the sons of Barodis, the sons of Sabat, the sons of Allom.

{5:35} All the ministers of the temple, and the sons of the servants of Solomon, were three hundred seventy and two.

{5:36} These came up from Thermeleth and Thelersas, Charaathalar leading them, and Aalar;

{5:37} Neither could they shew their families, nor their stock, how they were of Israel: the sons of Ladan, the son of Ban, the sons of Necodan, six hundred fifty and two.

{5:38} And of the priests that usurped the office of the priesthood, and were not found: the sons of Obdia, the sons of Accoz, the sons of Addus, who married Augia one of the daughters of Barzelus, and was named after his name.

{5:39} And when the description of the kindred of these men was sought in the register, and was not found, they were removed from executing the office of the priesthood:

{5:40} For unto them said Nehemias and Atharias, that they should not be partakers of the holy things, till there arose up an high priest clothed with doctrine and truth.

{5:41} So of Israel, from them of twelve years old and upward, they were all in number forty thousand, beside menservants and women servants two thousand three hundred and sixty.

{5:42} Their menservants and handmaids were seven thousand three hundred forty and seven: the singing men and singing women, two hundred forty and five:

{5:43} Four hundred thirty and five camels, seven thousand thirty and six horses, two hundred forty and five mules, five thousand five hundred twenty and five beasts used to the yoke.

{5:44} And certain of the chief of their families, when they came to the temple of God that is in Jerusalem, vowed to set up the house again in his own place according to their ability,

{5:45} And to give into the holy treasury of the works a thousand pounds of gold, five thousand of silver, and an hundred priestly vestments.

{5:46} And so dwelt the priests and the Levites and the people in Jerusalem, and in the country, the singers also and the porters; and all Israel in their villages.

{5:47} But when the seventh month was at hand, and when the children of Israel were every man in his own place, they came all together with one consent into the open place of the first gate which is toward the east.

{5:48} Then stood up Jesus the son of Josedec, and his brethren the priests and Zorobabel the son of Salathiel, and his brethren, and made ready the altar of the God of Israel,

{5:49} To offer burnt sacrifices upon it, according as it is expressly commanded in the book of Moses the man of God.

{5:50} And there were gathered unto them out of the other nations of the land, and they erected the altar upon his own place, because all the nations of the land were at enmity with them, and oppressed them; and they offered sacrifices according to the time, and burnt offerings to the Lord both morning and evening.

{5:51} Also they held the feast of tabernacles, as it is commanded in the law, and offered sacrifices daily, as was meet:

{5:52} And after that, the continual oblations, and the sacrifice of the sabbaths, and of the new moons, and of all holy feasts.

{5:53} And all they that had made any vow to God began to offer sacrifices to God from the first day of the seventh month, although the temple of the Lord was not yet built.

{5:54} And they gave unto the masons and carpenters money, meat, and drink, with cheerfulness.

{5:55} Unto them of Zidon also and Tyre they gave carrs, that they should bring cedar trees from Libanus, which should be brought by floats to the haven of Joppa, according as it was commanded them by Cyrus king of the Persians.

{5:56} And in the second year and second month after his coming to the temple of God at Jerusalem began Zorobabel the son of Salathiel, and Jesus the son of Josedec, and their brethren, and the priests, and the Levites, and all they that were come unto Jerusalem out of the captivity:

{5:57} And they laid the foundation of the house of God in the first day of the second month, in the second year after they were come to Jewry and Jerusalem.

{5:58} And they appointed the Levites from twenty years old over the works of the Lord. Then stood up Jesus, and his sons and brethren, and Cadmiel his brother, and the sons of Madiabun, with the sons of Joda the son of Eliadun, with their sons and brethren, all Levites, with one accord setters forward of the business, laboring to advance the works in the house of God. So the workmen built the temple of the Lord.

{5:59} And the priests stood arrayed in their vestments with musical instruments and trumpets; and the Levites the sons of Asaph had cymbals,

{5:60} Singing songs of thanksgiving, and praising the Lord, according as David the king of Israel had ordained.

{5:61} And they sung with loud voices songs to the praise of the Lord, because his mercy and glory is forever in all Israel.

{5:62} And all the people sounded trumpets, and shouted with a loud voice, singing songs of thanksgiving unto the Lord for the rearing up of the house of the Lord.

{5:63} Also of the priests and Levites, and of the chief of their families, the ancients who had seen the former house came to the building of this with weeping and great crying.

{5:64} But many with trumpets and joy shouted with loud voice,

{5:65} Insomuch that the trumpets might not be heard for the weeping of the people: yet the multitude sounded marvellously, so that it was heard afar off.

{5:66} Wherefore when the enemies of the tribe of Judah and Benjamin heard it, they came to know what that noise of trumpets should mean.

{5:67} And they perceived that they that were of the captivity did build the temple unto the Lord God of Israel.

{5:68} So they went to Zorobabel and Jesus, and to the chief of the families, and said unto them, we will build together with you.

{5:69} For we likewise, as ye, do obey your Lord, and do sacrifice unto him from the days of Azbazareth the king of the Assyrians, who brought us hither.

{5:70} Then Zorobabel and Jesus and the chief of the families of Israel said unto them, it is not for us and you to build together an house unto the Lord our God.

{5:71} We ourselves alone will build unto the Lord of Israel, according as Cyrus the king of the Persians hath commanded us.

{5:72} But the heathen of the land lying heavy upon the inhabitants of Judea, and holding them strait, hindered their building;

{5:73} And by their secret plots, and popular persuasions and commotions, they hindered the finishing of the building all the time that king Cyrus lived: so they were hindered from building for the space of two years, until the reign of Darius.

{6:1} Now in the second year of the reign of Darius Aggeus and Zacharias the son of Addo, the prophets, prophesied unto the Jews in Jewry and Jerusalem in the name of the Lord God of Israel, which was upon them.

{6:2} Then stood up Zorobabel the son of Salatiel, and Jesus the son of Josedec, and began to build the house of the Lord at Jerusalem, the prophets of the Lord being with them, and helping them.

{6:3} At the same time came unto them Sisinnes the governor of Syria and Phenice, with Sathrabuzanes and his companions, and said unto them,

{6:4} By whose appointment do ye build this house and this roof, and perform all the other things? and who are the workmen that perform these things?

{6:5} Nevertheless the elders of the Jews obtained favour, because the Lord had visited the captivity;

{6:6} And they were not hindered from building, until such time as signification was given unto Darius concerning them, and an answer received.

{6:7} The copy of the letters which Sisinnes, governor of Syria and Phenice, and Sathrabuzanes, with their companions, rulers in Syria and Phenice, wrote and sent unto Darius; To king Darius, greeting:

{6:8} Let all things be known unto our lord the king, that being come into the country of Judea, and entered into the city of Jerusalem we found in the city of Jerusalem the ancients of the Jews that were of the captivity

{6:9} Building an house unto the Lord, great and new, of hewn and costly stones, and the timber already laid upon the walls.

{6:10} And those works are done with great speed, and the work goeth on prosperously in their hands, and with all glory and diligence is it made.

{6:11} Then asked we these elders, saying, By whose commandment build ye this house, and lay the foundations of these works?

{6:12} Therefore to the intent that we might give knowledge unto thee by writing, we demanded of them who were the chief doers, and we required of them the names in writing of their principal men.

{6:13} So they gave us this answer, we are the servants of the Lord which made heaven and earth.

{6:14} And as for this house, it was builded many years ago by a king of Israel great and strong, and was finished.

{6:15} But when our fathers provoked God unto wrath, and sinned against the Lord of Israel which is in heaven, he gave them over into the power of Nabuchodonosor king of Babylon, of the Chaldees;

{6:16} Who pulled down the house, and burned it, and carried away the people captives unto Babylon.

{6:17} But in the first year that king Cyrus reigned over the country of Babylon Cyrus the king wrote to build up this house.

{6:18} And the holy vessels of gold and of silver, that Nabuchodonosor had carried away out of the house at Jerusalem, and had set them in his own temple those Cyrus the king brought forth again out of the temple at Babylon, and they were delivered to Zorobabel and to Sanabassarus the ruler,

{6:19} With commandment that he should carry away the same vessels, and put them in the temple at Jerusalem; and that the temple of the Lord should be built in his place.

{6:20} Then the same Sanabassarus, being come hither, laid the foundations of the house of the Lord at Jerusalem; and from that time to this being still a building, it is not yet fully ended.

{6:21} Now therefore, if it seem good unto the king, let search be made among the records of king Cyrus:

{6:22} And if it be found that the building of the house of the Lord at Jerusalem hath been done with the consent of king Cyrus, and if our lord the king be so minded, let him signify unto us thereof.

{6:23} Then commanded king Darius to seek among the records at Babylon: and so, at Ecbatane the palace, which is in the country of Media, there was found a roll wherein these things were recorded.

{6:24} In the first year of the reign of Cyrus king Cyrus commanded that the house of the Lord at Jerusalem should be built again, where they do sacrifice with continual fire:

{6:25} Whose height shall be sixty cubits and the breadth sixty cubits, with three rows of hewn stones, and one row of new wood of that country; and the expenses thereof to be given out of the house of king Cyrus:

{6:26} And that the holy vessels of the house of the Lord, both of gold and silver, that Nabuchodonosor took out of the house at Jerusalem, and brought to Babylon, should be restored to the house at Jerusalem, and be set in the place where they were before.

{6:27} And also, he commanded that Sisinnes the governor of Syria and Phenice, and Sathrabuzanes, and their companions, and those which were appointed rulers in Syria and Phenice, should be careful not to meddle with the place, but suffer Zorobabel, the servant of the Lord, and governor of Judea, and the elders of the Jews, to build the house of the Lord in that place.

{6:28} I have commanded also to have it built up whole again; and that they look diligently to help those that be of the captivity of the Jews, till the house of the Lord be finished:

{6:29} And out of the tribute of Celosyria and Phenice a portion carefully to be given these men for the sacrifices of the Lord, that is, to Zorobabel the governor, for bullocks, and rams, and lambs;

{6:30} And also corn, salt, wine, and oil, and that continually every year without further question, according as the priests that be in Jerusalem shall signify to be daily spent:

{6:31} That offerings may be made to the most high God for the king and for his children, and that they may pray for their lives.

{6:32} And he commanded that whosoever should transgress, yea, or make light of anything afore spoken or written, out of his own house should a tree be taken, and he thereon be hanged, and all his goods seized for the king.

{6:33} The Lord therefore, whose name is there called upon, utterly destroy every king and nation, that stretcheth out his hand to hinder or endamage that house of the Lord in Jerusalem.

{6:34} I Darius the king have ordained that according unto these things it be done with diligence.

{7:1} Then Sisinnes the governor of Celosyria and Phenice, and Sathrabuzanes, with their companions following the commandments of king Darius,

{7:2} Did very carefully oversee the holy works, assisting the ancients of the Jews and governors of the temple.

{7:3} And so the holy works prospered, when Aggeus and Zacharias the prophets prophesied.

{7:4} And they finished these things by the commandment of the Lord God of Israel, and with the consent of Cyrus, Darius, and Artexerxes, kings of Persia.

{7:5} And thus was the holy house finished in the three and twentieth day of the month Adar, in the sixth year of Darius king of the Persians

{7:6} And the children of Israel, the priests, and the Levites, and others that were of the captivity, that were added unto them, did according to the things written in the book of Moses.

{7:7} And to the dedication of the temple of the Lord they offered an hundred bullocks two hundred rams, four hundred lambs;

{7:8} And twelve goats for the sin of all Israel, according to the number of the chief of the tribes of Israel.

{7:9} The priests also and the Levites stood arrayed in their vestments, according to their kindreds, in the service of the Lord God of Israel, according to the book of Moses: and the porters at every gate.

{7:10} And the children of Israel that were of the captivity held the Passover the fourteenth day of the first month, after that the priests and the Levites were sanctified.

{7:11} They that were of the captivity were not all sanctified together: but the Levites were all sanctified together.

{7:12} And so they offered the Passover for all them of the captivity, and for their brethren the priests, and for themselves.

{7:13} And the children of Israel that came out of the captivity did eat, even all they that had separated themselves from the abominations of the people of the land, and sought the Lord.

{7:14} And they kept the feast of unleavened bread seven days, making merry before the Lord,

{7:15} For that he had turned the counsel of the king of Assyria toward them, to strengthen their hands in the works of the Lord God of Israel.

{8:1} And after these things, when Artexerxes the king of the Persians reigned came Esdras the son of Saraias, the son of Ezerias, the son of Helchiah, the son of Salum,

{8:2} The son of Sadduc, the son of Achitob, the son of Amarias, the son of Ezias, the son of Meremoth, the son of Zaraias, the son of Savias, the son of Boccas, the son of Abisum, the son of Phinees, the son of Eleazar, the son of Aaron the chief priest.

{8:3} This Esdras went up from Babylon, as a scribe, being very ready in the law of Moses, that was given by the God of Israel.

{8:4} And the king did him honour: for he found grace in his sight in all his requests.

{8:5} There went up with him also certain of the children of Israel, of the priest of the Levites, of the holy singers, porters, and ministers of the temple, unto Jerusalem,

{8:6} In the seventh year of the reign of Artexerxes, in the fifth month, this was the king's seventh year; for they went from Babylon in the first day of the first month, and came to Jerusalem, according to the prosperous journey which the Lord gave them.

{8:7} For Esdras had very great skill, so that he omitted nothing of the law and commandments of the Lord, but taught all Israel the ordinances and judgments.

{8:8} Now the copy of the commission, which was written from Artexerxes the king, and came to Esdras the priest and reader of the law of the Lord, is this that followeth;

{8:9} King Artexerxes unto Esdras the priest and reader of the law of the Lord sendeth greeting:

{8:10} Having determined to deal graciously, I have given order, that such of the nation of the Jews, and of the priests and Levites being within our realm, as are willing and desirous should go with thee unto Jerusalem.

{8:11} As many therefore as have a mind thereunto, let them depart with thee, as it hath seemed good both to me and my seven friends the counsellors;

{8:12} That they may look unto the affairs of Judea and Jerusalem, agreeably to that which is in the law of the Lord;

{8:13} And carry the gifts unto the Lord of Israel to Jerusalem, which I and my friends have vowed, and all the gold and silver that in the country of Babylon can be found, to the Lord in Jerusalem,

{8:14} With that also which is given of the people for the temple of the Lord their God at Jerusalem: and that silver and gold may be collected for bullocks, rams, and lambs, and things thereunto appertaining;

{8:15} To the end that they may offer sacrifices unto the Lord upon the altar of the Lord their God, which is in Jerusalem.

{8:16} And whatsoever thou and thy brethren will do with the silver and gold, that do, according to the will of thy God.

{8:17} And the holy vessels of the Lord, which are given thee for the use of the temple of thy God, which is in Jerusalem, thou shalt set before thy God in Jerusalem.

{8:18} And whatsoever thing else thou shalt remember for the use of the temple of thy God, thou shalt give it out of the king's treasury.

{8:19} And I king Artexerxes have also commanded the keepers of the treasures in Syria and Phenice, that whatsoever Esdras the priest and the reader of the law of the most high God shall send for, they should give it him with speed,

{8:20} To the sum of an hundred talents of silver, likewise also of wheat even to an hundred cors, and an hundred pieces of wine, and other things in abundance.

{8:21} Let all things be performed after the law of God diligently unto the most high God, that wrath come not upon the kingdom of the king and his sons.

{8:22} I command you also, that ye require no tax, nor any other imposition, of any of the priests, or Levites, or holy singers, or porters, or ministers of the temple, or of any that have doings in this temple, and that no man have authority to impose any thing upon them.

{8:23} And thou, Esdras, according to the wisdom of God ordain judges and justices, that they may judge in all Syria and Phenice all those that know the law of thy God; and those that know it not thou shalt teach.

{8:24} And whosoever shall transgress the law of thy God, and of the king, shall be punished diligently, whether it be by death, or other punishment, by penalty of money, or by imprisonment.

{8:25} Then said Esdras the scribe, blessed be the only Lord God of my fathers, who hath put these things into the heart of the king, to glorify his house that is in Jerusalem:

{8:26} And hath honoured me in the sight of the king, and his counsellors, and all his friends and nobles.

{8:27} Therefore was I encouraged by the help of the Lord my God, and gathered together men of Israel to go up with me.

{8:28} And these are the chief according to their families and several dignities, that went up with me from Babylon in the reign of king Artexerxes:

{8:29} Of the sons of Phinees, Gerson: of the sons of Ithamar, Gamael: of the sons of David, Lettus the son of Sechenias:

{8:30} Of the sons of Pharez, Zacharias; and with him were counted an hundred and fifty men:

{8:31} Of the sons of Pahath Moab, Eliaonias, the son of Zaraias, and with him two hundred men:

{8:32} Of the sons of Zathoe, Sechenias the son of Jezelus, and with him three hundred men: of the sons of Adin, Obeth the son of Jonathan, and with him two hundred and fifty men:

{8:33} Of the sons of Elam, Josias son of Gotholias, and with him seventy men:

{8:34} Of the sons of Saphatias, Zaraias son of Michael, and with him threescore and ten men:

{8:35} Of the sons of Joab, Abadias son of Jezelus, and with him two hundred and twelve men:

{8:36} Of the sons of Banid, Assalimoth son of Josaphias, and with him an hundred and threescore men:

{8:37} Of the sons of Babi, Zacharias son of Bebai, and with him twenty and eight men:

{8:38} Of the sons of Astath, Johannes son of Acatan, and with him an hundred and ten men:

{8:39} Of the sons of Adonikam the last, and these are the names of them, Eliphalet, Jewel, and Samaias, and with them seventy men:

{8:40} Of the sons of Bago, Uthi the son of Istalcurus, and with him seventy men.

{8:41} And these I gathered together to the river called Theras, where we pitched our tents three days: and then I surveyed them.

{8:42} But when I had found there none of the priests and Levites,

{8:43} Then sent I unto Eleazar, and Iduel, and Masman,

{8:44} And Alnathan, and Mamaias, and Joribas, and Nathan, Eunatan, Zacharias, and Mosollamon, principal men and learned.

{8:45} And I bade them that they should go unto Saddeus the captain, who was in the place of the treasury:

{8:46} And commanded them that they should speak unto Daddeus, and to his brethren, and to the treasurers in that place, to send us such men as might execute the priests' office in the house of the Lord.

{8:47} And by the mighty hand of our Lord they brought unto us skillful men of the sons of Moli the son of Levi, the son of Israel, Asebebia, and his sons, and his brethren, who were eighteen.

{8:48} And Asebia, and Annus, and Osaias his brother, of the sons of Channuneus, and their sons, were twenty men.

{8:49} And of the servants of the temple whom David had ordained, and the principal men for the service of the Levites to wit, the servants of the temple two hundred and twenty, the catalogue of whose names were shewed.

{8:50} And there I vowed a fast unto the young men before our Lord, to desire of him a prosperous journey both for us and them that were with us, for our children, and for the cattle:

{8:51} For I was ashamed to ask the king footmen, and horsemen, and conduct for safeguard against our adversaries.

{8:52} For we had said unto the king, that the power of the Lord our God should be with them that seek him, to support them in all ways.

{8:53} And again we besought our Lord as touching these things, and found him favourable unto us.

{8:54} Then I separated twelve of the chief of the priests, Esebrias, and Assanias, and ten men of their brethren with them:

{8:55} And I weighed them the gold, and the silver, and the holy vessels of the house of our Lord, which the king, and his council, and the princes, and all Israel, had given.

{8:56} And when I had weighed it, I delivered unto them six hundred and fifty talents of silver, and silver vessels of an hundred talents, and an hundred talents of gold,

{8:57} And twenty golden vessels, and twelve vessels of brass, even of fine brass, glittering like gold.

{8:58} And I said unto them, both ye are holy unto the Lord, and the vessels are holy, and the gold and the silver is a vow unto the Lord, the Lord of our fathers.

{8:59} Watch ye, and keep them till ye deliver them to the chief of the priests and Levites, and to the principal men of the families of Israel, in Jerusalem, into the chambers of the house of our God.

{8:60} So the priests and the Levites, who had received the silver and the gold and the vessels, brought them unto Jerusalem, into the temple of the Lord.

{8:61} And from the river there as we departed the twelfth day of the first month, and came to Jerusalem by the mighty hand of our Lord, which was with us: and from the beginning of our journey the Lord delivered us from every enemy, and so we came to Jerusalem.

{8:62} And when we had been there three days, the gold and silver that was weighed was delivered in the house of our Lord on the fourth day unto Marmoth the priest the son of Iri.

{8:63} And with him was Eleazar the son of Phinees, and with them were Josabad the son of Jesu and Moeth the son of Sabban, Levites: all was delivered them by number and weight.

{8:64} And all the weight of them was written up the same hour.

{8:65} Moreover they that were come out of the captivity offered sacrifice unto the Lord God of Israel, even twelve bullocks for all Israel, fourscore and sixteen rams,

{8:66} Threescore and twelve lambs, goats for a peace offering, twelve; all of them a sacrifice to the Lord.

{8:67} And they delivered the king's commandments unto the king's stewards' and to the governors of Celosyria and Phenice; and they honoured the people and the temple of God.

{8:68} Now when these things were done, the rulers came unto me, and said,

{8:69} The nation of Israel, the princes, the priests and Levites, have not put away from them the strange people of the land, nor the pollutions of the Gentiles to wit, of the Canaanites, Hittites, Pheresites, Jebusites, and the Moabites, Egyptians, and Edomites.

{8:70} For both they and their sons have married with their daughters, and the holy seed is mixed with the strange people of the land; and from the beginning of this matter the rulers and the great men have been partakers of this iniquity.

{8:71} And as soon as I had heard these things, I rent my clothes, and the holy garment, and pulled off the hair from off my head and beard, and sat me down sad and very heavy.

{8:72} So all they that were then moved at the word of the Lord God of Israel assembled unto me, whilst I mourned for the iniquity: but I sat still full of heaviness until the evening sacrifice.

{8:73} Then rising up from the fast with my clothes and the holy garment rent, and bowing my knees, and stretching forth my hands unto the Lord,

{8:74} I said, O Lord, I am confounded and ashamed before thy face;

{8:75} For our sins are multiplied above our heads, and our ignorances have reached up unto heaven.

{8:76} For ever since the time of our fathers we have been and are in great sin, even unto this day.

{8:77} And for our sins and our fathers' we with our brethren and our kings and our priests were given up unto the kings of the earth, to the sword, and to captivity, and for a prey with shame, unto this day.

{8:78} And now in some measure hath mercy been shewed unto us from thee, O Lord, that there should be left us a root and a name in the place of thy sanctuary;

{8:79} And to discover unto us a light in the house of the Lord our

God, and to give us food in the time of our servitude.

{8:80} Yea, when we were in bondage, we were not forsaken of our Lord; but he made us gracious before the kings of Persia, so that they gave us food;

{8:81} Yea, and honoured the temple of our Lord, and raised up the desolate Sion, that they have given us a sure abiding in Jewry and Jerusalem.

{8:82} And now, O Lord, what shall we say, having these things? for we have transgressed thy commandments, which thou gavest by the hand of thy servants the prophets, saying,

{8:83} That the land, which ye enter into to possess as an heritage, is a land polluted with the pollutions of the strangers of the land, and they have filled it with their uncleanness.

{8:84} Therefore now shall ye not join your daughters unto their sons, neither shall ye take their daughters unto your sons.

{8:85} Moreover ye shall never seek to have peace with them, that ye may be strong, and eat the good things of the land, and that ye may leave the inheritance of the land unto your children for evermore.

{8:86} And all that is befallen is done unto us for our wicked works and great sins; for thou, O Lord, didst make our sins light,

{8:87} And didst give unto us such a root: but we have turned back again to transgress thy law, and to mingle ourselves with the uncleanness of the nations of the land.

{8:88} Mightest not thou be angry with us to destroy us, till thou hadst left us neither root, seed, nor name?

{8:89} O Lord of Israel, thou art true: for we are left a root this day.

{8:90} Behold, now are we before thee in our iniquities, for we cannot stand any longer by reason of these things before thee.

{8:91} And as Esdras in his prayer made his confession, weeping, and lying flat upon the ground before the temple, there gathered unto him from Jerusalem a very great multitude of men and women and children: for there was great weeping among the multitude.

{8:92} Then Jechonias the son of Jeelus, one of the sons of Israel, called out, and said, O Esdras, we have sinned against the Lord God, we have married strange women of the nations of the land, and now is all Israel aloft.

{8:93} Let us make an oath to the Lord, that we will put away all our wives, which we have taken of the heathen, with their children,

{8:94} Like as thou hast decreed, and as many as do obey the law of the Lord.

{8:95} Arise and put in execution: for to thee doth this matter appertain, and we will be with thee: do valiantly.

{8:96} So Esdras arose, and took an oath of the chief of the priests and Levites of all Israel to do after these things; and so they sware.

{9:1} Then Esdras rising from the court of the temple went to the chamber of Joanan the son of Eliasib,

{9:2} And remained there, and did eat no meat nor drink water, mourning for the great iniquities of the multitude.

{9:3} And there was a proclamation in all Jewry and Jerusalem to all them that were of the captivity, that they should be gathered together at Jerusalem:

{9:4} And that whosoever met not there within two or three days according as the elders that bare rule appointed, their cattle should be seized to the use of the temple, and himself cast out from them that were of the captivity.

{9:5} And in three days were all they of the tribe of Judah and Benjamin gathered together at Jerusalem the twentieth day of the ninth month.

{9:6} And all the multitude sat trembling in the broad court of the temple because of the present foul weather.

{9:7} So Esdras arose up, and said unto them, Ye have transgressed the law in marrying strange wives, thereby to increase the sins of Israel.

{9:8} And now by confessing give glory unto the Lord God of our fathers,

{9:9} And do his will, and separate yourselves from the heathen of the land, and from the strange women.

{9:10} Then cried the whole multitude, and said with a loud voice, Like as thou hast spoken, so will we do.

{9:11} But forasmuch as the people are many, and it is foul weather, so that we cannot stand without, and this is not a work of a day or two, seeing our sin in these things is spread far:

{9:12} Therefore let the rulers of the multitude stay, and let all them of our habitations that have strange wives come at the time appointed,

{9:13} And with them the rulers and judges of every place, till we turn away the wrath of the Lord from us for this matter.

{9:14} Then Jonathan the son of Azael and Ezechias the son of Theocanus accordingly took this matter upon them: and Mosollam and Levis and Sabbatheus helped them.

{9:15} And they that were of the captivity did according to all these things.

{9:16} And Esdras the priest chose unto him the principal men of their families, all by name: and in the first day of the tenth month they sat together to examine the matter.

{9:17} So their cause that held strange wives was brought to an end in the first day of the first month.

{9:18} And of the priests that were come together, and had strange wives, there were found:

{9:19} Of the sons of Jesus the son of Josedec, and his brethren; Matthelas and Eleazar, and Joribus and Joadanus.

{9:20} And they gave their hands to put away their wives and to offer rams to make reconcilement for their errors.

{9:21} And of the sons of Emmer; Ananias, and Zabdeus, and Eanes, and Sameius, and Hiereel, and Azarias.

{9:22} And of the sons of Phaisur; Elionas, Massias Israel, and Nathanael, and Ocidelus and Talsas.

{9:23} And of the Levites; Jozabad, and Semis, and Colius, who was called Calitas, and Patheus, and Judas, and Jonas.

{9:24} Of the holy singers; Eleazurus, Bacchurus.

{9:25} Of the porters; Sallumus, and Tolbanes.

{9:26} Of them of Israel, of the sons of Phoros; Hiermas, and Eddias, and Melchias, and Maelus, and Eleazar, and Asibias, and Baanias.

{9:27} Of the sons of Ela; Matthanias, Zacharias, and Hierielus, and Hieremoth, and Aedias.

{9:28} And of the sons of Zamoth; Eliadas, Elisimus, Othonias, Jarimoth, and Sabatus, and Sardeus.

{9:29} Of the sons of Babai; Johannes, and Ananias and Josabad, and Amatheis.

{9:30} Of the sons of Mani; Olamus, Mamuchus, Jedeus, Jasubus, Jasael, and Hieremoth.

{9:31} And of the sons of Addi; Naathus, and Moosias, Lacunus, and Naidus, and Mathanias, and Sesthel, Balnuus, and Manasseas.

{9:32} And of the sons of Annas; Elionas and Aseas, and Melchias, and Sabbeus, and Simon Chosameus.

{9:33} And of the sons of Asom; Altaneus, and Matthias, and Baanaia, Eliphalet, and Manasses, and Semei.

{9:34} And of the sons of Maani; Jeremias, Momdis, Omaerus, Juel, Mabdai, and Pelias, and Anos, Carabasion, and Enasibus, and Mamnitanaimus, Eliasis, Bannus, Eliali, Samis, Selemias, Nathanias: and of the sons of Ozora; Sesis, Esril, Azaelus, Samatus, Zambis, Josephus.

{9:35} And of the sons of Ethma; Mazitias, Zabadaias, Edes, Juel, Banaias.

{9:36} All these had taken strange wives, and they put them away with their children.

{9:37} And the priests and Levites, and they that were of Israel, dwelt in Jerusalem, and in the country, in the first day of the seventh month: so the children of Israel were in their habitations.

{9:38} And the whole multitude came together with one accord into the broad place of the holy porch toward the east:

{9:39} And they spake unto Esdras the priest and reader, that he would bring the law of Moses, that was given of the Lord God of Israel.

{9:40} So Esdras the chief priest brought the law unto the whole multitude from man to woman, and to all the priests, to hear law in the first day of the seventh month.

{9:41} And he read in the broad court before the holy porch from morning unto midday, before both men and women; and the multitude gave heed unto the law.

{9:42} And Esdras the priest and reader of the law stood up upon a pulpit of wood, which was made for that purpose.

{9:43} And there stood up by him Mattathias, Sammus, Ananias, Azarias, Urias, Ezecias, Balasamus, upon the right hand:

{9:44} And upon his left hand stood Phaldaius, Misael, Melchias, Lothasubus, and Nabarias.

{9:45} Then took Esdras the book of the law before the multitude: for he sat honourably in the first place in the sight of them all.

{9:46} And when he opened the law, they stood all straight up. So Esdras blessed the Lord God most High, the God of hosts, Almighty.

{9:47} And all the people answered, Amen; and lifting up their hands they fell to the ground, and worshipped the Lord.

{9:48} Also Jesus, Anus, Sarabias, Adinus, Jacubus, Sabateas, Auteas, Maianeas, and Calitas, Asrias, and Joazabdus, and Ananias, Biatas, the Levites, taught the law of the Lord, making them withal to understand it.

{9:49} Then spake Attharates unto Esdras the chief priest. and reader, and to the Levites that taught the multitude, even to all, saying,

{9:50} This day is holy unto the Lord; (for they all wept when they heard the law:)

{9:51} Go then, and eat the fat, and drink the sweet, and send part to them that have nothing;

{9:52} For this day is holy unto the Lord: and be not sorrowful; for the Lord will bring you to honour.

{9:53} So the Levites published all things to the people, saying, This day is holy to the Lord; be not sorrowful.

{9:54} Then went they their way, everyone to eat and drink, and make merry, and to give part to them that had nothing, and to make great cheer;

{9:55} Because they understood the words wherein they were instructed, and for the which they had been assembled.

The Second Book of Esdras

{1:1} The second book of the prophet Esdras, the son of Saraias, the son of Azarias, the son of Helchias, the son of Sadamias, the sou of Sadoc, the son of Achitob,

{1:2} The son of Achias, the son of Phinees, the son of Heli, the son of Amarias, the son of Aziei, the son of Marimoth, the son of And he spake unto the of Borith, the son of Abisei, the son of Phinees, the son of Eleazar,

{1:3} The son of Aaron, of the tribe of Levi; which was captive in the land of the Medes, in the reign of Artexerxes king of the Persians.

{1:4} And the word of the Lord came unto me, saying,

{1:5} Go thy way, and shew my people their sinful deeds, and their children their wickedness which they have done against me; that they may tell their children's children:

{1:6} Because the sins of their fathers are increased in them: for they have forgotten me, and have offered unto strange gods.

{1:7} Am not I even he that brought them out of the land of Egypt, from the house of bondage? but they have provoked me unto wrath, and despised my counsels.

{1:8} Pull thou off then the hair of thy head, and cast all evil upon them, for they have not been obedient unto my law, but it is a rebellious people.

{1:9} How long shall I forbear them, into whom I have done so much good?

{1:10} Many kings have I destroyed for their sakes; Pharaoh with his servants and all his power have I smitten down.

{1:11} All the nations have I destroyed before them, and in the east I have scattered the people of two provinces, even of Tyrus and Sidon, and have slain all their enemies.

{1:12} Speak thou therefore unto them, saying, Thus saith the Lord,

{1:13} I led you through the sea and in the beginning gave you a large and safe passage; I gave you Moses for a leader, and Aaron for a priest.

{1:14} I gave you light in a pillar of fire, and great wonders have I done among you; yet have ye forgotten me, saith the Lord.

{1:15} Thus saith the Almighty Lord, the quails were as a token to you; I gave you tents for your safeguard: nevertheless ye murmured there,

{1:16} And triumphed not in my name for the destruction of your enemies, but ever to this day do ye yet murmur.

{1:17} Where are the benefits that I have done for you? when ye were hungry and thirsty in the wilderness, did ye not cry unto me,

{1:18} Saying, why hast thou brought us into this wilderness to kill us? it had been better for us to have served the Egyptians, than to die in this wilderness.

{1:19} Then had I pity upon your mourning's, and gave you manna to eat; so ye did eat angels' bread.

{1:20} When ye were thirsty, did I not cleave the rock, and waters flowed out to your fill? for the heat I covered you with the leaves of the trees.

{1:21} I divided among you a fruitful land, I cast out the Canaanites, the Pherezites, and the Philistines, before you: what shall I yet do more for you? saith the Lord.

{1:22} Thus saith the Almighty Lord, When ye were in the wilderness, in the river of the Amorites, being athirst, and blaspheming my name,

{1:23} I gave you not fire for your blasphemies, but cast a tree in the water, and made the river sweet.

{1:24} What shall I do unto thee, O Jacob? thou, Juda, wouldest not obey me: I will turn me to other nations, and unto those will I give my name, that they may keep my statutes.

{1:25} Seeing ye have forsaken me, I will forsake you also; when ye desire me to be gracious unto you, I shall have no mercy upon you.

{1:26} Whensoever ye shall call upon me, I will not hear you: for ye have defiled your hands with blood, and your feet are swift to commit manslaughter.

{1:27} Ye have not as it were forsaken me, but your own selves, saith the Lord.

{1:28} Thus saith the Almighty Lord, Have I not prayed you as a father his sons, as a mother her daughters, and a nurse her young babes,

{1:29} That ye would be my people, and I should be your God; that ye would be my children, and I should be your father?

{1:30} I gathered you together, as a hen gathereth her chickens under her wings: but now, what shall I do unto you? I will cast you out from my face.

{1:31} When ye offer unto me, I will turn my face from you: for your solemn feast days, your new moons, and your circumcisions, have I forsaken.

{1:32} I sent unto you my servants the prophets, whom ye have taken and slain, and torn their bodies in pieces, whose blood I will require of your hands, saith the Lord.

{1:33} Thus saith the Almighty Lord, your house is desolate, I will cast you out as the wind doth stubble.

{1:34} And your children shall not be fruitful; for they have despised my commandment, and done the thing that is an evil before me.

{1:35} Your houses will I give to a people that shall come; which not having heard of me yet shall believe me; to whom I have shewed no signs, yet they shall do that I have commanded them.

{1:36} They have seen no prophets, yet they shall call their sins to remembrance, and acknowledge them.

{1:37} I take to witness the grace of the people to come, whose little ones rejoice in gladness: and though they have not seen me with bodily eyes, yet in spirit they believe the thing that I say.

{1:38} And now, brother, behold what glory; and see the people that come from the east:

{1:39} Unto whom I will give for leaders, Abraham, Isaac, and Jacob, Oseas, Amos, and Micheas, Joel, Abdias, and Jonas,

{1:40} Nahum, and Abacuc, Sophonias, Aggeus, Zachary, and Malachy, which is called also an angel of the Lord.

{2:1} Thus saith the Lord, I brought this people out of bondage, and I gave them my commandments by menservants the prophets; whom they would not hear, but despised my counsels.

{2:2} The mother that bare them saith unto them, Go your way, ye children; for I am a widow and forsaken.

{2:3} I brought you up with gladness; but with sorrow and heaviness have I lost you: for ye have sinned before the Lord your God, and done that thing that is evil before him.

{2:4} But what shall I now do unto you? I am a widow and forsaken: go your way, O my children, and ask mercy of the Lord.

{2:5} As for me, O father, I call upon thee for a witness over the mother of these children, which would not keep my covenant,

{2:6} That thou bring them to confusion, and their mother to a spoil, that there may be no offspring of them.

{2:7} Let them be scattered abroad among the heathen, let their names be put out of the earth: for they have despised my covenant.

{2:8} Woe be unto thee, Assur, thou that hidest the unrighteous in thee! O thou wicked people, remember what I did unto Sodom and Gomorrha;

{2:9} Whose land lieth in clods of pitch and heaps of ashes: even so also will I do unto them that hear me not, saith the Almighty Lord.

{2:10} Thus saith the Lord unto Esdras, Tell my people that I will give them the kingdom of Jerusalem, which I would have given unto Israel.

{2:11} Their glory also will I take unto me, and give these the everlasting tabernacles, which I had prepared for them.

{2:12} They shall have the tree of life for an ointment of sweet savour; they shall neither labour, nor be weary.

{2:13} Go, and ye shall receive: pray for few days unto you, that they may be shortened: the kingdom is already prepared for you: watch.

{2:14} Take heaven and earth to witness; for I have broken the evil in pieces, and created the good: for I live, saith the Lord.

{2:15} Mother, embrace thy children, and bring them up with gladness, make their feet as fast as a pillar: for I have chosen thee, saith the Lord.

{2:16} And those that be dead will I raise up again from their places, and bring them out of the graves: for I have known my name in Israel.

{2:17} Fear not, thou mother of the children: for I have chosen thee, saith the Lord.

{2:18} For thy help will I send my servants Esau and Jeremy, after whose counsel I have sanctified and prepared for thee twelve trees laden with divers fruits,

{2:19} And as many fountains flowing with milk and honey, and seven mighty mountains, whereupon there grow roses and lilies, whereby I will fill thy children with joy.

{2:20} Do right to the widow, judge for the fatherless, give to the poor, defend the orphan, clothe the naked,

{2:21} Heal the broken and the weak, laugh not a lame man to scorn, defend the maimed, and let the blind man come into the sight of my clearness.

{2:22} Keep the old and young within thy walls.

{2:23} Wheresoever thou findest the dead, take them and bury them, and I will give thee the first place in my resurrection.

{2:24} Abide still, O my people, and take thy rest, for thy quietness still comes.

{2:25} Nourish thy children, O thou good nurse; stablish their feet.

{2:26} As for the servants whom I have given thee, there shall not one of them perish; for I will require them from among thy number.

{2:27} Be not weary: for when the day of trouble and heaviness cometh, others shall weep and be sorrowful, but thou shalt be merry and have abundance.

{2:28} The heathen shall envy thee, but they shall be able to do nothing against thee, saith the Lord.

{2:29} My hands shall cover thee, so that thy children shall not see hell.

{2:30} Be joyful, O thou mother, with thy children; for I will deliver thee, saith the Lord.

{2:31} Remember thy children that sleep, for I shall bring them out of the sides of the earth, and shew mercy unto them: for I am merciful, saith the Lord Almighty.

{2:32} Embrace thy children until I come and shew mercy unto them: for my wells run over, and my grace shall not fail.

{2:33} I Esdras received a charge of the Lord upon the mount Oreb, that I should go unto Israel; but when I came unto them, they set me at nought, and despised the commandment of the Lord.

{2:34} And therefore I say unto you, O ye heathen, that hear and understand, look for your Shepherd, he shall give you everlasting rest; for he is nigh at hand, that shall come in the end of the world.

{2:35} Be ready to the reward of the kingdom, for the everlasting light shall shine upon you for evermore.

{2:36} Flee the shadow of this world, receive the joyfulness of your glory: I testify my Savior openly.

{2:37} O receive the gift that is given you, and be glad, giving thanks unto him that hath led you to the heavenly kingdom.

{2:38} Arise up and stand, behold the number of those that be sealed in the feast of the Lord;

{2:39} Which are departed from the shadow of the world, and have received glorious garments of the Lord.

{2:40} Take thy number, O Sion, and shut up those of thine that are clothed in white, which have fulfilled the law of the Lord.

{2:41} The number of thy children, whom thou longedst for, is fulfilled: beseech the power of the Lord, that thy people, which have been called from the beginning, may be hallowed.

{2:42} I Esdras saw upon the mount Sion a great people, whom I could not number, and they all praised the Lord with songs.

{2:43} And in the midst of them there was a young man of a high stature, taller than all the rest, and upon every one of their heads he set crowns, and was more exalted; which I marveled at greatly.

{2:44} So I asked the angel, and said, Sir, what are these?

{2:45} He answered and said unto me, these be they that have put off the mortal clothing, and put on the immortal, and have confessed the name of God: now are they crowned, and receive palms.

{2:46} Then said I unto the angel, what young person is it that crowneth them, and giveth them palms in their hands?

{2:47} So he answered and said unto me, It is the Son of God, whom they have confessed in the world. Then began I greatly to commend them that stood so stiffly for the name of the Lord.

{2:48} Then the angel said unto me, go thy way, and tell my people what manner of things, and how great wonders of the Lord thy God, thou hast seen.

{3:1} In the thirtieth year after the ruin of the city I was in Babylon, and lay troubled upon my bed, and my thoughts came up over my heart:

{3:2} For I saw the desolation of Sion, and the wealth of them that dwelt at Babylon.

{3:3} And my spirit was sore moved, so that I began to speak words full of fear to the most High, and said,

{3:4} O Lord, who bearest rule, thou spakest at the beginning, when thou didst plant the earth, and that thyself alone, and commandedst the people,

{3:5} And gavest a body unto Adam without soul, which was the workmanship of thine hands, and didst breathe into him the breath of life, and he was made living before thee.

{3:6} And thou leadest him into paradise, which thy right hand had planted, before ever the earth came forward.

{3:7} And unto him thou gavest commandment to love thy way: which he transgressed, and immediately thou appointedst death in him and in his generations, of whom came nations, tribes, people, and kindreds, out of number.

{3:8} And every people walked after their own will, and did wonderful things before thee, and despised thy commandments.

{3:9} And again in process of time thou broughtest the flood upon those that dwelt in the world, and destroyedst them.

{3:10} And it came to pass in every of them, that as death was to Adam, so was the flood to these.

{3:11} Nevertheless one of them thou leftest, namely, Noah with his household, of whom came all righteous men.

{3:12} And it happened, that when they that dwelt upon the earth began to multiply, and had gotten them many children, and were a great people, they began again to be more ungodly than the first.

{3:13} Now when they lived so wickedly before thee, thou didst choose thee a man from among them, whose name was Abraham.

{3:14} Him thou lovedst, and unto him only thou shewedst thy will:

{3:15} And madest an everlasting covenant with him, promising him that thou wouldest never forsake his seed.

{3:16} And unto him thou gavest Isaac, and unto Isaac also thou gavest Jacob and Esau. As for Jacob, thou didst choose him to thee, and put by Esau: and so Jacob became a great multitude.

{3:17} And it came to pass, that when thou leadest his seed out of Egypt, thou broughtest them up to the mount Sinai.

{3:18} And bowing the heavens, thou didst set fast the earth, movedst the whole world, and madest the depths to tremble, and troubledst the men of that age.

{3:19} And thy glory went through four gates, of fire, and of earthquake, and of wind, and of cold; that thou mightest give the law unto the seed of Jacob, and diligence unto the generation of Israel.

{3:20} And yet tookest thou not away from them a wicked heart, that thy law might bring forth fruit in them.

{3:21} For the first Adam bearing a wicked heart transgressed, and was overcome; and so be all they that are born of him.

{3:22} Thus infirmity was made permanent; and the law (also) in the heart of the people with the malignity of the root; so that the good departed away, and the evil abode still.

{3:23} So the times passed away, and the years were brought to an end: then didst thou raise thee up a servant, called David:

{3:24} Whom thou commandedst to build a city unto thy name, and to offer incense and oblations unto thee therein.

{3:25} When this was done many years, then they that inhabited the city forsook thee,

{3:26} And in all things, did even as Adam and all his generations had done: for they also had a wicked heart:

{3:27} And so thou gavest thy city over into the hands of thine enemies.

{3:28} Are their deeds then any better that inhabit Babylon, that they should therefore have the dominion over Sion?

{3:29} For when I came thither, and had seen impieties without number, then my soul saw many evildoers in this thirtieth year, so that my heart failed me.

{3:30} For I have seen how thou sufferest them sinning, and hast spared wicked doers: and hast destroyed thy people, and hast preserved thine enemies, and hast not signified it.

{3:31} I do not remember how this way may be left: Are they then of Babylon better than they of Sion?

{3:32} Or is there any other people that knoweth thee beside Israel? or what generation hath so believed thy covenants as Jacob?

{3:33} And yet their reward appeareth not, and their labour hath no fruit: for I have gone here and there through the heathen, and I see that they flow in wealth, and think not upon thy commandments.

{3:34} Weigh thou therefore our wickedness now in the balance, and their's also that dwell the world; and so, shall thy name nowhere be found but in Israel.

{3:35} Or when was it that they which dwell upon the earth have not sinned in thy sight? or what people have so kept thy commandments?

{3:36} Thou shalt find that Israel by name hath kept thy precepts; but not the heathen.

{4:1} And the angel that was sent unto me, whose name was Uriel, gave me an answer,

{4:2} And said, Thy heart hath gone to far in this world, and thinkest thou to comprehend the way of the most High?

{4:3} Then said I, Yea, my lord. And he answered me, and said, I am sent to shew thee three ways, and to set forth three similitudes before thee:

{4:4} Whereof if thou canst declare me one, I will shew thee also the way that thou desirest to see, and I shall shew thee from whence the wicked heart cometh.

{4:5} And I said, Tell on, my lord. Then said he unto me, Go thy way, weigh me the weight of the fire, or measure me the blast of the wind, or call me again the day that is past.

{4:6} Then answered I and said, what man is able to do that, that thou shouldest ask such things of me?

{4:7} And he said unto me, If I should ask thee how great dwellings are in the midst of the sea, or how many springs are in the beginning of the deep, or how many springs are above the firmament, or which are the outgoings of paradise:

{4:8} Peradventure thou wouldest say unto me, I never went down into the deep, nor as yet into hell, neither did I ever climb up into heaven.

{4:9} Nevertheless now have I asked thee but only of the fire and wind, and of the day where through thou hast passed, and of things from which thou canst not be separated, and yet canst thou give me no answer of them.

{4:10} He said moreover unto me, thine own things, and such as are grown up with thee, canst thou not know;

{4:11} How should thy vessel then be able to comprehend the way of the Highest, and, the world being now outwardly corrupted to understand the corruption that is evident in my sight?

{4:12} Then said I unto him, it were better that we were not at all, than that we should live still in wickedness, and to suffer, and not to know wherefore.

{4:13} He answered me, and said, I went into a forest into a plain, and the trees took counsel,

{4:14} And said, Come, let us go and make war against the sea that it may depart away before us, and that we may make us more woods.

{4:15} The floods of the sea also in like manner took counsel, and said, Come, let us go up and subdue the woods of the plain, that there also we may make us another country.

{4:16} The thought of the wood was in vain, for the fire came and consumed it.

{4:17} The thought of the floods of the sea came likewise to nought, for the sand stood up and stopped them.

{4:18} If thou wert judge now betwixt these two, whom wouldest thou begin to justify? or whom wouldest thou condemn?

{4:19} I answered and said, verily it is a foolish thought that they both have devised, for the ground is given unto the wood, and the sea also hath his place to bear his floods.

{4:20} Then answered he me, and said, thou hast given a right judgment, but why judgest thou not thyself also?

{4:21} For like as the ground is given unto the wood, and the sea to his floods: even so they that dwell upon the earth may understand nothing but that which is upon the earth: and he that dwelleth above the heavens may only understand the things that are above the height of the heavens.

{4:22} Then answered I and said, I beseech thee, O Lord, let me have understanding:

{4:23} For it was not my mind to be curious of the high things, but of such as pass by us daily, namely, wherefore Israel is given up as a reproach to the heathen, and for what cause the people whom thou hast loved is given over unto ungodly nations, and why the law of our forefathers is brought to nought, and the written covenants come to none effect,

{4:24} And we pass away out of the world as grasshoppers, and our life is astonishment and fear, and we are not worthy to obtain mercy.

{4:25} What will he then do unto his name whereby we are called? of these things have I asked.

{4:26} Then answered he me, and said, The more thou searchest, the more thou shalt marvel; for the world hasteth fast to pass away,

{4:27} And cannot comprehend the things that are promised to the righteous in time to come: for this world is full of unrighteousness and infirmities.

{4:28} But as concerning the things whereof thou askest me, I will tell thee; for the evil is sown, but the destruction thereof is not yet come.

{4:29} If therefore that which is sown be not turned upside down, and if the place where the evil is sown pass not away, then cannot it come that is sown with good.

{4:30} For the grain of evil seed hath been sown in the heart of Adam from the beginning, and how much ungodliness hath it brought up unto this time? and how much shall it yet bring forth until the time of threshing come?

{4:31} Ponder now by thyself, how great fruit of wickedness the grain of evil seed hath brought forth.

{4:32} And when the ears shall be cut down, which are without number, how great a floor shall they fill?

{4:33} Then I answered and said, How, and when shall these things come to pass? wherefore are our years few and evil?

{4:34} And he answered me, saying, do not thou hasten above the most Highest: for thy haste is in vain to be above him, for thou hast much exceeded.

{4:35} Did not the souls also of the righteous ask question of these things in their chambers, saying, how long shall I hope on this fashion? when cometh the fruit of the floor of our reward?

{4:36} And unto these things Uriel the archangel gave them answer, and said, even when the number of seeds is filled in you: for he hath weighed the world in the balance.

{4:37} By measure hath he measured the times; and by number hath he numbered the times; and he doth not move nor stir them, until the said measure be fulfilled.

{4:38} Then answered I and said, O Lord that bearest rule, even we all are full of impiety.

{4:39} And for our sakes peradventure it is that the floors of the righteous are not filled, because of the sins of them that dwell upon the earth.

{4:40} So he answered me, and said, Go thy way to a woman with child, and ask of her when she hath fulfilled her nine months, if her womb may keep the birth any longer within her.

{4:41} Then said I, No, Lord, that can she not. And he said unto me, In the grave, the chambers of souls are like the womb of a woman:

{4:42} For like as a woman that travaileth maketh haste to escape the necessity of the travail: even so do these places haste to deliver those things that are committed unto them.

{4:43} From the beginning, look, what thou desirest to see, it shall be shewed thee.

{4:44} Then answered I and said, If I have found favour in thy sight, and if it be possible, and if I be meet therefore,

{4:45} Shew me then whether there be more to come than is past, or more past than is to come.

{4:46} What is past I know, but what is for to come I know not.

{4:47} And he said unto me, Stand up upon the right side, and I shall expound the similitude unto thee.

{4:48} So I stood, and saw, and, behold, an hot burning oven passed by before me: and it happened that when the flame was gone by I looked, and, behold, the smoke remained still.

{4:49} After this there passed by before me a watery cloud, and sent down much rain with a storm; and when the stormy rain was past, the drops remained still.

{4:50} Then said he unto me, consider with thyself; as the rain is more than the drops, and as the fire is greater than the smoke; but the drops and the smoke remain behind. so the quantity which is past did more exceed.

{4:51} Then I prayed, and said, May I live, thinkest thou, until that time? or what shall happen in those days?

{4:52} He answered me, and said, As for the tokens whereof thou askest me, I may tell thee of them in part: but as touching thy life, I am not sent to shew thee; for I do not know it.

{5:1} Nevertheless as coming the tokens, behold, the days shall come, that they which dwell upon earth shall be taken in a great number, and the way of truth shall be hidden, and the land shall be barren of faith.

{5:2} But iniquity shall be increased above that which now thou seest, or that thou hast heard long ago.

{5:3} And the land, that thou seest now to have root, shalt thou see wasted suddenly.

{5:4} But if the most High grant thee to live, thou shalt see after the third trumpet that the sun shall suddenly shine again in the night, and the moon thrice in the day:

{5:5} And blood shall drop out of wood, and the stone shall give his voice, and the people shall be troubled:

{5:6} And even he shall rule, whom they look not for that dwell upon the earth, and the fowls shall take their flight away together:

{5:7} And the Sodomitish sea shall cast out fish, and make a noise in the night, which many have not known: but they shall all hear the voice thereof.

{5:8} There shall be a confusion also in many places, and the fire shall be oft sent out again, and the wild beasts shall change their places, and menstruous women shall bring forth monsters:

{5:9} And salt waters shall be found in the sweet, and all friends shall destroy one another; then shall wit hide itself, and understanding withdraw itself into his secret chamber,

{5:10} And shall be sought of many, and yet not be found: then shall unrighteousness and incontinency be multiplied upon earth.

{5:11} One land also shall ask another, and say, Is righteousness that maketh a man righteous gone through thee? And it shall say, No.

{5:12} At the same time shall men hope, but nothing obtain: they shall labour, but their ways shall not prosper.

{5:13} To shew thee such tokens I have leave; and if thou wilt pray again, and weep as now, and fast even days, thou shalt hear yet greater things.

{5:14} Then I awaked, and an extreme fearfulness went through all my body, and my mind was troubled, so that it fainted.

{5:15} So the angel that was come to talk with me held me, comforted me, and set me up upon my feet.

{5:16} And in the second night it came to pass, that Salathiel the captain of the people came unto me, saying, where hast thou been? and why is thy countenance so heavy?

{5:17} Knowest thou not that Israel is committed unto thee in the land of their captivity?

{5:18} Up then, and eat bread, and forsake us not, as the shepherd that leaveth his flock in the hands of cruel wolves.

{5:19} Then said I unto him, go thy ways from me, and come not nigh me. And he heard what I said, and went from me.

{5:20} And so I fasted seven days, mourning and weeping, like as Uriel the angel commanded me.

{5:21} And after seven days so it was, that the thoughts of my heart were very grievous unto me again,

{5:22} And my soul recovered the spirit of understanding, and I began to talk with the most High again,

{5:23} And said, O Lord that bearest rule, of every wood of the earth, and of all the trees thereof, thou hast chosen thee one only vine:

{5:24} And of all lands of the whole world thou hast chosen thee one pit: and of all the flowers thereof one lily:

{5:25} And of all the depths of the sea thou hast filled thee one river: and of all builded cities thou hast hallowed Sion unto thyself:

{5:26} And of all the fowls that are created thou hast named thee one dove: and of all the cattle that are made thou hast provided thee one sheep:

{5:27} And among all the multitudes of people thou hast gotten thee one people: and unto this people, whom thou lovedst, thou gavest a law that is approved of all.

{5:28} And now, O Lord, why hast thou given this one people over unto many? and upon the one root hast thou prepared others, and why hast thou scattered thy only one people among many?

{5:29} And they which did gainsay thy promises, and believed not thy covenants, have trodden them down.

{5:30} If thou didst so much hate thy people, yet shouldest thou punish them with thine own hands.

{5:31} Now when I had spoken these words, the angel that came to me the night afore was sent unto me,

{5:32} And said unto me, hear me, and I will instruct thee; hearken to the thing that I say, and I shall tell thee more.

{5:33} And I said, Speak on, my Lord. Then said he unto me, Thou art sore troubled in mind for Israel's sake: lovest thou that people better than he that made them?

{5:34} And I said, No, Lord: but of very grief have I spoken: for my reins pain me every hour, while I labour to comprehend the way of the most High, and to seek out part of his judgment.

{5:35} And he said unto me, Thou canst not. And I said, Wherefore,

Lord? whereunto was I born then? or why was not my mother's womb then my grave, that I might not have seen the travail of Jacob, and the wearisome toil of the stock of Israel?

{5:36} And he said unto me, Number me the things that are not yet come, gather me together the dross that are scattered abroad, make me the flowers green again that are withered,

{5:37} Open me the places that are closed, and bring me forth the winds that in them are shut up, shew me the image of a voice: and then I will declare to thee the thing that thou labourest to know.

{5:38} And I said, O Lord that bearest rule, who may know these things, but he that hath not his dwelling with men?

{5:39} As for me, I am unwise: how may I then speak of these things whereof thou askest me?

{5:40} Then said he unto me, like as thou canst do none of these things that I have spoken of, even so canst thou not find out my judgment, or in the end the love that I have promised unto my people.

{5:41} And I said, Behold, O Lord, yet art thou nigh unto them that be reserved till the end. and what shall they do that have been before me, or we that be now, or they that shall come after us?

{5:42} And he said unto me, I will liken my judgment unto a ring: like as there is no slackness of the last, even so there is no swiftness of the first.

{5:43} So I answered and said, couldest thou not make those that have been made, and be now, and that are for to come, at once; that thou mightest shew thy judgment the sooner?

{5:44} Then answered he me, and said, the creature may not haste above the maker; neither may the world hold them at once that shall be created therein.

{5:45} And I said, as thou hast said unto thy servant, that thou, which givest life to all, hast given life at once to the creature that thou hast created, and the creature bare it: even so it might now also bear them that now be present at once.

{5:46} And he said unto me, Ask the womb of a woman, and say unto her, If thou bringest forth children, why dost thou it not together, but one after another? pray her therefore to bring forth ten children at once.

{5:47} And I said, she cannot: but must do it by distance of time.

{5:48} Then said he unto me, even so have I given the womb of the earth to those that be sown in it in their times.

{5:49} For like as a young child may not bring forth the things that belong to the aged, even so have I disposed the world which I created.

{5:50} And I asked, and said, seeing thou hast now given me the way, I will proceed to speak before thee: for our mother, of whom thou hast told me that she is young, draweth now nigh unto age.

{5:51} He answered me, and said, Ask a woman that beareth children, and she shall tell thee.

{5:52} Say unto her, wherefore are unto they whom thou hast now brought forth like those that were before, but less of stature?

{5:53} And she shall answer thee, they that be born in the the strength of youth are of one fashion, and they that are born in the time of age, when the womb faileth, are otherwise.

{5:54} Consider thou therefore also, how that ye are less of stature than those that were before you.

{5:55} And so are they that come after you less than ye, as the creatures which now begin to be old, and have passed over the strength of youth.

{5:56} Then said I, Lord, I beseech thee, if I have found favour in thy sight, shew thy servant by whom thou visitest thy creature.

{6:1} And he said unto me, In the beginning, when the earth was made, before the borders of the world stood, or ever the winds blew,

{6:2} Before it thundered and lightened, or ever the foundations of paradise were laid,

{6:3} Before the fair flowers were seen, or ever the moveable powers were established, before the innumerable multitude of angels were gathered together,

{6:4} Or ever the heights of the air were lifted up, before the measures of the firmament were named, or ever the chimneys in Sion were hot,

{6:5} And ere the present years were sought out, and or ever the inventions of them that now sin were turned, before they were sealed that have gathered faith for a treasure:

{6:6} Then did I consider these things, and they all were made through me alone, and through none other: by me also they shall be ended, and by none other.

{6:7} Then answered I and said, what shall be the parting asunder of the times? or when shall be the end of the first, and the beginning of it that followeth?

{6:8} And he said unto me, From Abraham unto Isaac, when Jacob and Esau were born of him, Jacob's hand held first the heel of Esau.

{6:9} For Esau is the end of the world, and Jacob is the beginning of it that followeth.

{6:10} The hand of man is betwixt the heel and the hand: other question, Esdras, ask thou not.

{6:11} I answered then and said, O Lord that bearest rule, if I have found favour in thy sight,

{6:12} I beseech thee, shew thy servant the end of thy tokens, whereof thou shewedst me part the last night.

{6:13} So he answered and said unto me, stand up upon thy feet, and hear a mighty sounding voice.

{6:14} And it shall be as it were a great motion; but the place where thou standest shall not be moved.

{6:15} And therefore when it speaketh be not afraid: for the word is of the end, and the foundation of the earth is understood.

{6:16} And why? because the speech of these things trembleth and is moved: for it knoweth that the end of these things must be changed.

{6:17} And it happened, that when I had heard it I stood up upon my feet, and hearkened, and, behold, there was a voice that spake, and the sound of it was like the sound of many waters.

{6:18} And it said, Behold, the days come, that I will begin to draw nigh, and to visit them that dwell upon the earth,

{6:19} And will begin to make inquisition of them, what they be that have hurt unjustly with their unrighteousness, and when the affliction of Sion shall be fulfilled;

{6:20} And when the world, that shall begin to vanish away, shall be finished, then will I shew these tokens: the books shall be opened before the firmament, and they shall see all together:

{6:21} And the children of a year old shall speak with their voices, the women with child shall bring forth untimely children of three or four months old, and they shall live, and be raised up.

{6:22} And suddenly shall the sown places appear unsown, the full storehouses shall suddenly be found empty:

{6:23} And tha trumpet shall give a sound, which when every man heareth, they shall be suddenly afraid.

{6:24} At that time shall friends fight one against another like enemies, and the earth shall stand in fear with those that dwell therein, the springs of the fountains shall stand still, and in three hours they shall not run.

{6:25} Whosoever remaineth from all these that I have told thee shall escape, and see my salvation, and the end of your world.

{6:26} And the men that are received shall see it, who have not tasted death from their birth: and the heart of the inhabitants shall be changed, and turned into another meaning.

{6:27} For evil shall be put out, and deceit shall be quenched.

{6:28} As for faith, it shall flourish, corruption shall be overcome, and the truth, which hath been so long without fruit, shall be declared.

{6:29} And when he talked with me, behold, I looked by little and little upon him before whom I stood.

{6:30} And these words said he unto me; I am come to shew thee the time of the night to come.

{6:31} If thou wilt pray yet more, and fast seven days again, I shall tell thee greater things by day than I have heard.

{6:32} For thy voice is heard before the most High: for the Mighty hath seen thy righteous dealing, he hath seen also thy chastity, which thou hast had ever since thy youth.

{6:33} And therefore hath he sent me to shew thee all these things, and to say unto thee, Be of good comfort and fear not

{6:34} And hasten not with the times that are past, to think vain things, that thou mayest not hasten from the latter times.

{6:35} And it came to pass after this, that I wept again, and fasted seven days in like manner, that I might fulfil the three weeks which he told me.

{6:36} And in the eighth night was my heart vexed within me again, and I began to speak before the most High.

{6:37} For my spirit was greatly set on fire, and my soul was in distress.

{6:38} And I said, O Lord, thou spakest from the beginning of the creation, even the first day, and saidst thus; Let heaven and earth be made; and thy word was a perfect work.

{6:39} And then was the spirit, and darkness and silence were on every side; the sound of man's voice was not yet formed.

{6:40} Then commandedst thou a fair light to come forth of thy treasures, that thy work might appear.

{6:41} Upon the second day thou madest the spirit of the firmament, and commandedst it to part asunder, and to make a division betwixt the waters, that the one part might go up, and the other remain beneath.

{6:42} Upon the third day thou didst command that the waters should be gathered in the seventh part of the earth: six pats hast thou dried up, and kept them, to the intent that of these some being planted of God and tilled might serve thee.

{6:43} For as soon as thy word went forth the work was made.

{6:44} For immediately there was great and innumerable fruit, and many and divers pleasures for the taste, and flowers of unchangeable colour, and odours of wonderful smell: and this was done the third day.

{6:45} Upon the fourth day thou commandedst that the sun should shine, and the moon give her light, and the stars should be in order:

{6:46} And gavest them a charge to do service unto man, that was to be made.

{6:47} Upon the fifth day thou saidst unto the seventh part, where the waters were gathered that it should bring forth living creatures, fowls and fishes: and so it came to pass.

{6:48} For the dumb water and without life brought forth living things at the commandment of God, that all people might praise thy wondrous works.

{6:49} Then didst thou ordain two living creatures, the one thou calledst Enoch, and the other Leviathan;

{6:50} And didst separate the one from the other: for the seventh part, namely, where the water was gathered together, might not hold them both.

{6:51} Unto Enoch thou gavest one part, which was dried up the third day, that he should dwell in the same part, wherein are a thousand hills:

{6:52} But unto Leviathan thou gavest the seventh part, namely, the moist; and hast kept him to be devoured of whom thou wilt, and when.

{6:53} Upon the sixth day thou gavest commandment unto the earth, that before thee it should bring forth beasts, cattle, and creeping things:

{6:54} And after these, Adam also, whom thou madest lord of all thy creatures: of him come we all, and the people also whom thou hast chosen.

{6:55} All this have I spoken before thee, O Lord, because thou madest the world for our sakes

{6:56} As for the other people, which also come of Adam, thou hast said that they are nothing, but be like unto spittle: and hast likened the abundance of them unto a drop that falleth from a vessel.

{6.57} And now, O Lord, behold, these heathen, which have ever been reputed as nothing, have begun to be lords over us, and to devour us.

{6:58} But we thy people, whom thou hast called thy firstborn, thy only begotten, and thy fervent lover, are given into their hands.

{6:59} If the world now be made for our sakes, why do we not possess an inheritance with the world? how long shall this endure?

{7:1} And when I had made an end of speaking these words, there was sent unto me the angel which had been sent unto me the nights afore:

{7:2} And he said unto me, Up, Esdras, and hear the words that I am come to tell thee.

{7:3} And I said, Speak on, my God. Then said he unto me, The sea is set in a wide place, that it might be deep and great.

{7:4} But put the case the entrance were narrow, and like a river;

{7:5} Who then could go into the sea to look upon it, and to rule it? if he went not through the narrow, how could he come into the broad?

{7:6} There is also another thing; A city is builded, and set upon a broad field, and is full of all good things:

{7:7} The entrance thereof is narrow, and is set in a dangerous

place to fall, like as if there were a fire on the right hand, and on
the left a deep water:

{7:8} And one only path between them both, even between the fire and
the water, so small that there could but one man goes there at once.

{7:9} If this city now were given unto a man for an inheritance, if
he never shall pass the danger set before it, how shall he receive this
inheritance?

{7:10} And I said, it is so, Lord. Then said he unto me, even so
also is Israel's portion.

{7:11} Because for their sakes I made the world: and when Adam
transgressed my statutes, then was decreed that now is done.

{7:12} Then were the entrances of this world made narrow, full of
sorrow and travail: they are but few and evil, full of perils, and
very painful.

{7:13} For the entrances of the elder world were wide and sure, and
brought immortal fruit.

{7:14} If then they that live labour not to enter these strait and
vain things, they can never receive those that are laid up for them.

{7:15} Now therefore why disquietest thou thyself, seeing thou art but a corruptible man? and why art thou moved, whereas thou art but mortal?

{7:16} Why hast thou not considered in thy mind this thing that is to come, rather than that which is present?

{7:17} Then answered I and said, O Lord that bearest rule, thou hast ordained in thy law, that the righteous should inherit these things, but that the ungodly should perish.

{7:18} Nevertheless the righteous shall suffer strait things, and hope for wide: for they that have done wickedly have suffered the strait things, and yet shall not see the wide.

{7:19} And he said unto me. There is no judge above God, and none that hath understanding above the Highest.

{7:20} For there be many that perish in this life, because they despise the law of God that is set before them.

{7:21} For God hath given strait commandment to such as came, what they should do to live, even as they came, and what they should observe to avoid punishment.

{7:22} Nevertheless they were not obedient unto him; but spake against him, and imagined vain things;

{7:23} And deceived themselves by their wicked deeds; and said of the most High, that he is not; and knew not his ways:

{7:24} But his law have they despised, and denied his covenants; in his statutes have they not been faithful, and have not performed his works.

{7:25} And therefore, Esdras, for the empty are empty things, and for the full are the full things.

{7:26} Behold, the time shall come, that these tokens which I have told thee shall come to pass, and the bride shall appear, and she coming forth shall be seen, that now is withdrawn from the earth.

{7:27} And whosoever is delivered from the foresaid evils shall see my wonders.

{7:28} For my son Jesus shall be revealed with those that be with him, and they that remain shall rejoice within four hundred years.

{7:29} After these years shall my son Christ die, and all men that have life.

{7:30} And the world shall be turned into the old silence seven days, like as in the former judgments: so that no man shall remain.

{7:31} And after seven days the world, that yet awaketh not, shall be raised up, and that shall die that is corrupt

{7:32} And the earth shall restore those that are asleep in her, and so shall the dust those that dwell in silence, and the secret places shall deliver those souls that were committed unto them.

{7:33} And the most High shall appear upon the seat of judgment, and misery shall pass away, and the long suffering shall have an end:

{7:34} But judgment only shall remain, truth shall stand, and faith shall wax strong:

{7:35} And the work shall follow, and the reward shall be shewed, and the good deeds shall be of force, and wicked deeds shall bear no rule.

{7:36} Then said I, Abraham prayed first for the Sodomites, and Moses for the fathers that sinned in the wilderness:

{7:37} And Jesus after him for Israel in the time of Achan:

{7:38} And Samuel and David for the destruction: and Solomon for them that should come to the sanctuary:

{7:39} And Helias for those that received rain; and for the dead, that he might live:

{7:40} And Ezechias for the people in the time of Sennacherib: and many for many.

{7:41} Even so now, seeing corruption is grown up, and wickedness increased, and the righteous have prayed for the ungodly: wherefore shall it not be so now also?

{7:42} He answered me, and said, this present life is not the end where much glory doth abide; therefore have they prayed for the weak.

{7:43} But the day of doom shall be the end of this time, and the beginning of the immortality for to come, wherein corruption is past,

{7:44} Intemperance is at an end, infidelity is cut off, righteousness is grown, and truth is sprung up.

{7:45} Then shall no man be able to save him that is destroyed, nor to oppress him that hath gotten the victory.

{7:46} I answered then and said, this is my first and last saying, that it had been better not to have given the earth unto Adam: or else, when it was given him, to have restrained him from sinning.

{7:47} For what profit is it for men now in this present time to live in heaviness, and after death to look for punishment?

{7:48} O thou Adam, what hast thou done? for though it was thou that sinned, thou art not fallen alone, but we all that come of thee.

{7:49} For what profit is it unto us, if there be promised us an immortal time, whereas we have done the works that bring death?

{7:50} And that there is promised us an everlasting hope, whereas ourselves being most wicked are made vain?

{7:51} And that there are laid up for us dwellings of health and safety, whereas we have lived wickedly?

{7:52} And that the glory of the most High is kept to defend them which have led a wary life, whereas we have walked in the most wicked ways of all?

{7:53} And that there should be shewed a paradise, whose fruit endureth for ever, wherein is security and medicine, since we shall not enter into it?

{7:54} (For we have walked in unpleasant places.)

{7:55} And that the faces of them which have used abstinence shall shine above the stars, whereas our faces shall be blacker than darkness?

{7:56} For while we lived and committed iniquity, we considered not that we should begin to suffer for it after death.

{7:57} Then answered he me, and said, this is the condition of the battle, which man that is born upon the earth shall fight;

{7:58} That, if he be overcome, he shall suffer as thou hast said: but if he get the victory, he shall receive the thing that I say.

{7:59} For this is the life whereof Moses spake unto the people while he lived, saying, Choose thee life, that thou mayest live.

{7:60} Nevertheless they believed not him, nor yet the prophets after him, no nor me which have spoken unto them,

{7:61} That there should not be such heaviness in their destruction, as shall be joy over them that are persuaded to salvation.

{7:62} I answered then, and said, I know, Lord, that the most High is called merciful, in that he hath mercy upon them which are not yet come into the world,

{7:63} And upon those also that turn to his law;

{7:64} And that he is patient, and long suffereth those that have sinned, as his creatures;

{7:65} And that he is bountiful, for he is ready to give where it needeth;

{7:66} And that he is of great mercy, for he multiplieth more and more mercies to them that are present, and that are past, and also to them which are to come.

{7:67} For if he shall not multiply his mercies, the world would not continue with them that inherit therein.

{7:68} And he pardoneth; for if he did not so of his goodness, that they which have committed iniquities might be eased of them, the ten thousandth part of men should not remain living.

{7:69} And being judge, if he should not forgive them that are cured with his word, and put out the multitude of contentions,

{7:70} There should be very few left peradventure in an innumerable multitude.

{8:1} And he answered me, saying, the most High hath made this world for many, but the world to come for few.

{8:2} I will tell thee a similitude, Esdras; As when thou askest the earth, it shall say unto thee, that it giveth much mould whereof earthen vessels are made, but little dust that gold cometh of: even so is the course of this present world.

{8:3} There be many created, but few shall be saved.

{8:4} So answered I and said, Swallow then down, O my soul, understanding, and devour wisdom.

{8:5} For thou hast agreed to give ear, and art willing to prophesy: for thou hast no longer space than only to live.

{8:6} O Lord, if thou suffer not thy servant, that we may pray before thee, and thou give us seed unto our heart, and culture to our understanding, that there may come fruit of it; how shall each man live that is corrupt, who beareth the place of a man?

{8:7} For thou art alone, and we all one workmanship of thine hands, like as thou hast said.

{8:8} For when the body is fashioned now in the mother's womb, and thou givest it members, thy creature is preserved in fire and water, and nine months doth thy workmanship endure thy creature which is created in her.

{8:9} But that which keepeth and is kept shall both be preserved: and when the time cometh, the womb preserved delivereth up the things that grew in it.

{8:10} For thou hast commanded out of the parts of the body, that is to say, out of the breasts, milk to be given, which is the fruit of the breasts,

{8:11} That the thing which is fashioned may be nourished for a time, till thou disposest it to thy mercy.

{8:12} Thou broughtest it up with thy righteousness, and nurturedst it in thy law, and reformedst it with thy judgment.

{8:13} And thou shalt mortify it as thy creature, and quicken it as thy work.

{8:14} If therefore thou shalt destroy him which with so great labour was fashioned, it is an easy thing to be ordained by thy commandment, that the thing which was made might be preserved.

{8:15} Now therefore, Lord, I will speak; touching man in general, thou knowest best; but touching thy people, for whose sake I am sorry;

{8:16} And for thine inheritance, for whose cause I mourn; and for Israel, for whom I am heavy; and for Jacob, for whose sake I am troubled;

{8:17} Therefore will I begin to pray before thee for myself and for them: for I see the falls of us that dwell in the land.

{8:18} But I have heard the swiftness of the judge which is to come.

{8:19} Therefore hear my voice, and understand my words, and I shall speak before thee. This is the beginning of the words of Esdras, before he was taken up: and I said,

{8:20} O Lord, thou that dwellest in everlastingness which beholdest from above things in the heaven and in the air;

{8:21} Whose throne is inestimable; whose glory may not be comprehended; before whom the hosts of angels stand with trembling,

{8:22} Whose service is conversant in wind and fire; whose word is true, and sayings constant; whose commandment is strong, and ordinance fearful;

{8:23} Whose look drieth up the depths, and indignation maketh the mountains to melt away; which the truth witnesseth:

{8:24} O hear the prayer of thy servant, and give ear to the petition of thy creature.

{8:25} For while I live I will speak, and so long as I have understanding I will answer.

{8:26} O look not upon the sins of thy people; but on them which serve thee in truth.

{8:27} Regard not the wicked inventions of the heathen, but the desire of those that keep thy testimonies in afflictions.

{8:28} Think not upon those that have walked feignedly before thee: but remember them, which according to thy will have known thy fear.

{8:29} Let it not be thy will to destroy them which have lived like beasts; but to look upon them that have clearly taught thy law.

{8:30} Take thou no indignation at them which are deemed worse than beasts; but love them that always put their trust in thy righteousness and glory.

{8:31} For we and our fathers do languish of such diseases: but because of us sinners thou shalt be called merciful.

{8:32} For if thou hast a desire to have mercy upon us, thou shalt be called merciful, to us namely, that have no works of righteousness.

{8:33} For the just, which have many good works laid up with thee, shall out of their own deeds receive reward.

{8:34} For what is man, that thou shouldest take displeasure at him? or what is a corruptible generation, that thou shouldest be so bitter toward it?

{8:35} For in truth them is no man among them that be born, but he hath dealt wickedly; and among the faithful there is none which hath not done amiss.

{8:36} For in this, O Lord, thy righteousness and thy goodness shall be declared, if thou be merciful unto them which have not the confidence of good works.

{8:37} Then answered he me, and said, some things hast thou spoken aright, and according unto thy words it shall be.

{8:38} For indeed I will not think on the disposition of them which have sinned before death, before judgment, before destruction:

{8:39} But I will rejoice over the disposition of the righteous, and I will remember also their pilgrimage, and the salvation, and the reward, that they shall have.

{8:40} Like as I have spoken now, so shall it come to pass.

{8:41} For as the husbandman soweth much seed upon the ground, and planteth many trees, and yet the thing that is sown good in his season cometh not up, neither doth all that is planted take root: even so is it of them that are sown in the world; they shall not all be saved.

{8:42} I answered then and said, If I have found grace, let me speak.

{8:43} Like as the husbandman's seed perisheth, if it come not up, and receive not thy rain in due season; or if there come too much rain, and corrupt it:

{8:44} Even so perisheth man also, which is formed with thy hands, and is called thine own image, because thou art like unto him, for whose sake thou hast made all things, and likened him unto the husbandman's seed.

{8:45} Be not wroth with us but spare thy people, and have mercy upon thine own inheritance: for thou art merciful unto thy creature.

{8:46} Then answered he me, and said, Things present are for the present, and things to cometh for such as be to come.

{8:47} For thou comest far short that thou shouldest be able to love my creature more than I: but I have ofttimes drawn nigh unto thee, and unto it, but never to the unrighteous.

{8:48} In this also thou art marvelous before the most High:

{8:49} In that thou hast humbled thyself, as it becometh thee, and hast not judged thyself worthy to be much glorified among the righteous.

{8:50} For many great miseries shall be done to them that in the latter time shall dwell in the world, because they have walked in great pride.

{8:51} But understand thou for thyself, and seek out the glory for such as be like thee.

{8:52} For unto you is paradise opened, the tree of life is planted, the time to come is prepared, plenteousness is made ready, a city is builded, and rest is allowed, yea, perfect goodness and wisdom.

{8:53} The root of evil is sealed up from you, weakness and the moth is hid from you, and corruption is fled into hell to be forgotten:

{8:54} Sorrows are passed, and in the end is shewed the treasure of immortality.

{8:55} And therefore ask thou no more questions concerning the multitude of them that perish.

{8:56} For when they had taken liberty, they despised the most High, thought scorn of his law, and forsook his ways.

{8:57} Moreover they have trodden down his righteous,

{8:58} And said in their heart, that there is no God; yea, and that knowing they must die.

{8:59} For as the things aforesaid shalt receive you, so thirst and pain are prepared for them: for it was not his will that men should come to nought:

{8:60} But they which be created have defiled the name of him that made them, and were unthankful unto him which prepared life for them.

{8:61} And therefore is my judgment now at hand.

{8:62} These things have I not shewed unto all men, but unto thee, and a few like thee. Then answered I and said,

{8:63} Behold, O Lord, now hast thou shewed me the multitude of the wonders, which thou wilt begin to do in the last times: but at what time, thou hast not shewed me.

{9:1} He answered me then, and said, Measure thou the time diligently in itself: and when thou seest part of the signs past, which I have told thee before,

{9:2} Then shalt thou understand, that it is the very same time, wherein the Highest will begin to visit the world which he made.

{9:3} Therefore when there shall be seen earthquakes and uproars of the people in the world.

{9:4} Then shalt thou well understand, that the most High spake of those things from the days that were before thee, even from the beginning.

{9:5} For like as all that is made in the world hath a beginning and an end, and the end is manifest:

{9:6} Even so the times also of the Highest have plain beginnings in wonder and powerful works, and endings in effects and signs.

{9:7} And every one that shall be saved, and shall be able to escape by his works, and by faith, whereby ye have believed,

{9:8} Shall be preserved from the said perils, and shall see my salvation in my land, and within my borders: for I have sanctified them for me from the beginning.

{9:9} Then shall they be in pitiful case, which now have abused my ways: and they that have cast them away despitefully shall dwell in torments.

{9:10} For such as in their life have received benefits, and have not known me;

{9:11} And they that have loathed my law, while they had yet liberty, and, when as yet place of repentance was open unto them, understood not, but despised it;

{9:12} The same must know it after death by pain.

{9:13} And therefore be thou not curious how the ungodly shall be punished, and when: but enquire how the righteous shall be saved, whose the world is, and for whom the world is created.

{9:14} Then answered I and said,

{9:15} I have said before, and now do speak, and will speak it also hereafter, that there be many more of them which perish, than of them which shall be saved:

{9:16} Like as a wave is greater than a drop.

{9:17} And he answered me, saying, like as the field is, so is also the seed; as the flowers be, such are the colours also; such as the workman is, such also is the work; and as the husbandman Is himself, so is his husbandry also: for it was the time of the world.

{9:18} And now when I prepared the world, which was not yet made, even for them to dwell in that now live, no man spake against me.

{9:19} For then everyone obeyed: but now the manners of them which are created in this world that is made are corrupted by a perpetual seed, and by a law which is unsearchable rid themselves.

{9:20} So I considered the world, and, behold, there was peril because of the devices that were come into it.

{9:21} And I saw, and spared it greatly, and have kept me a grape of the cluster, and a plant of a great people.

{9:22} Let the multitude perish then, which was born in vain; and let my grape be kept, and my plant; for with great labour have I made it perfect.

{9:23} Nevertheless, if thou wilt cease yet seven days more, (but thou shalt not fast in them,

{9:24} But go into a field of flowers, where no house is builded, and eat only the flowers of the field; taste no flesh, drink no wine, but eat flowers only;)

{9:25} And pray unto the Highest continually, then will I come and talk with thee.

{9:26} So I went my way into the field which is called Ardath, like as he commanded me; and there I sat among the flowers, and did eat of the herbs of the field, and the meat of the same satisfied me.

{9:27} After seven days I sat upon the grass, and my heart was vexed within me, like as before:

{9:28} And I opened my mouth, and began to talk before the most High, and said,

{9:29} O Lord, thou that shewest thyself unto us, thou wast shewed unto our fathers in the wilderness, in a place where no man treadeth, in a barren place, when they came out of Egypt.

{9:30} And thou spakest saying, hear me, O Israel; and mark my words, thou seed of Jacob.

{9:31} For, behold, I sow my law in you, and it shall bring fruit in you, and ye shall be honoured in it for ever.

{9:32} But our fathers, which received the law, kept it not, and observed not thy ordinances: and though the fruit of thy law did not perish, neither could it, for it was thine;

{9:33} Yet they that received it perished, because they kept not the thing that was sown in them.

{9:34} And, lo, it is a custom, when the ground hath received seed, or the sea a ship, or any vessel meat or drink, that, that being perished wherein it was sown or cast into,

{9:35} That thing also which was sown, or cast therein, or received, doth perish, and remaineth not with us: but with us it hath not happened so.

{9:36} For we that have received the law perish by sin, and our heart also which received it

{9:37} Notwithstanding the law perisheth not, but remaineth in his force.

{9:38} And when I spake these things in my heart, I looked back with mine eyes, and upon the right side I saw a woman, and, behold, she mourned and wept with a loud voice, and was much grieved in heart, and her clothes were rent, and she had ashes upon her head.

{9:39} Then let I my thoughts go that I was in, and turned me unto her,

{9:40} And said unto her, Wherefore weepest thou? why art thou so grieved in thy mind?

{9:41} And she said unto me, Sir, let me alone, that I may bewail myself, and add unto my sorrow, for I am sore vexed in my mind, and brought very low.

{9:42} And I said unto her, what aileth thee? tell me.

{9:43} She said unto me, I thy servant have been barren, and had no child, though I had an husband thirty years,

{9:44} And those thirty years I did nothing else day and night, and every hour, but make my, prayer to the Highest.

{9:45} After thirty years God heard me thine handmaid, looked upon my misery, considered my trouble, and gave me a son: and I was very glad of him, so was my husband also, and all my neighbours: and we gave great honour unto the Almighty.

{9:46} And I nourished him with great travail.

{9:47} So when he grew up, and came to the time that he should have a wife, I made a feast.

{10.1} And it so came to pass, that when my son was entered into his wedding chamber, he fell down, and died.

{10:2} Then we all overthrew the lights, and all my neighbours rose up to comfort me: so I took my rest unto the second day at night.

{10:3} And it came to pass, when they had all left off to comfort me, to the end I might be quiet; then rose I up by night and fled, and came hither into this field, as thou seest.

{10:4} And I do now purpose not to return into the city, but here to stay, and neither to eat nor drink, but continually to mourn and to fast until I die.

{10:5} Then left I the meditations wherein I was, and spake to her in anger, saying,

{10:6} Thou foolish woman above all other, seest thou not our mourning, and what happeneth unto us?

{10:7} How that Sion our mother is full of all heaviness, and much humbled, mourning very sore?

{10:8} And now, seeing we all mourn and are sad, for we are all in heaviness, art thou grieved for one son?

{10:9} For ask the earth, and she shall tell thee, that it is she which ought to mourn for the fall of so many that grow upon her.

{10:10} For out of her came all at the first, and out of her shall all others come, and, behold, they walk almost all into destruction, and a multitude of them is utterly rooted out.

{10:11} Who then should make more mourning than she, that hath lost so great a multitude; and not thou, which art sorry but for one?

{10:12} But if thou sayest unto me, my lamentation is not like the earth's, because I have lost the fruit of my womb, which I brought forth with pains, and bear with sorrows;

{10:13} But the earth not so: for the multitude present in it according to the course of the earth is gone, as it came:

{10:14} Then say I unto thee, like as thou hast brought forth with labour; even so the earth also hath given her fruit, namely, man, ever since the beginning unto him that made her.

{10:15} Now therefore keep thy sorrow to thyself, and bear with a good courage that which hath befallen thee.

{10:16} For if thou shalt acknowledge the determination of God to be just, thou shalt both receive thy son in time, and shalt be commended among women.

{10:17} Go thy way then into the city to thine husband.

{10:18} And she said unto me, that will I not do: I will not go into the city, but here will I die.

{10:19} So I proceeded to speak further unto her, and said,

{10:20} Do not so, but be counselled. by me: for how many are the adversities of Sion? be comforted in regard of the sorrow of Jerusalem.

{10:21} For thou seest that our sanctuary is laid waste, our altar broken down, our temple destroyed;

{10:22} Our psaltery is laid on the ground, our song is put to silence, our rejoicing is at an end, the light of our candlestick is put out, the ark of our covenant is spoiled, our holy things are defiled, and the name that is called upon us is almost profaned: our children are put to shame, our priests are burnt, our Levites are gone into captivity, our virgins are defiled, and our wives ravished; our righteous men carried away, our little ones destroyed, our young men are brought in bondage, and our strong men are become weak;

{10:23} And, which is the greatest of all, the seal of Sion hath now lost her honour; for she is delivered into the hands of them that hate us.

{10:24} And therefore shake off thy great heaviness, and put away the multitude of sorrows, that the Mighty may be merciful unto thee again, and the Highest shall give thee rest and ease from thy labour.

{10:25} And it came to pass while I was talking with her, behold, her face upon a sudden shined exceedingly, and her countenance glistered, so that I was afraid of her, and mused what it might be.

{10:26} And, behold, suddenly she made a great cry very fearful: so that the earth shook at the noise of the woman.

{10:27} And I looked, and, behold, the woman appeared unto me no more, but there was a city builded, and a large place shewed itself from the foundations: then was I afraid, and cried with a loud voice, and said,

{10:28} Where is Uriel the angel, who came unto me at the first? for he hath caused me to fall into many trances, and mine end is turned into corruption, and my prayer to rebuke.

{10.29} And as I was speaking these words behold, he came unto me, and looked upon me.

{10:30} And, lo, I lay as one that had been dead, and mine understanding was taken from me: and he took me by the right hand, and comforted me, and set me upon my feet, and said unto me,

{10:31} What aileth thee? and why art thou so disquieted? and why is thine understanding troubled, and the thoughts of thine heart?

{10:32} And I said, because thou hast forsaken me, and yet I did according to thy words, and I went into the field, and, lo, I have seen, and yet see, that I am not able to express.

{10:33} And he said unto me, stand up manfully, and I will advise thee.

{10:34} Then said I, speak on, my lord, in me; only forsake me not, lest I die frustrate of my hope.

{10:35} For I have seen that I knew not, and hear that I do not know.

{10:36} Or is my sense deceived, or my soul in a dream?

{10:37} Now therefore I beseech thee that thou wilt shew thy servant of this vision.

{10:38} He answered me then, and said, hear me, and I shall inform thee, and tell thee wherefore thou art afraid: for the Highest will reveal many secret things unto thee.

{10:39} He hath seen that thy way is right: for that thou sorrowest continually for thy people, and makest great lamentation for Sion.

{10:40} This therefore is the meaning of the vision which thou lately sawest:

{10:41} Thou sawest a woman mourning, and thou begannest to comfort her:

{10:42} But now seest thou the likeness of the woman no more, but there appeared unto thee a city builded.

{10:43} And whereas she told thee of the death of her son, this is the solution:

{10:44} This woman, whom thou sawest is Sion: and whereas she said unto thee, even she whom thou seest as a city builded,

{10:45} Whereas, I say, she said unto thee, that she hath been thirty years barren: those are the thirty years wherein there was no offering made in her.

{10:46} But after thirty years Solomon builded the city and offered offerings: and then bare the barren a son.

{10:47} And whereas she told thee that she nourished him with labour: that was the dwelling in Jerusalem.

{10:48} But whereas she said unto thee, that my son coming into his marriage chamber happened to have a fail, and died: this was the destruction that came to Jerusalem.

{10:49} And, behold, thou sawest her likeness, and because she mourned for her son, thou begannest to comfort her: and of these things which have chanced, these are to be opened unto thee.

{10:50} For now the most High seeth that thou art grieved unfeignedly, and sufferest from thy whole heart for her, so hath he shewed thee the brightness of her glory, and the comeliness of her beauty:

{10:51} And therefore I bade thee remain in the field where no house was builded:

{10:52} For I knew that the Highest would shew this unto thee.

{10:53} Therefore I commanded thee to go into the field, where no foundation of any building was.

{10:54} For in the place wherein the Highest beginneth to shew his city, there can no man's building be able to stand.

{10:55} And therefore fear not, let not thine heart be affrighted, but go thy way in, and see the beauty and greatness of the building, as much as thine eyes be able to see:

{10:56} And then shalt thou hear as much as thine ears may comprehend.

{10:57} For thou art blessed above many other, and art called with the Highest; and so are but few.

{10:58} But tomorrow at night thou shalt remain here;

{10:59} And so shall the Highest shew thee visions of the high things, which the most High will do unto them that dwell upon the earth in the last days. So I slept that night and another, like as he commanded me.

{11:1} Then saw I a dream, and, behold, there came up from the sea an eagle, which had twelve feathered wings, and three heads.

{11:2} And I saw, and, behold, she spread her wings over all the earth, and all the winds of the air blew on her, and were gathered together.

{11:3} And I beheld, and out of her feathers there grew other contrary feathers; and they became little feathers and small.

{11:4} But her heads were at rest: the head in the midst was greater than the other, yet rested it with the residue.

{11:5} Moreover I beheld, and, lo, the eagle flew with her feathers, and reigned upon earth, and over them that dwelt therein.

{11:6} And I saw that all things under heaven were subject unto her, and no man spake against her, no, not one creature upon earth.

{11:7} And I beheld, and, lo, the eagle rose upon her talons, and spake to her feathers, saying,

{11:8} Watch not all at once: sleep everyone in his own place, and watch by course:

{11:9} But let the heads be preserved for the last.

{11:10} And I beheld, and, lo, the voice went not out of her heads, but from the midst of her body.

{11:11} And I numbered her contrary feathers, and, behold, there were eight of them.

{11:12} And I looked, and, behold, on the right side there arose one feather, and reigned over all the earth;

{11:13} And so it was, that when it reigned, the end of it came, and the place thereof appeared no more: so the next following stood up. and reigned, and had a great time;

{11:14} And it happened, that when it reigned, the end of it came also, like as the first, so that it appeared no more.

{11:15} Then came there a voice unto it, and said,

{11:16} Hear thou that hast borne rule over the earth so long: this I say unto thee, before thou beginnest to appear no more,

{11:17} There shall none after thee attain unto thy time, neither unto the half thereof.

{11:18} Then arose the third, and reigned as the other before, and appeared no more also.

{11:19} So went it with all the residue one after another, as that every one reigned, and then appeared no more.

{11:20} Then I beheld, and, lo, in process of time the feathers that followed stood up upon the right side, that they might rule also; and some of them ruled, but within a while they appeared no more:

{11:21} For some of them were set up, but ruled not.

{11:22} After this I looked, and, behold, the twelve feathers appeared no more, nor the two little feathers:

{11:23} And there was no more upon the eagle's body, but three heads that rested, and six little wings.

{11:24} Then saw I also that two little feathers divided themselves from the six, and remained under the head that was upon the right side: for the four continued in their place.

{11:25} And I beheld, and, lo, the feathers that were under the wing thought to set up themselves and to have the rule.

{11:26} And I beheld, and, lo, there was one set up, but shortly it appeared no more.

{11:27} And the second was sooner away than the first.

{11:28} And I beheld, and, lo, the two that remained thought also in themselves to reign:

{11:29} And when they so thought, behold, there awaked one of the heads that were at rest, namely, it that was in the midst; for that was greater than the two other heads.

{11:30} And then I saw that the two other heads were joined with it.

{11:31} And, behold, the head was turned with them that were with it, and did eat up the two feathers under the wing that would have reigned.

{11:32} But this head put the whole earth in fear, and bare rule in it over all those that dwelt upon the earth with much oppression; and it had the governance of the world more than all the wings that had been.

{11:33} And after this I beheld, and, lo, the head that was in the midst suddenly appeared no more, like as the wings.

{11:34} But there remained the two heads, which also in like sort ruled upon the earth, and over those that dwelt therein.

{11:35} And I beheld, and, lo, the head upon the right side devoured it that was upon the left side.

{11:36} Then I heard a voice, which said unto me, Look before thee, and consider the thing that thou seest.

{11:37} And I beheld, and lo, as it were a roaring lion chased out of the wood: and I saw that he sent out a man's voice unto the eagle, and said,

{11:38} Hear thou, I will talk with thee, and the Highest shall say unto thee,

{11:39} Art not thou it that remainest of the four beasts, whom I made to reign in my world, that the end of their times might come through them?

{11:40} And the fourth came, and overcame all the beasts that were past, and had power over the world with great fearfulness, and over the whole compass of the earth with much wicked oppression; and so long time dwelt he upon the earth with deceit.

{11:41} For the earth hast thou not judged with truth.

{11:42} For thou hast afflicted the meek, thou hast hurt the peaceable, thou hast loved liars, and destroyed the dwellings of them that brought forth fruit, and hast cast down the walls of such as did thee no harm.

{11:43} Therefore is thy wrongful dealing come up unto the Highest, and thy pride unto the Mighty.

{11:44} The Highest also hath looked upon the proud times, and, behold, they are ended, and his abominations are fulfilled.

{11:45} And therefore appear no more, thou eagle, nor thy horrible wings, nor thy wicked feathers nor thy malicious heads, nor thy hurtful claws, nor all thy vain body:

{11:46} That all the earth may be refreshed, and may return, being delivered from thy violence, and that she may hope for the judgment and mercy of him that made her.

{12:1} And it came to pass, whiles the lion spake these words unto the eagle, I saw,

{12:2} And, behold, the head that remained and the four wings appeared no more, and the two went unto it and set themselves up to reign, and their kingdom was small, and fill of uproar.

{12:3} And I saw, and, behold, they appeared no more, and the whole body of the eagle was burnt so that the earth was in great fear: then awaked I out of the trouble and trance of my mind, and from great fear, and said unto my spirit,

{12:4} Lo, this hast thou done unto me, in that thou searchest out the ways of the Highest.

{12:5} Lo, yet am I weary in my mind, and very weak in my spirit; and little strength is there in me, for the great fear wherewith I was afflicted this night.

{12:6} Therefore will I now beseech the Highest, that he will comfort me unto the end.

{12:7} And I said, Lord that bearest rule, if I have found grace before thy sight, and if I am justified with thee before many others, and if my prayer indeed be come up before thy face;

{12:8} Comfort me then, and shew me thy servant the interpretation and plain difference of this fearful vision, that thou mayest perfectly comfort my soul.

{12:9} For thou hast judged me worthy to shew me the last times.

{12:10} And he said unto me, this is the interpretation of the vision:

{12:11} The eagle, whom thou sawest come up from the sea, is the kingdom which was seen in the vision of thy brother Daniel.

{12:12} But it was not expounded unto him, therefore now I declare it unto thee.

{12:13} Behold, the days will come, that there shall rise up a kingdom upon earth, and it shall be feared above all the kingdoms that were before it.

{12:14} In the same shall twelve kings reign, one after another:

{12:15} Whereof the second shall begin to reign, and shall have more time than any of the twelve.

{12:16} And this do the twelve wings signify, which thou sawest.

{12.17} As for the voice which thou heardest speak, and that thou sawest not to go out from the heads but from the midst of the body thereof, this is the interpretation:

{12:18} That after the time of that kingdom there shall arise great strivings, and it shall stand in peril of failing: nevertheless it shall not then fall, but shall be restored again to his beginning.

{12:19} And whereas thou sawest the eight small under feathers sticking to her wings, this is the interpretation:

{12:20} That in him there shall arise eight kings, whose times shall be but small, and their years swift.

{12:21} And two of them shall perish, the middle time approaching: four shall be kept until their end begin to approach: but two shall be kept unto the end.

{12:22} And whereas thou sawest three heads resting, this is the interpretation:

{12:23} In his last days shall the most High raise up three kingdoms, and renew many things therein, and they shall have the dominion of the earth,

{12:24} And of those that dwell therein, with much oppression, above all those that were before them: therefore are they called the heads of the eagle.

{12:25} For these are they that shall accomplish his wickedness, and that shall finish his last end.

{12:26} And whereas thou sawest that the great head appeared no more, it signifieth that one of them shall die upon his bed, and yet with pain.

{12:27} For the two that remain shall be slain with the sword.

{12:28} For the sword of the one shall devour the other: but at the last shall he fall through the sword himself.

{12:29} And whereas thou sawest two feathers under the wings passing over the head that is on the right side;

{12:30} It signifieth that these are they, whom the Highest hath kept unto their end: this is the small kingdom and full of trouble, as thou sawest.

{12:31} And the lion, whom thou sawest rising up out of the wood, and roaring, and speaking to the eagle, and rebuking her for her unrighteousness with all the words which thou hast heard;

{12:32} This is the anointed, which the Highest hath kept for them and for their wickedness unto the end: he shall reprove them, and shall upbraid them with their cruelty.

{12:33} For he shall set them before him alive in judgment, and shall rebuke them, and correct them.

{12:34} For the rest of my people shall he deliver with mercy, those that have been pressed upon my borders, and he shall make them joyful until the coming of the day of judgment, whereof I have spoken unto thee from the the beginning.

{12:35} This is the dream that thou sawest, and these are the interpretations.

{12:36} Thou only hast been meet to know this secret of the Highest.

{12:37} Therefore write all these things that thou hast seen in a book, and hide them:

{12:38} And teach them to the wise of the people, whose hearts thou knowest may comprehend and keep these secrets.

{12:39} But wait thou here thyself yet seven days more, that it may be shewed thee, whatsoever it pleaseth the Highest to declare unto thee. And with that he went his way.

{12:40} And it came to pass, when all the people saw that the seven days were past, and I not come again into the city, they gathered them all together, from the least unto the greatest, and came unto me, and said,

{12:41} What have we offended thee? and what evil have we done against thee, that thou forsakest us, and sittest here in this place?

{12:42} For of all the prophets thou only art left us, as a cluster of the vintage, and as a candle in a dark place, and as a haven or ship preserved from the tempest.

{12:43} Are not the evils which are come to us sufficient?

{12:44} If thou shalt forsake us, how much better had it been for us, if we also had been burned in the midst of Sion?

{12:45} For we are not better than they that died there. And they wept with a loud voice. Then answered I them, and said,

{12:46} Be of good comfort, O Israel; and be not heavy, thou house of Jacob:

{12:47} For the Highest hath you in remembrance, and the Mighty hath not forgotten you in temptation.

{12:48} As for me, I have not forsaken you, neither am I departed from you: but am come into this place, to pray for the desolation of Sion, and that I might seek mercy for the low estate of your sanctuary.

{12:49} And now go your way home every man, and after these days will I come unto you.

{12:50} So the people went their way into the city, like as I commanded them:

{12:51} But I remained still in the field seven days, as the angel commanded me; and did eat only in those days of the flowers of the field, and had my meat of the herbs

{13:1} And it came to pass after seven days, I dreamed a dream by night:

{13:2} And, lo, there arose a wind from the sea, that it moved all the waves thereof.

{13:3} And I beheld, and, lo, that man waxed strong with the thousands of heaven: and when he turned his countenance to look, all the things trembled that were seen under him.

{13:4} And whensoever the voice went out of his mouth, all they burned that heard his voice, like as the earth faileth when it feeleth the fire.

{13:5} And after this I beheld, and, lo, there was gathered together a multitude of men, out of number, from the four winds of the heaven, to subdue the man that came out of the sea

{13:6} But I beheld, and, lo, he had graved himself a great mountain, and flew up upon it.

{13:7} But I would have seen the region or place whereout the hill was graven, and I could not.

{13:8} And after this I beheld, and, lo, all they which were gathered together to subdue him were sore afraid, and yet durst fight.

{13:9} And, lo, as he saw the violence of the multitude that came, he neither lifted up his hand, nor held sword, nor any instrument of war:

{13:10} But only I saw that he sent out of his mouth as it had been a blast of fire, and out of his lips a flaming breath, and out of his tongue he cast out sparks and tempests.

{13:11} And they were all mixed together; the blast of fire, the flaming breath, and the great tempest; and fell with violence upon the multitude which was prepared to fight, and burned them up every one, so that upon a sudden of an innumerable multitude nothing was to be perceived, but only dust and smell of smoke: when I saw this I was afraid.

{13:12} Afterward saw I the same man come down from the mountain, and call unto him another peaceable Multitude.

{13:13} And there came much people unto him, whereof some were glad, some were sorry, and some of them were bound, and other some brought of
them that were offered: then was I sick through great fear, and I awaked, and said,

{13:14} Thou hast shewed thy servant these wonders from the beginning, and hast counted me worthy that thou shouldest receive my prayer:

{13:15} Shew me now yet the interpretation of this dream.

{13:16} For as I conceive in mine understanding, woe unto them that shall be left in those days and much more woe unto them that are not left behind!

{13:17} For they that were not left were in heaviness.

{13:18} Now understand I the things that are laid up in the latter days, which shall happen unto them, and to those that are left behind.

{13:19} Therefore are they come into great perils and many necessities, like as these dreams declare.

{13:20} Yet is it easier for him that is in danger to come into these things, than to pass away as a cloud out of the world, and not to see the things that happen in the last days. And he answered unto me, and said,

{13:21} The interpretation of the vision shall I shew thee, and I will open unto thee the thing that thou hast required.

{13:22} Whereas thou hast spoken of them that are left behind, this is the interpretation:

{13:23} He that shall endure the peril in that time hath kept himself: they that be fallen into danger are such as have works, and faith toward the Almighty.

{13:24} Know this therefore, that they which be left behind are more blessed than they that be dead.

{13:25} This is the meaning of the vision: Whereas thou sawest a man coming up from the midst of the sea:

{13:26} The same is he whom God the Highest hath kept a great season, which by his own self shall deliver his creature: and he shall order them that are left behind.

{13:27} And whereas thou sawest, that out of his mouth there came as a blast of wind, and fire, and storm;

{13:28} And that he held neither sword, nor any instrument of war, but that the rushing in of him destroyed the whole multitude that came to subdue him; this is the interpretation:

{13:29} Behold, the days come, when the most High will begin to deliver them that are upon the earth.

{13:30} And he shall come to the astonishment of them that dwell on the earth.

{13:31} And one shall undertake to fight against another, one city against another, one place against another, one people against another, and one realm against another.

{13:32} And the time shall be when these things shall come to pass, and the signs shall happen which I shewed thee before, and then shall my Son be declared, whom thou sawest as a man ascending.

{13:33} And when all the people hear his voice, every man shall in their own land leave the battle they have one against another.

{13:34} And an innumerable multitude shall be gathered together, as thou sawest them, willing to come, and to overcome him by fighting.

{13:35} But he shall stand upon the top of the mount Sion.

{13:36} And Sion shall come, and shall be shewed to all men, being prepared and builded, like as thou sawest the hill graven without hands.

{13:37} And this my Son shall rebuke the wicked inventions of those nations, which for their wicked life are fallen into the tempest;

{13:38} And shall lay before them their evil thoughts, and the torments wherewith they shall begin to be tormented, which are like unto a flame: and he shall destroy them without labour by the law which is like unto me.

{13:39} And whereas thou sawest that he gathered another peaceable multitude unto him;

{13:40} Those are the ten tribes, which were carried away prisoners out of their own land in the time of Osea the king, whom Salmanasar the king of Assyria led away captive, and he carried them over the waters, and so came they into another land.

{13:41} But they took this counsel among themselves, that they would leave the multitude of the heathen, and go forth into a further country, where never mankind dwelt,

{13:42} That they might there keep their statutes, which they never kept in their own land.

{13:43} And they entered into Euphrates by the narrow places of the river.

{13:44} For the most High then shewed signs for them, and held still the flood, till they were passed over.

{13:45} For through that country there was a great way to go, namely, of a year and a half: and the same region is called Arsareth.

{13:46} Then dwelt they there until the latter time; and now when they shall begin to come,

{13:47} The Highest shall stay the springs of the stream again, that they may go through: therefore sawest thou the multitude with peace.

{13:48} But those that be left behind of thy people are they that are found within my borders.

{13:49} Now when he destroyeth the multitude of the nations that are gathered together, he shall defend his people that remain.

{13:50} And then shall he shew them great wonders.

{13:51} Then said I, O Lord that bearest rule, shew me this: Wherefore have I seen the man coming up from the midst of the sea?

{13:52} And he said unto me, like as thou canst neither seek out nor know the things that are in the deep of the sea: even so can no man upon earth see my Son, or those that be with him, but in the day time.

{13:53} This is the interpretation of the dream which thou sawest, and whereby thou only art here lightened.

{13:54} For thou hast forsaken thine own way, and applied thy diligence unto my law, and sought it.

{13:55} Thy life hast thou ordered in wisdom, and hast called understanding thy mother.

{13:56} And therefore have I shewed thee the treasures of the Highest: after other three days, I will speak other things unto thee, and declare unto thee mighty and wondrous things.

{13:57} Then went I forth into the field, giving praise and thanks greatly unto the most High because of his wonders which he did in time;

{13:58} And because he governeth the same, and such things as fall in their seasons: and there I sat three days.

{14:1} And it came to pass upon the third day, I sat under an oak, and, behold, there came a voice out of a bush over against me, and said, Esdras, Esdras.

{14:2} And I said, here am I, Lord And I stood up upon my feet.

{14:3} Then said he unto me, In the bush I did manifestly reveal myself unto Moses, and talked with him, when my people served in Egypt:

{14:4} And I sent him and led my people out of Egypt, and brought him up to the mount of where I held him by me a long season,

{14:5} And told him many wondrous things, and shewed him the secrets of the times, and the end; and commanded him, saying,

{14:6} These words shalt thou declare, and these shalt thou hide.

{14:7} And now I say unto thee,

{14:8} That thou lay up in thy heart the signs that I have shewed, and the dreams that thou hast seen, and the interpretations which thou hast heard:

{14:9} For thou shalt be taken away from all, and from henceforth thou shalt remain with my Son, and with such as be like thee, until the times be ended.

{14:10} For the world hath lost his youth, and the times begin to wax old.

{14:11} For the world is divided into twelve parts, and the ten parts of it are gone already, and half of a tenth part:

{14:12} And there remaineth that which is after the half of the tenth part.

{14:13} Now therefore set thine house in order, and reprove thy people, comfort such of them as be in trouble, and now renounce corruption,

{14:14} Let go from thee mortal thoughts, cast away the burdens of man, put off now the weak nature,

{14:15} And set aside the thoughts that are most heavy unto thee, and haste thee to flee from these times.

{14:16} For yet greater evils than those which thou hast seen happen shall be done hereafter.

{14:17} For look how much the world shall be weaker through age, so much the more shall evils increase upon them that dwell therein.

{14:18} For the time is fled far away, and leasing is hard at hand: for now hasteth the vision to come, which thou hast seen.

{14:19} Then answered I before thee, and said,

{14:20} Behold, Lord, I will go, as thou hast commanded me, and reprove the people which are present: but they that shall be born afterward, who shall admonish them? thus the world is set in darkness, and they that dwell therein are without light.

{14:21} For thy law is burnt, therefore no man knoweth the things that are done of thee, or the work that shall begin.

{14:22} But if I have found grace before thee, send the Holy Ghost into me, and I shall write all that hath been done in the world since the beginning, which were written in thy law, that men may find thy path, and that they which will live in the latter days may live.

{14:23} And he answered me, saying, go thy way, gather the people together, and say unto them, that they seek thee not for forty days.

{14:24} But look thou prepare thee many box trees, and take with thee Sarea, Dabria, Selemia, Ecanus, and Asiel, these five which are ready to write swiftly;

{14:25} And come hither, and I shall light a candle of understanding in thine heart, which shall not be put out, till the things be performed which thou shalt begin to write.

{14:26} And when thou hast done, some things shalt thou publish, and some things shalt thou shew secretly to the wise: tomorrow this hour shalt thou begin to write.

{14:27} Then went I forth, as he commanded, and gathered all the people together, and said,

{14:28} Hear these words, O Israel.

{14:29} Our fathers at the beginning were strangers in Egypt, from whence they were delivered:

{14:30} And received the law of life, which they kept not, which ye also have transgressed after them.

{14:31} Then was the land, even the land of Sion, parted among you by lot: but your fathers, and ye yourselves, have done unrighteousness, and have not kept the ways which the Highest commanded you.

{14:32} And forasmuch as he is a righteous judge, he took from you in time the thing that he had given you.

{14:33} And now are ye here, and your brethren among you.

{14:34} Therefore if so be that ye will subdue your own understanding, and reform your hearts, ye shall be kept alive and after death ye shall obtain mercy.

{14:35} For after death shall the judgment come, when we shall live again: and then shall the names of the righteous be manifest, and the works of the ungodly shall be declared.

{14:36} Let no man therefore come unto me now, nor seek after me these forty days.

{14:37} So I took the five men, as he commanded me, and we went into the field, and remained there.

{14:38} And the next day, behold, a voice called me, saying, Esdras, open thy mouth, and drink that I give thee to drink.

{14:39} Then opened I my mouth, and, behold, he reached me a full cup, which was full as it were with water, but the colour of it was like fire.

{14:40} And I took it, and drank: and when I had drunk of it, my heart uttered understanding, and wisdom grew in my breast, for my spirit strengthened my memory:

{14:41} And my mouth was opened, and shut no more.

{14:42} The Highest gave understanding unto the five men, and they wrote the wonderful visions of the night that were told, which they knew not. and they sat forty days, and they wrote in the day, and at night they ate bread.

{14:43} As for me. I spake in the day, and I held not my tongue by night.

{14:44} In forty days they wrote two hundred and four books.

{14:45} And it came to pass, when the forty days were filled, that the Highest spake, saying, the first that thou hast written publish openly, that the worthy and unworthy may read it:

{14:46} But keep the seventy last, that thou mayest deliver them only to such as be wise among the people:

{14:47} For in them is the spring of understanding, the fountain of wisdom, and the stream of knowledge.

{14:48} And I did so.

{15:1} Behold, speak thou in the ears of my people the words of prophecy, which I will put in thy mouth, saith the Lord:

{15:2} And cause them to be written in paper: for they are faithful and true.

{15:3} Fear not the imaginations against thee, let not the

incredulity of them trouble thee, that speak against thee.

{15:4} For all the unfaithful shall die in their unfaithfulness.

{15:5} Behold, saith the Lord, I will bring plagues upon the world; the sword, famine, death, and destruction.

{15:6} For wickedness hath exceedingly polluted the whole earth, and their hurtful works are fulfilled.

{15:7} Therefore saith the Lord,

{15:8} I will hold my tongue no more as touching their wickedness, which they profanely commit, neither will I suffer them in those things, in which they wickedly exercise themselves: behold, the innocent and righteous blood crieth unto me, and the souls of the just complain continually.

{15:9} And therefore, saith the Lord, I will surely avenge them, and receive unto me all the innocent blood from among them.

{15:10} Behold, my people is led as a flock to the slaughter: I will not suffer them now to dwell in the land of Egypt:

{15:11} But I will bring them with a mighty hand and a stretched out arm, and smite Egypt with plagues, as before, and will destroy all the land thereof.

{15:12} Egypt shall mourn, and the foundation of it shall be smitten with the plague and punishment that God shall bring upon it.

{15:13} They that till the ground shall mourn: for their seeds shall fail through the blasting and hail, and with a fearful constellation.

{15:14} Woe to the world and them that dwell therein!

{15:15} For the sword and their destruction draweth nigh, and one people shall stand up and fight against another, and swords in their hands.

{15:16} For there shall be sedition among men, and invading one another; they shall not regard their kings nor princes, and the course of their actions shall stand in their power.

{15:17} A man shall desire to go into a city, and shall not be able.

{15:18} For because of their pride the cities shall be troubled, the houses shall be destroyed, and men shall be afraid.

{15:19} A man shall have no pity upon his neighbour, but shall destroy their houses with the sword, and spoil their goods, because of the lack of bread, and for great tribulation.

{15:20} Behold, saith God, I will call together all the kings of the earth to reverence me, which are from the rising of the sun, from the south, from the east, and Libanus; to turn themselves one against another, and repay the things that they have done to them.

{15:21} Like as they do yet this day unto my chosen, so will I do also, and recompense in their bosom. Thus saith the Lord God;

{15:22} My right hand shall not spare the sinners, and my sword shall not cease over them that shed innocent blood upon the earth.

{15:23} The fire is gone forth from his wrath, and hath consumed the foundations of the earth, and the sinners, like the straw that is kindled.

{15:24} Woe to them that sin, and keep not my commandments! saith the Lord.

{15:25} I will not spare them: go your way, ye children, from the power, defile not my sanctuary.

{15:26} For the Lord knoweth all them that sin against him, and therefore delivereth he them unto death and destruction.

{15:27} For now are the plagues come upon the whole earth and ye shall remain in them: for God shall not deliver you, because ye have sinned against him.

{15:28} Behold an horrible vision, and the appearance thereof from the east:

{15:29} Where the nations of the dragons of Arabia shall come out with many chariots, and the multitude of them shall be carried as the wind upon earth, that all they which hear them may fear and tremble.

{15:30} Also the Carmanians raging in wrath shall go forth as the wild boars of the wood, and with great power shall they come, and join battle with them, and shall waste a portion of the land of the Assyrians.

{15:31} And then shall the dragons have the upper hand, remembering their nature; and if they shall turn themselves, conspiring together in great power to persecute them,

{15:32} Then these shall be troubled bled, and keep silence through their power, and shall flee.

{15:33} And from the land of the Assyrians shall the enemy besiege them, and consume some of them, and in their host shall be fear and dread, and strife among their kings.

{15:34} Behold clouds from the east and from the north unto the south, and they are very horrible to look upon, full of wrath and storm.

{15:35} They shall smite one upon another, and they shall smite down a great multitude of stars upon the earth, even their own star; and blood shall be from the sword unto the belly,

{15:36} And dung of men unto the camel's hough.

{15:37} And there shall be great fearfulness and trembling upon earth: and they that see the wrath shall be afraid, and trembling shall come upon them.

{15:38} And then shall there come great storms from the south, and from the north, and another part from the west.

{15:39} And strong winds shall arise from the east, and shall open it; and the cloud which he raised up in wrath, and the star stirred to cause fear toward the east and west wind, shall be destroyed.

{15:40} The great and mighty clouds shall be puffed up full of wrath, and the star, that they may make all the earth afraid, and them that dwell therein; and they shall pour out over every high and eminent place an horrible star,

{15:41} Fire, and hail, and flying swords, and many waters, that all fields may be full, and all rivers, with the abundance of great waters.

{15:42} And they shall break down the cities and walls, mountains and hills, trees of the wood, and grass of the meadows, and their corn.

{15:43} And they shall go stedfastly unto Babylon, and make her afraid.

{15:44} They shall come to her, and besiege her, the star and all wrath shall they pour out upon her: then shall the dust and smoke go up unto the heaven, and all they that be about her shall bewail her.

{15:45} And they that remain under her shall do service unto them that have put her in fear.

{15:46} And thou, Asia, that art partaker of the hope of Babylon, and art the glory of her person:

{15:47} Woe be unto thee, thou wretch, because thou hast made thyself like unto her; and hast decked thy daughters in whoredom, that they might please and glory in thy lovers, which have always desired to commit whoredom with thee.

{15:48} Thou hast followed her that is hated in all her works and inventions: therefore saith God,

{15:49} I will send plagues upon thee; widowhood, poverty, famine, sword, and pestilence, to waste thy houses with destruction and death.

{15:50} And the glory of thy Power shall be dried up as a flower, the heat shall arise that is sent over thee.

{15:51} Thou shalt be weakened as a poor woman with stripes, and as one chastised with wounds, so that the mighty and lovers shall not be able to receive thee.

{15:52} Would I with jealousy have so proceeded against thee, saith the Lord,

{15:53} If thou hadst not always slain my chosen, exalting the stroke of thine hands, and saying over their dead, when thou wast drunken,

{15.54} Set forth the beauty of thy countenance?

{15:55} The reward of thy whoredom shall be in thy bosom, therefore shalt thou receive recompence.

{15:56} Like as thou hast done unto my chosen, saith the Lord, even so shall God do unto thee, and shall deliver thee into mischief

{15:57} Thy children shall die of hunger, and thou shalt fall through the sword: thy cities shall be broken down, and all thine shall perish with the sword in the field.

{15:58} They that be in the mountains shall die of hunger, and eat their own flesh, and drink their own blood, for very hunger of bread, and thirst of water.

{15:59} Thou as unhappy shalt come through the sea, and receive plagues again.

{15:60} And in the passage, they shall rush on the idle city, and shall destroy some portion of thy land, and consume part of thy glory, and shall return to Babylon that was destroyed.

{15:61} And thou shalt be cast down by them as stubble, and they shall be unto thee as fire;

{15:62} And shall consume thee, and thy cities, thy land, and thy mountains; all thy woods and thy fruitful trees shall they burn up with fire.

{15:63} Thy children shall they carry away captive, and, look, what thou hast, they shall spoil it, and mar the beauty of thy face.

{16:1} Woe be unto thee, Babylon, and Asia! woe be unto thee, Egypt and Syria!

{16:2} Gird up yourselves with cloths of sack and hair, bewail your children, and be sorry; for your destruction is at hand.

{16:3} A sword is sent upon you, and who may turn it back?

{16:4} A fire is sent among you, and who may quench it?

{16:5} Plagues are sent unto you, and what is he that may drive them away?

{16:6} May any man drive away an hungry lion in the wood? or may any one quench the fire in stubble, when it hath begun to burn?

{16:7} May one turn again the arrow that is shot of a strong archer?

{16:8} The mighty Lord sendeth the plagues and who is he that can drive them away?

{16:9} A fire shall go forth from his wrath, and who is he that may quench it?

{16:10} He shall cast lightnings, and who shall not fear? he shall thunder, and who shall not be afraid?

{16:11} The Lord shall threaten, and who shall not be utterly beaten to powder at his presence?

{16:12} The earth quaketh, and the foundations thereof; the sea ariseth up with waves from the deep, and the waves of it are troubled, and the fishes thereof also, before the Lord, and before the glory of his power:

{16:13} For strong is his right hand that bendeth the bow, his arrows that he shooteth are sharp, and shall not miss, when they begin to be shot into the ends of the world.

{16:14} Behold, the plagues are sent, and shall not return again, until they come upon the earth.

{16:15} The fire is kindled, and shall not be put out, till it consume the foundation of the earth.

{16:16} Like as an arrow which is shot of a mighty archer returneth not backward: even so the plagues that shall be sent upon earth shall not return again.

{16:17} Woe is me! woe is me! who will deliver me in those days?

{16:18} The beginning of sorrows and great mourning's; the beginning of famine and great death; the beginning of wars, and the powers shall stand in fear; the beginning of evils! what shall I do when these evils shall come?

{16:19} Behold, famine and plague, tribulation and anguish, are sent as scourges for amendment.

{16:20} But for all these things they shall not turn from their wickedness, nor be always mindful of the scourges.

{16:21} Behold, victuals shall be so good cheap upon earth, that they shall think themselves to be in good case, and even then shall evils grow upon earth, sword, famine, and great confusion.

{16:22} For many of them that dwell upon earth shall perish of famine; and the other, that escape the hunger, shall the sword destroy.

{16:23} And the dead shall be cast out as dung, and there shall be no man to comfort them: for the earth shall be wasted, and the cities shall be cast down.

{16:24} There shall be no man left to till the earth, and to sow it

{16:25} The trees shall give fruit, and who shall gather them?

{16:26} The grapes shall ripen, and who shall tread them? for all places shall be desolate of men:

{16:27} So that one man shall desire to see another, and to hear his voice.

{16:28} For of a city there shall be ten left, and two of the field, which shall hide themselves in the thick groves, and in the clefts of the rocks.

{16:29} As in an orchard of Olives upon every tree there are left three or four olives;

{16:30} Or as when a vineyard is gathered, there are left some clusters of them that diligently seek through the vineyard:

{16:31} Even so in those days there shall be three or four left by them that search their houses with the sword.

{16:32} And the earth shall be laid waste, and the fields thereof shall wax old, and her ways and all her paths shall grow full of thorns, because no man shall travel therethrough.

{16:33} The virgins shall mourn, having no bridegrooms; the women shall mourn, having no husbands; their daughters shall mourn, having no helpers.

{16:34} In the wars shall their bridegrooms be destroyed, and their husbands shall perish of famine.

{16:35} Hear now these things and understand them, ye servants of the Lord.

{16:36} Behold, the word of the Lord, receive it: believe not the gods of whom the Lord spake.

{16:37} Behold, the plagues draw nigh, and are not slack.

{16:38} As when a woman with child in the ninth month bringeth forth her son, with two or three hours of her birth great pains compass her womb, which pains, when the child cometh forth, they slack not a moment:

{16:39} Even so shall not the plagues be slack to come upon the earth, and the world shall mourn, and sorrows shall come upon it on every side.

{16:40} O my people, hear my word: make you ready to thy battle, and in those evils be even as pilgrims upon the earth.

{16:41} He that selleth, let him be as he that fleeth away: and he that buyeth, as one that will lose:

{16:42} He that occupieth merchandise, as he that hath no profit by it: and he that buildeth, as he that shall not dwell therein:

{16:43} He that soweth, as if he should not reap: so also he that planteth the vineyard, as he that shall not gather the grapes:

{16:44} They that marry, as they that shall get no children; and they that marry not, as the widowers.

{16:45} And therefore they that labour labour in vain:

{16:46} For strangers shall reap their fruits, and spoil their goods, overthrow their houses, and take their children captives, for in captivity and famine shall they get children.

{16:47} And they that occupy their merchandise with robbery, the more they deck their cities, their houses, their possessions, and their own persons:

{16:48} The more will I be angry with them for their sin, saith the Lord.

{16:49} Like as a whore envieth a right honest and virtuous woman:

{16:50} So shall righteousness hate iniquity, when she decketh herself, and shall accuse her to her face, when he cometh that shall defend him that diligently searcheth out every sin upon earth.

{16:51} And therefore be ye not like thereunto, nor to the works thereof.

{16:52} For yet a little, and iniquity shall be taken away out of the earth, and righteousness shall reign among you.

{16:53} Let not the sinner say that he hath not sinned: for God shall burn coals of fire upon his head, which saith before the Lord God and his glory, I have not sinned.

{16:54} Behold, the Lord knoweth all the works of men, their imaginations, their thoughts, and their hearts:

{16:55} Which spake but the word, Let the earth be made; and it was made: Let the heaven be made; and it was created.

{16:56} In his word were the stars made, and he knoweth the number of them.

{16:57} He searcheth the deep, and the treasures thereof; he hath measured the sea, and what it containeth.

{16:58} He hath shut the sea in the midst of the waters, and with his word hath he hanged the earth upon the waters.

{16:59} He spreadeth out the heavens like a vault; upon the waters hath he founded it.

{16:60} In the desert hath he made springs of water, and pools upon the tops of the mountains, that the floods might pour down from the high rocks to water the earth.

{16:61} He made man, and put his heart in the midst of the body, and gave him breath, life, and understanding.

{16:62} Yea and the Spirit of Almighty God, which made all things, and searcheth out all hidden things in the secrets of the earth,

{16:63} Surely he knoweth your inventions, and what ye think in your hearts, even them that sin, and would hide their sin.

{16:64} Therefore hath the Lord exactly searched out all your works, and he will put you all to shame.

{16:65} And when your sins are brought forth, ye shall be ashamed before men, and your own sins shall be your accusers in that day.

{16:66} What will ye do? or how will ye hide your sins before God and his angels?

{16:67} Behold, God himself is the judge, fear him: leave off from your sins, and forget your iniquities, to meddle no more with them for ever: so shall God lead you forth, and deliver you from all trouble.

{16:68} For, behold, the burning wrath of a great multitude is kindled over you, and they shall take away certain of you, and feed you, being idle, with things offered unto idols.

{16:69} And they that consent unto them shall be had in derision and in reproach, and trodden under foot.

{16:70} For there shall be in every place, and in the next cities, a great insurrection upon those that fear the Lord.

{16:71} They shall be like mad men, sparing none, but still spoiling and destroying those that fear the Lord.

{16:72} For they shall waste and take away their goods, and cast them out of their houses.

{16:73} Then shall they be known, who are my chosen; and they shall be tried as the gold in the fire.

{16:74} Hear, O ye my beloved, saith the Lord: behold, the days of trouble are at hand, but I will deliver you from the same.

{16:75} Be ye not afraid neither doubt; for God is your guide,

{16:76} And the guide of them who keep my commandments and precepts,
saith the Lord God: let not your sins weigh you down, and let not your iniquities lift up themselves.

{16:77} Woe be unto them that are bound with their sins, and covered with their iniquities like as a field is covered over with bushes, and the path thereof covered with thorns, that no man may travel through! {16:78} It is left undressed, and is cast into the fire to be consumed therewith.

The First Book of the Maccabees

{1:1} And it happened, after that Alexander son of Philip, the Macedonian, who came out of the land of Chettiim, had smitten Darius king of the Persians and Medes, that he reigned in his stead, the first over Greece,

{1:2} And made many wars, and won many strong holds, and slew the kings of the earth,

{1:3} And went through to the ends of the earth, and took spoils of many nations, insomuch that the earth was quiet before him; whereupon he was exalted and his heart was lifted up.

{1:4} And he gathered a mighty strong host and ruled over countries, and nations, and kings, who became tributaries unto him.

{1:5} And after these things he fell sick, and perceived that he should die.

{1:6} Wherefore he called his servants, such as were honourable, and had been brought up with him from his youth, and parted his kingdom among them, while he was yet alive.

{1:7} So Alexander reigned twelve years, and then died.

{1:8} And his servants bare rule everyone in his place.

{1:9} And after his death they all put crowns upon themselves; so did their sons after them many years: and evils were multiplied in the earth.

{1:10} And there came out of them a wicked root Antiochus surnamed Epiphanes, son of Antiochus the king, who had been an hostage at Rome, and he reigned in the hundred and thirty and seventh year of the kingdom of the Greeks.

{1:11} In those days went there out of Israel wicked men, who persuaded many, saying, let us go and make a covenant with the heathen that are round about us: for since we departed from them we have had much sorrow.

{1:12} So this device pleased them well.

{1:13} Then certain of the people were so forward herein, that they went to the king, who gave them licence to do after the ordinances of the heathen:

{1:14} Whereupon they built a place of exercise at Jerusalem according to the customs of the heathen:

{1:15} And made themselves uncircumcised, and forsook the holy covenant, and joined themselves to the heathen, and were sold to do mischief.

{1:16} Now when the kingdom was established before Antiochus, he thought to reign over Egypt that he might have the dominion of two realms.

{1:17} Wherefore he entered into Egypt with a great multitude, with chariots, and elephants, and horsemen, and a great navy,

{1:18} And made war against Ptolemee king of Egypt: but Ptolemee was afraid of him, and fled; and many were wounded to death.

{1:19} Thus they got the strong cities in the land of Egypt and he took the spoils thereof.

{1:20} And after that Antiochus had smitten Egypt, he returned again in the hundred forty and third year, and went up against Israel and Jerusalem with a great multitude,

{1:21} And entered proudly into the sanctuary, and took away the golden altar, and the candlestick of light, and all the vessels thereof,

{1:22} And the table of the shewbread, and the pouring vessels, and the vials. and the censers of gold, and the veil, and the crown, and the golden ornaments that were before the temple, all which he pulled off.

{1:23} He took also the silver and the gold, and the precious vessels: also he took the hidden treasures which he found.

{1:24} And when he had taken all away, he went into his own land, having made a great massacre, and spoken very proudly.

{1:25} Therefore there was a great mourning in Israel, in every place where they were;

{1:26} So that the princes and elders mourned, the virgins and young men were made feeble, and the beauty of women was changed.

{1:27} Every bridegroom took up lamentation, and she that sat in the marriage chamber was in heaviness,

{1:28} The land also was moved for the inhabitants thereof, and all the house of Jacob was covered with confusion.

{1:29} And after two years fully expired the king sent his chief collector of tribute unto the cities of Juda, who came unto Jerusalem with a great multitude,

{1:30} And spake peaceable words unto them, but all was deceit: for when they had given him credence, he fell suddenly upon the city, and smote it very sore, and destroyed much people of Israel.

{1:31} And when he had taken the spoils of the city, he set it on fire, and pulled down the houses and walls thereof on every side.

{1:32} But the women and children took they captive, and possessed the cattle.

{1:33} Then builded they the city of David with a great and strong wall, and with mighty towers, and made it a strong hold for them.

{1:34} And they put therein a sinful nation, wicked men, and fortified themselves therein.

{1:35} They stored it also with armour and victuals, and when they had gathered together the spoils of Jerusalem, they laid them up there, and so they became a sore snare:

{1:36} For it was a place to lie in wait against the sanctuary, and an evil adversary to Israel.

{1:37} Thus they shed innocent blood on every side of the sanctuary, and defiled it:

{1:38} Insomuch that the inhabitants of Jerusalem fled because of them: whereupon the city was made an habitation of strangers, and became strange to those that were born in her; and her own children left her.

{1:39} Her sanctuary was laid waste like a wilderness, her feasts were turned into mourning, her sabbaths into reproach her honour into contempt.

{1:40} As had been her glory, so was her dishonour increased, and her excellency was turned into mourning.

{1:41} Moreover king Antiochus wrote to his whole kingdom, that all should be one people,

{1:42} And everyone should leave his laws: so all the heathen agreed according to the commandment of the king.

{1:43} Yea, many also of the Israelites consented to his religion, and sacrificed unto idols, and profaned the sabbath.

{1:44} For the king had sent letters by messengers unto Jerusalem and the cities of Juda that they should follow the strange laws of the land,

{1:45} And forbid burnt offerings, and sacrifice, and drink offerings, in the temple; and that they should profane the sabbaths and festival days:

{1:46} And pollute the sanctuary and holy people:

{1:47} Set up altars, and groves, and chapels of idols, and sacrifice swine's flesh, and unclean beasts:

{1:48} That they should also leave their children uncircumcised, and make their souls abominable with all manner of uncleanness and profanation:

{1:49} To the end they might forget the law, and change all the ordinances.

{1:50} And whosoever would not do according to the commandment of the king, he said, he should die.

{1:51} In the selfsame manner wrote he to his whole kingdom, and appointed overseers over all the people, commanding the cities of Juda to sacrifice, city by city.

{1:52} Then many of the people were gathered unto them, to wit every one that forsook the law; and so they committed evils in the land;

{1:53} And drove the Israelites into secret places, even wheresoever they could flee for succour.

{1:54} Now the fifteenth day of the month Casleu, in the hundred forty and fifth year, they set up the abomination of desolation upon the altar, and builded idol altars throughout the cities of Juda on every side;

{1:55} And burnt incense at the doors of their houses, and in the streets.

{1:56} And when they had rent in pieces the books of the law which they found, they burnt them with fire.

{1:57} And whosoever was found with any the book of the testament, or if any committed to the law, the king's commandment was, that they should put him to death.

{1:58} Thus did they by their authority unto the Israelites every month, to as many as were found in the cities.

{1:59} Now the five and twentieth day of the month they did sacrifice upon the idol altar, which was upon the altar of God.

{1:60} At which time according to the commandment they put to death certain women, that had caused their children to be circumcised.

{1:61} And they hanged the infants about their necks, and rifled their houses, and slew them that had circumcised them.

{1:62} Howbeit many in Israel were fully resolved and confirmed in themselves not to eat any unclean thing.

{1:63} Wherefore the rather to die, that they might not be defiled with meats, and that they might not profane the holy covenant: so then they died.

{1:64} And there was very great wrath upon Israel.

{2:1} In those days arose Mattathias the son of John, the son of Simeon, a priest of the sons of Joarib, from Jerusalem, and dwelt in Modin.

{2:2} And he had five sons, Joannan, called Caddis:

{2:3} Simon; called Thassi:

{2:4} Judas, who was called Maccabeus:

{2:5} Eleazar, called Avaran: and Jonathan, whose surname was Apphus.

{2:6} And when he saw the blasphemies that were committed in Juda and Jerusalem,

{2:7} He said, Woe is me! wherefore was I born to see this misery of my people, and of the holy city, and to dwell there, when it was delivered into the hand of the enemy, and the sanctuary into the hand of strangers?

{2:8} Her temple is become as a man without glory.

{2:9} Her glorious vessels are carried away into captivity, her infants are slain in the streets, her young men with the sword of the enemy.

{2:10} What nation hath not had a part in her kingdom and gotten of her spoils?

{2:11} All her ornaments are taken away; of a free woman she is become a bond slave.

{2:12} And, behold, our sanctuary, even our beauty and our glory, is laid waste, and the Gentiles have profaned it.

{2:13} To what end therefore shall we live any longer?

{2:14} Then Mattathias and his sons rent their clothes, and put on sackcloth, and mourned very sore.

{2:15} In the mean while the king's officers, such as compelled the people to revolt, came into the city Modin, to make them sacrifice.

{2:16} And when many of Israel came unto them, Mattathias also and his sons came together.

{2:17} Then answered the king's officers, and said to Mattathias on this wise, Thou art a ruler, and an honourable and great man in this city, and strengthened with sons and brethren:

{2:18} Now therefore come thou first, and fulfil the king's commandment, like as all the heathen have done, yea, and the men of Juda also, and such as remain at Jerusalem: so shalt thou and thy house be in the number of the king's friends, and thou and thy children shall be honoured with silver and gold, and many rewards.

{2:19} Then Mattathias answered and spake with a loud voice, Though all the nations that are under the king's dominion obey him, and fall away everyone from the religion of their fathers, and give consent to his commandments:

{2:20} Yet will I and my sons and my brethren walk in the covenant of our fathers.

{2:21} God forbid that we should forsake the law and the ordinances.

{2:22} We will not hearken to the king's words, to go from our religion, either on the right hand, or the left.

{2:23} Now when he had left speaking these words, there came one of the Jews in the sight of all to sacrifice on the altar which was at Modin, according to the king's commandment.

{2:24} Which thing when Mattathias saw, he was inflamed with zeal, and his reins trembled, neither could he forbear to shew his anger according to judgment: wherefore he ran, and slew him upon the altar.

{2:25} Also the king's commissioner, who compelled men to sacrifice, he killed at that time, and the altar he pulled down.

{2:26} Thus dealt he zealously for the law of God like as Phinees did unto Zambri the son of Salom.

{2:27} And Mattathias cried throughout the city with a loud voice, saying, Whosoever is zealous of the law, and maintaineth the covenant, let him follow me.

{2:28} So he and his sons fled into the mountains, and left all that ever they had in the city.

{2:29} Then many that sought after justice and judgment went down into the wilderness, to dwell there:

{2:30} Both they, and their children, and their wives; and their cattle; because afflictions increased sore upon them.

{2:31} Now when it was told the king's servants, and the host that was at Jerusalem, in the city of David, that certain men, who had broken the king's commandment, were gone down into the secret places in the wilderness,

{2:32} They pursued after them a great number, and having overtaken them, they camped against them, and made war against them on the sabbath day.

{2:33} And they said unto them, let that which ye have done hitherto suffice; come forth, and do according to the commandment of the king, and ye shall live.

{2:34} But they said, we will not come forth, neither will we do the king's commandment, to profane the sabbath day.

{2:35} So then they gave them the battle with all speed.

{2:36} Howbeit they answered them not, neither cast they a stone at them, nor stopped the places where they lay hid;

{2:37} But said, let us die all in our innocence: heaven and earth will testify for us, that ye put us to death wrongfully.

{2:38} So they rose up against them in battle on the sabbath, and they slew them, with their wives and children and their cattle, to the number of a thousand people.

{2:39} Now when Mattathias and his friends understood hereof, they mourned for them right sore.

{2:40} And one of them said to another, if we all do as our brethren have done, and fight not for our lives and laws against the heathen, they will now quickly root us out of the earth.

{2:41} At that time therefore they decreed, saying, Whosoever shall come to make battle with us on the sabbath day, we will fight against him; neither will we die all, as our brethren that were murdered im the secret places.

{2:42} Then came there unto him a company of Assideans who were mighty men of Israel, even all such as were voluntarily devoted unto the law.

{2:43} Also all they that fled for persecution joined themselves unto them, and were a stay unto them.

{2:44} So they joined their forces, and smote sinful men in their anger, and wicked men in their wrath: but the rest fled to the heathen for succour.

{2:45} Then Mattathias and his friends went round about, and pulled down the altars:

{2:46} And what children soever they found within the coast of Israel uncircumcised, those they circumcised valiantly.

{2:47} They pursued also after the proud men, and the work prospered in their hand.

{2:48} So they recovered the law out of the hand of the Gentiles, and out of the hand of kings, neither suffered they the sinner to triumph.

{2:49} Now when the time drew near that Mattathias should die, he said unto his sons, now hath pride and rebuke gotten strength, and the time of destruction, and the wrath of indignation:

{2:50} Now therefore, my sons, be ye zealous for the law, and give your lives for the covenant of your fathers.

{2:51} Call to remembrance what acts our fathers did in their time; so shall ye receive great honour and an everlasting name.

{2:52} Was not Abraham found faithful in temptation, and it was imputed unto him for righteousness?

{2:53} Joseph in the time of his distress kept the commandment and was made lord of Egypt.

{2:54} Phinees our father in being zealous and fervent obtained the covenant of an everlasting priesthood.

{2:55} Jesus for fulfilling the word was made a judge in Israel.

{2:56} Caleb for bearing witness before the congregation received the heritage of the land.

{2:57} David for being merciful possessed the throne of an everlasting kingdom.

{2:58} Elias for being zealous and fervent for the law was taken up into heaven.

{2:59} Ananias, Azarias, and Misael, by believing were saved out of the flame.

{2:60} Daniel for his innocence was delivered from the mouth of lions.

{2:61} And thus consider ye throughout all ages, that none that put their trust in him shall be overcome.

{2:62} Fear not then the words of a sinful man: for his glory shall be dung and worms.

{2:63} To day he shall be lifted up and tomorrow he shall not be found, because he is returned into his dust, and his thought is come to nothing.

{2:64} Wherefore, ye my sons, be valiant and shew yourselves men in the behalf of the law; for by it shall ye obtain glory.

{2:65} And behold, I know that your brother Simon is a man of counsel, give ear unto him always: he shall be a father unto you.

{2:66} As for Judas Maccabeus, he hath been mighty and strong, even from his youth up: let him be your captain, and fight the battle of the people.

{2:67} Take also unto you all those that observe the law, and avenge ye the wrong of your people.

{2:68} Recompense fully the heathen, and take heed to the commandments of the law.

{2:69} So he blessed them, and was gathered to his fathers.

{2:70} And he died in the hundred forty and sixth year, and his sons buried him in the sepulchres of his fathers at Modin, and all Israel made great lamentation for him.

{3:1} Then his son Judas, called Maccabeus, rose up in his stead.

{3:2} And all his brethren helped him, and so did all they that held with his father, and they fought with cheerfulness the battle of Israel.

{3:3} So he gat his people great honour, and put on a breastplate as a giant, and girt his warlike harness about him, and he made battles, protecting the host with his sword.

{3:4} In his acts he was like a lion, and like a lion's whelp roaring for his prey.

{3:5} For He pursued the wicked, and sought them out, and burnt up those that vexed his people.

{3:6} Wherefore the wicked shrunk for fear of him, and all the workers of iniquity were troubled, because salvation prospered in his hand.

{3:7} He grieved also many kings, and made Jacob glad with his acts, and his memorial is blessed forever.

{3:8} Moreover he went through the cities of Juda, destroying the ungodly out of them, and turning away wrath from Israel:

{3:9} So that he was renowned unto the utmost part of the earth, and he received unto him such as were ready to perish.

{3:10} Then Apollonius gathered the Gentiles together, and a great host out of Samaria, to fight against Israel.

{3:11} Which thing when Judas perceived, he went forth to meet him, and so he smote him, and slew him: many also fell down slain, but the rest fled.

{3:12} Wherefore Judas took their spoils, and Apollonius' sword also, and therewith he fought all his life long.

{3:13} Now when Seron, a prince of the army of Syria, heard say that Judas had gathered unto him a multitude and company of the faithful to go out with him to war;

{3:14} He said, I will get me a name and honour in the kingdom; for I will go fight with Judas and them that are with him, who despise the king's commandment.

{3:15} So he made him ready to go up, and there went with him a mighty host of the ungodly to help him, and to be avenged of the children of Israel.

{3:16} And when he came near to the going up of Bethhoron, Judas went forth to meet him with a small company:

{3:17} Who, when they saw the host coming to meet them, said unto

Judas, how shall we be able, being so few, to fight against so great a multitude and so strong, seeing we are ready to faint with fasting all this day?

{3:18} Unto whom Judas answered, it is no hard matter for many to be shut up in the hands of a few; and with the God of heaven it is all one, to deliver with a great multitude, or a small company:

{3:19} For the victory of battle standeth not in the multitude of an host; but strength cometh from heaven.

{3:20} They come against us in much pride and iniquity to destroy us, and our wives and children, and to spoil us:

{3:21} But we fight for our lives and our laws.

{3:22} Wherefore the Lord himself will overthrow them before our face: and as for you, be ye not afraid of them.

{3:23} Now as soon as he had left off speaking, he leapt suddenly upon them, and so Seron and his host was overthrown before him.

{3:24} And they pursued them from the going down of Bethhoron unto the plain, where were slain about eight hundred men of them; and the residue fled into the land of the Philistines.

{3:25} Then began the fear of Judas and his brethren, and an exceeding great dread, to fall upon the nations round about them:

{3:26} Insomuch as his fame came unto the king, and all nations talked of the battles of Judas.

{3:27} Now when king Antiochus heard these things, he was full of indignation: wherefore he sent and gathered together all the forces of his realm, even a very strong army.

{3:28} He opened also his treasure, and gave his soldiers pay for a year, commanding them to be ready whensoever he should need them.

{3:29} Nevertheless, when he saw that the money of his treasures failed and that the tributes in the country were small, because of the dissension and plague, which he had brought upon the land in taking away the laws which had been of old time;

{3:30} He feared that he should not be able to bear the charges any longer, nor to have such gifts to give so liberally as he did before: for he had abounded above the kings that were before him.

{3:31} Wherefore, being greatly perplexed in his mind, he determined to go into Persia, there to take the tributes of the countries, and to gather much money.

{3:32} So he left Lysias, a nobleman, and one of the blood royal, to oversee the affairs of the king from the river Euphrates unto the borders of Egypt:

{3:33} And to bring up his son Antiochus, until he came again.

{3:34} Moreover he delivered unto him the half of his forces, and the elephants, and gave him charge of all things that he would have done, as also concerning them that dwelt in Juda and Jerusalem:

{3:35} To wit, that he should send an army against them, to destroy and root out the strength of Israel, and the remnant of Jerusalem, and to take away their memorial from that place;

{3:36} And that he should place strangers in all their quarters, and divide their land by lot.

{3:37} So the king took the half of the forces that remained, and departed from Antioch, his royal city, the hundred forty and seventh year; and having passed the river Euphrates, he went through the high countries.

{3:38} Then Lysias chose Ptolemee the son of Dorymenes, Nicanor, and

Gorgias, mighty men of the king's friends:

{3:39} And with them he sent forty thousand footmen, and seven thousand horsemen, to go into the land of Juda, and to destroy it, as the king commanded.

{3:40} So they went forth with all their power, and came and pitched by Emmaus in the plain country.

{3:41} And the merchants of the country, hearing the fame of them, took silver and gold very much, with servants, and came into the camp to buy the children of Israel for slaves: a power also of Syria and of the land of the Philistines joined themselves unto them.

{3:42} Now when Judas and his brethren saw that miseries were multiplied, and that the forces did encamp themselves in their borders: for they knew how the king had given commandment to destroy the people, and utterly abolish them;

{3:43} They said one to another, let us restore the decayed fortune of our people, and let us fight for our people and the sanctuary.

{3:44} Then was the congregation gathered together, that they might be ready for battle, and that they might pray, and ask mercy and compassion.

{3:45} Now Jerusalem lay void as a wilderness, there was none of her children that went in or out: the sanctuary also was trodden down, and aliens kept the strong hold; the heathen had their habitation in that place; and joy was taken from Jacob, and the pipe with the harp ceased.

{3:46} Wherefore the Israelites assembled themselves together, and came to Maspha, over against Jerusalem; for in Maspha was the place where they prayed aforetime in Israel.

{3:47} Then they fasted that day, and put on sackcloth, and cast ashes upon their heads, and rent their clothes,

{3:48} And laid open the book of the law, wherein the heathen had sought to paint the likeness of their images.

{3:49} They brought also the priests' garments, and the firstfruits, and the tithes: and the Nazarites they stirred up, who had accomplished their days.

{3:50} Then cried they with a loud voice toward heaven, saying, What shall we do with these, and whither shall we carry them away?

{3:51} For thy sanctuary is trodden down and profaned, and thy priests are in heaviness, and brought low.

{3:52} And lo, the heathen are assembled together against us to destroy us: what things they imagine against us, thou knowest.

{3:53} How shall we be able to stand against them, except thou, O God, be our help?

{3:54} Then sounded they with trumpets, and cried with a loud voice.

{3:55} And after this Judas ordained captains over the people, even captains over thousands, and over hundreds, and over fifties, and over tens.

{3:56} But as for such as were building houses, or had betrothed wives, or were planting vineyards, or were fearful, those he commanded that they should return, every man to his own house, according to the law.

{3:57} So the camp removed, and pitched upon the south side of Emmaus.

{3:58} And Judas said, arm yourselves, and be valiant men, and see that ye be in readiness against the morning, that ye may fight with these nations, that are assembled together against us to destroy us and our sanctuary:

{3:59} For it is better for us to die in battle, than to behold the calamities of our people and our sanctuary.

{3:60} Nevertheless, as the will of God is in heaven, so let him do.

{4:1} Then took Gorgias five thousand footmen, and a thousand of the best horsemen, and removed out of the camp by night;

{4:2} To the end he might rush in upon the camp of the Jews, and smite them suddenly. And the men of the fortress were his guides.

{4:3} Now when Judas heard thereof he himself removed, and the valiant men with him, that he might smite the king's army which was at Emmaus,

{4:4} While as yet the forces were dispersed from the camp.

{4:5} In the mean season came Gorgias by night into the camp of Judas: and when he found no man there, he sought them in the mountains: for said he, these fellows flee from us

{4:6} But as soon as it was day, Judas shewed himself in the plain with three thousand men, who nevertheless had neither armour nor swords to their minds.

{4:7} And they saw the camp of the heathen, that it was strong and well harnessed, and compassed round about with horsemen; and these were expert of war.

{4:8} Then said Judas to the men that were with him, Fear ye not their multitude, neither be ye afraid of their assault.

{4:9} Remember how our fathers were delivered in the Red sea, when Pharaoh pursued them with an army.

{4:10} Now therefore let us cry unto heaven, if peradventure the Lord will have mercy upon us, and remember the covenant of our fathers, and destroy this host before our face this day:

{4:11} That so all the heathen may know that there is one who delivereth and saveth Israel.

{4:12} Then the strangers lifted up their eyes, and saw them coming over against them.

{4:13} Wherefore they went out of the camp to battle; but they that were with Judas sounded their trumpets.

{4:14} So they joined battle, and the heathen being discomfited fled into the plain.

{4:15} Howbeit all the hindmost of them were slain with the sword: for they pursued them unto Gazera, and unto the plains of Idumea, and Azotus, and Jamnia, so that there were slain of them upon a three thousand men.

{4:16} This done, Judas returned again with his host from pursuing them,

{4:17} And said to the people, Be not greedy of the spoil inasmuch as there is a battle before us,

{4:18} And Gorgias and his host are here by us in the mountain: but stand ye now against our enemies, and overcome them, and after this ye may boldly take the spoils.

{4:19} As Judas was yet speaking these words, there appeared a part of them looking out of the mountain:

{4:20} Who when they perceived that the Jews had put their host to flight and were burning the tents; for the smoke that was seen declared what was done:

{4:21} When therefore they perceived these things, they were sore afraid, and seeing also the host of Judas in the plain ready to fight,

{4:22} They fled everyone into the land of strangers.

{4:23} Then Judas returned to spoil the tents, where they got much gold, and silver, and blue silk, and purple of the sea, and great riches.

{4:24} After this they went home, and sung a song of thanksgiving, and praised the Lord in heaven: because it is good, because his mercy endureth forever.

{4:25} Thus Israel had a great deliverance that day.

{4:26} Now all the strangers that had escaped came and told Lysias what had happened:

{4:27} Who, when he heard thereof, was confounded and discouraged, because neither such things as he would were done unto Israel, nor such things as the king commanded him were come to pass.

{4:28} The next year therefore following Lysias gathered together threescore thousand choice men of foot, and five thousand horsemen, that he might subdue them.

{4:29} So they came into Idumea, and pitched their tents at Bethsura, and Judas met them with ten thousand men.

{4:30} And when he saw that mighty army, he prayed and said, Blessed art thou, O Saviour of Israel, who didst quell the violence of the mighty man by the hand of thy servant David, and gavest the host of strangers into the hands of Jonathan the son of Saul, and his armourbearer;

{4:31} Shut up this army in the hand of thy people Israel, and let them be confounded in their power and horsemen:

{4:32} Make them to be of no courage, and cause the boldness of their strength to fall away, and let them quake at their destruction:

{4:33} Cast them down with the sword of them that love thee, and let all those that know thy name praise thee with thanksgiving.

{4:34} So they joined battle; and there were slain of the host of Lysias about five thousand men, even before them were they slain.

{4:35} Now when Lysias saw his army put to flight, and the manliness of Judas' soldiers, and how they were ready either to live or die valiantly, he went into Antiochia, and gathered together a company of strangers, and having made his army greater than it was, he purposed to come again into Judea.

{4:36} Then said Judas and his brethren, behold, our enemies are discomfited: let us go up to cleanse and dedicate the sanctuary.

{4:37} Upon this all the host assembled themselves together, and went up into mount Sion.

{4:38} And when they saw the sanctuary desolate, and the altar profaned, and the gates burned up, and shrubs growing in the courts as in a forest, or in one of the mountains, yea, and the priests' chambers pulled down;

{4:39} They rent their clothes, and made great lamentation, and cast ashes upon their heads,

{4:40} And fell down flat to the ground upon their faces, and blew an alarm with the trumpets, and cried toward heaven.

{4:41} Then Judas appointed certain men to fight against those that were in the fortress, until he had cleansed the sanctuary.

{4:42} So he chose priests of blameless conversation, such as had pleasure in the law:

{4:43} Who cleansed the sanctuary, and bare out the defiled stones into an unclean place.

{4:44} And when as they consulted what to do with the altar of burnt offerings, which was profaned;

{4:45} They thought it best to pull it down, lest it should be a reproach to them, because the heathen had defiled it: wherefore they pulled it down,

{4:46} And laid up the stones in the mountain of the temple in a convenient place, until there should come a prophet to shew what should be done with them.

{4:47} Then they took whole stones according to the law, and built a new altar according to the former;

{4:48} And made up the sanctuary, and the things that were within the temple, and hallowed the courts.

{4:49} They made also new holy vessels, and into the temple they brought the candlestick, and the altar of burnt offerings, and of incense, and the table.

{4:50} And upon the altar they burned incense, and the lamps that were upon the candlestick they lighted, that they might give light in the temple.

{4:51} Furthermore they set the loaves upon the table, and spread out the veils, and finished all the works which they had begun to make.

{4:52} Now on the five and twentieth day of the ninth month, which is called the month Casleu, in the hundred forty and eighth year, they rose up betimes in the morning,

{4:53} And offered sacrifice according to the law upon the new altar of burnt offerings, which they had made.

{4:54} Look, at what time and what day the heathen had profaned it, even in that was it dedicated with songs, and citherns, and harps, and cymbals.

{4:55} Then all the people fell upon their faces, worshipping and praising the God of heaven, who had given them good success.

{4:56} And so they kept the dedication of the altar eight days and offered burnt offerings with gladness, and sacrificed the sacrifice of deliverance and praise.

{4:57} They decked also the forefront of the temple with crowns of gold, and with shields; and the gates and the chambers they renewed, and hanged doors upon them.

{4:58} Thus was there very great gladness among the people, for that the reproach of the heathen was put away.

{4:59} Moreover Judas and his brethren with the whole congregation of Israel ordained, that the days of the dedication of the altar should be kept in their season from year to year by the space of eight days, from the five and twentieth day of the month Casleu, with mirth and gladness.

{4:60} At that time also they builded up the mount Sion with high walls and strong towers round about, lest the Gentiles should come and tread it down as they had done before.

{4:61} And they set there a garrison to keep it, and fortified Bethsura to preserve it; that the people might have a defence against Idumea.

{5:1} Now when the nations round about heard that the altar was built and the sanctuary renewed as before, it displeased them very much.

{5:2} Wherefore they thought to destroy the generation of Jacob that was among them, and thereupon they began to slay and destroy the people.

{5:3} Then Judas fought against the children of Esau in Idumea at Arabattine, because they besieged Gael: and he gave them a great overthrow, and abated their courage, and took their spoils.

{5:4} Also he remembered the injury of the children of Bean, who had been a snare and an offence unto the people, in that they lay in wait for them in the ways.

{5:5} He shut them up therefore in the towers, and encamped against them, and destroyed them utterly, and burned the towers of that place with fire, and all that were therein.

{5:6} Afterward he passed over to the children of Ammon, where he found a mighty power, and much people, with Timotheus their captain.

{5:7} So he fought many battles with them, till at length they were discomfited before him; and he smote them.

{5:8} And when he had taken Jazar, with the towns belonging thereto, he returned into Judea.

{5:9} Then the heathen that were at Galaad assembled themselves together against the Israelites that were in their quarters, to destroy them; but they fled to the fortress of Dathema.

{5:10} And sent letters unto Judas and his brethren, The heathen that are round about us are assembled together against us to destroy us:

{5:11} And they are preparing to come and take the fortress whereunto we are fled, Timotheus being captain of their host.

{5:12} Come now therefore, and deliver us from their hands, for many of us are slain:

{5:13} Yea, all our brethren that were in the places of Tobie are put to death: their wives and their children also they have carried away captives, and borne away their stuff; and they have destroyed there about a thousand men.

{5:14} While these letters were yet reading, behold, there came other messengers from Galilee with their clothes rent, who reported on this wise,

{5:15} And said, They of Ptolemais, and of Tyrus, and Sidon, and all Galilee of the Gentiles, are assembled together against us to consume us.

{5:16} Now when Judas and the people heard these words, there assembled a great congregation together, to consult what they should do for their brethren, that were in trouble, and assaulted of them.

{5:17} Then said Judas unto Simon his brother, Choose thee out men, and go and deliver thy brethren that are in Galilee, for I and Jonathan my brother will go into the country of Galaad.

{5:18} So he left Joseph the son of Zacharias, and Azarias, captains of the people, with the remnant of the host in Judea to keep it.

{5:19} Unto whom he gave commandment, saying, Take ye the charge of this people, and see that ye make not war against the heathen until the time that we come again.

{5:20} Now unto Simon were given three thousand men to go into Galilee, and unto Judas eight thousand men for the country of Galaad.

{5:21} Then went Simon into Galilee, where he fought many battles with the heathen, so that the heathen were discomfited by him.

{5:22} And he pursued them unto the gate of Ptolemais; and there were slain of the heathen about three thousand men, whose spoils he took.

{5:23} And those that were in Galilee, and in Arbattis, with their wives and their children, and all that they had, took he away with him, and brought them into Judea with great joy.

{5:24} Judas Maccabeus also and his brother Jonathan went over Jordan, and travelled three days' journey in the wilderness,

{5:25} Where they met with the Nabathites, who came unto them in a peaceable manner, and told them everything that had happened to their brethren in the land of Galaad:

{5:26} And how that many of them were shut up in Bosora, and Bosor, and Alema, Casphor, Maked, and Carnaim; all these cities are strong and great:

{5:27} And that they were shut up in the rest of the cities of the country of Galaad, and that against tomorrow they had appointed to bring their host against the forts, and to take them, and to destroy them all in one day.

{5:28} Hereupon Judas and his host turned suddenly by the way of the wilderness unto Bosora; and when he had won the city, he slew all the males with the edge of the sword, and took all their spoils, and burned the city with fire,

{5.29} From whence he removed by night, and went till he came to the fortress.

{5:30} And betimes in the morning they looked up, and, behold, there was an innumerable people bearing ladders and other engines of war, to take the fortress: for they assaulted them.

{5:31} When Judas therefore saw that the battle was begun, and that the cry of the city went up to heaven, with trumpets, and a great sound,

{5:32} He said unto his host, Fight this day for your brethren.

{5:33} So he went forth behind them in three companies, who sounded their trumpets, and cried with prayer.

{5:34} Then the host of Timotheus, knowing that it was Maccabeus, fled from him: wherefore he smote them with a great slaughter; so that there were killed of them that day about eight thousand men.

{5:35} This done, Judas turned aside to Maspha; and after he had assaulted it he took and slew all the males therein, and received the spoils thereof and and burnt it with fire.

{5:36} From thence went he, and took Casphon, Maged, Bosor, and the other cities of the country of Galaad.

{5:37} After these things gathered Timotheus another host and encamped against Raphon beyond the brook.

{5:38} So Judas sent men to espy the host, who brought him word, saying, All the heathen that be round about us are assembled unto them, even a very great host.

{5:39} He hath also hired the Arabians to help them and they have pitched their tents beyond the brook, ready to come and fight against thee. Upon this Judas went to meet them.

{5:40} Then Timotheus said unto the captains of his host, When Judas and his host come near the brook, if he pass over first unto us, we shall not be able to withstand him; for he will mightily prevail against us:

{5:41} But if he be afraid, and camp beyond the river, we shall go over unto him, and prevail against him.

{5:42} Now when Judas came near the brook, he caused the scribes of the people to remain by the brook: unto whom he gave commandment, saying, suffer no man to remain in the camp, but let all come to the battle.

{5:43} So he went first over unto them, and all the people after him: then all the heathen, being discomfited before him, cast away their weapons, and fled unto the temple that was at Carnaim.

{5:44} But they took the city, and burned the temple with all that were therein. Thus was Carnaim subdued, neither could they stand any longer before Judas.

{5:45} Then Judas gathered together all the Israelites that were in the country of Galaad, from the least unto the greatest, even their wives, and their children, and their stuff, a very great host, to the end they might come into the land of Judea.

{5:46} Now when they came unto Ephron, (this was a great city in the way as they should go, very well fortified) they could not turn from it, either on the right hand or the left, but must needs pass through the midst of it.

{5:47} Then they of the city shut them out, and stopped up the gates with stones.

{5:48} Whereupon Judas sent unto them in peaceable manner, saying, Let us pass through your land to go into our own country, and none shall do you any hurt; we will only pass through on foot: howbeit they would not open unto him.

{5:49} Wherefore Judas commanded a proclamation to be made

throughout the host, that every man should pitch his tent in the place where he was.

{5:50} So the soldiers pitched, and assaulted the city all that day and all that night, till at the length the city was delivered into his hands:

{5:51} Who then slew all the males with the edge of the sword, and rased the city, and took the spoils thereof, and passed through the city over them that were slain.

{5:52} After this went they over Jordan into the great plain before Bethsan.

{5:53} And Judas gathered together those that came behind, and exhorted the people all the way through, till they came into the land of Judea.

{5:54} So they went up to mount Sion with joy and gladness, where they offered burnt offerings, because not one of them were slain until they had returned in peace.

{5:55} Now what time as Judas and Jonathan were in the land of Galaad, and Simon his brother in Galilee before Ptolemais,

{5:56} Joseph the son of Zacharias, and Azarias, captains of the garrisons, heard of the valiant acts and warlike deeds which they had done.

{5:57} Wherefore they said, Let us also get us a name, and go fight against the heathen that are round about us.

{5:58} So when they had given charge unto the garrison that was with them, they went toward Jamnia.

{5:59} Then came Gorgias and his men out of the city to fight against them.

{5:60} And so it was, that Joseph and Azaras were put to flight, and pursued unto the borders of Judea: and there were slain that day of the people of Israel about two thousand men.

{5:61} Thus was there a great overthrow among the children of Israel, because they were not obedient unto Judas and his brethren, but thought to do some valiant act.

{5:62} Moreover these men came not of the seed of those, by whose hand deliverance was given unto Israel.

{5:63} Howbeit the man Judas and his brethren were greatly renowned in the sight of all Israel, and of all the heathen, wheresoever their name was heard of;

{5:64} Insomuch as the the people assembled unto them with joyful acclamations.

{5:65} Afterward went Judas forth with his brethren, and fought against the children of Esau in the land toward the south, where he smote Hebron, and the towns thereof, and pulled down the fortress of it, and burned the towers thereof round about.

{5:66} From thence he removed to go into the land of the Philistines, and passed through Samaria.

{5:67} At that time certain priests, desirous to shew their valour, were slain in battle, for that they went out to fight unadvisedly.

{5:68} So Judas turned to Azotus in the land of the Philistines, and when he had pulled down their altars, and burned their carved images with fire, and spoiled their cities, he returned into the land of Judea.

{6:1} About that time king Antiochus travelling through the high countries heard say, that Elymais in the country of Persia was a city greatly renowned for riches, silver, and gold;

{6:2} And that there was in it a very rich temple, wherein were coverings of gold, and breastplates, and shields, which Alexander, son of Philip, the Macedonian king, who reigned first among the Grecians, had left there.

{6:3} Wherefore he came and sought to take the city, and to spoil it; but he was not able, because they of the city, having had warning thereof,

{6:4} Rose up against him in battle: so he fled, and departed thence with great heaviness, and returned to Babylon.

{6:5} Moreover there came one who brought him tidings into Persia, that the armies, which went against the land of Judea, were put to flight:

{6:6} And that Lysias, who went forth first with a great power was driven away of the Jews; and that they were made strong by the armour, and power, and store of spoils, which they had gotten of the armies, whom they had destroyed:

{6:7} Also that they had pulled down the abomination, which he had set up upon the altar in Jerusalem, and that they had compassed about the sanctuary with high walls, as before, and his city Bethsura.

{6:8} Now when the king heard these words, he was astonished and sore moved: whereupon he laid him down upon his bed, and fell sick for grief, because it had not befallen him as he looked for.

{6:9} And there he continued many days: for his grief was ever more and more, and he made account that he should die.

{6:10} Wherefore he called for all his friends, and said unto them, The sleep is gone from mine eyes, and my heart faileth for very care.

{6:11} And I thought with myself, into what tribulation am I come, and how great a flood of misery is it, wherein now I am! for I was bountiful and beloved in my power.

{6:12} But now I remember the evils that I did at Jerusalem, and that I took all the vessels of gold and silver that were therein, and sent to destroy the inhabitants of Judea without a cause.

{6:13} I perceive therefore that for this cause these troubles are come upon me, and, behold, I perish through great grief in a strange land.

{6:14} Then called he for Philip, one of his friends, who he made ruler over all his realm,

{6:15} And gave him the crown, and his robe, and his signet, to the end he should bring up his son Antiochus, and nourish him up for the kingdom.

{6:16} So king Antiochus died there in the hundred forty and ninth year.

{6:17} Now when Lysias knew that the king was dead, he set up Antiochus his son, whom he had brought up being young, to reign in his stead, and his name he called Eupator.

{6:18} About this time they that were in the tower shut up the Israelites round about the sanctuary, and sought always their hurt, and the strengthening of the heathen.

{6:19} Wherefore Judas, purposing to destroy them, called all the people together to besiege them.

{6:20} So they came together, and besieged them in the hundred and fiftieth year, and he made mounts for shot against them, and other engines.

{6:21} Howbeit certain of them that were besieged got forth, unto whom some ungodly men of Israel joined themselves:

{6:22} And they went unto the king, and said, How long will it be ere thou execute judgment, and avenge our brethren?

{6:23} We have been willing to serve thy father, and to do as he would have us, and to obey his commandments;

{6:24} For which cause they of our nation besiege the tower, and are alienated from us: moreover as many of us as they could light on they slew, and spoiled our inheritance.

{6:25} Neither have they stretched out their hand against us only, but also against their borders.

{6:26} And, behold, this day are they besieging the tower at Jerusalem, to take it: the sanctuary also and Bethsura have they fortified.

{6:27} Wherefore if thou dost not prevent them quickly, they will do the greater things than these, neither shalt thou be able to rule them.

{6:28} Now when the king heard this, he was angry, and gathered together all his friends, and the captains of his army, and those that had charge of the horse.

{6:29} There came also unto him from other kingdoms, and from isles of the sea, bands of hired soldiers.

{6:30} So that the number of his army was an hundred thousand footmen, and twenty thousand horsemen, and two and thirty elephants exercised in battle.

{6:31} These went through Idumea, and pitched against Bethsura, which they assaulted many days, making engines of war; but they of Bethsura came out, and burned them with fire, and fought valiantly.

{6:32} Upon this Judas removed from the tower, and pitched in Bathzacharias, over against the king's camp.

{6:33} Then the king rising very early marched fiercely with his host toward Bathzacharias, where his armies made them ready to battle, and sounded the trumpets.

{6:34} And to the end they might provoke the elephants to fight, they shewed them the blood of grapes and mulberries.

{6:35} Moreover they divided the beasts among the armies, and for every elephant they appointed a thousand men, armed with coats of mail, and with helmets of brass on their heads; and beside this, for every beast were ordained five hundred horsemen of the best.

{6:36} These were ready at every occasion: wheresoever the beast was, and whithersoever the beast went, they went also, neither departed they from him.

{6:37} And upon the beasts were there strong towers of wood, which covered every one of them, and were girt fast unto them with devices: there were also upon everyone two and thirty strong men, that fought upon them, beside the Indian that ruled him.

{6:38} As for the remnant of the horsemen, they set them on this side and that side at the two parts of the host giving them signs what to do, and being harnessed all over amidst the ranks.

{6:39} Now when the sun shone upon the shields of gold and brass, the mountains glistered therewith, and shined like lamps of fire.

{6:40} So part of the king's army being spread upon the high mountains, and part on the valleys below, they marched on safely and in order.

{6:41} Wherefore all that heard the noise of their multitude, and the marching of the company, and the rattling of the harness, were moved: for the army was very great and mighty.

{6:42} Then Judas and his host drew near, and entered into battle, and there were slain of the king's army six hundred men.

{6:43} Eleazar also, surnamed Savaran, perceiving that one of the beasts, armed with royal harness, was higher than all the rest, and supposing that the king was upon him,

{6:44} Put himself in jeopardy, to the end he might deliver his people, and get him a perpetual name:

{6:45} Wherefore he ran upon him courageously through the midst of the battle, slaying on the right hand and on the left, so that they were divided from him on both sides.

{6:46} Which done, he crept under the elephant, and thrust him under, and slew him: whereupon the elephant fell down upon him, and there he died.

{6:47} Howbeit the rest of the Jews seeing the strength of the king, and the violence of his forces, turned away from them.

{6:48} Then the king's army went up to Jerusalem to meet them, and the king pitched his tents against Judea, and against mount Sion.

{6:49} But with them that were in Bethsura he made peace: for they came out of the city, because they had no victuals there to endure the siege, it being a year of rest to the land.

{6:50} So the king took Bethsura, and set a garrison there to keep it.

{6:51} As for the sanctuary, he besieged it many days: and set there artillery with engines and instruments to cast fire and stones, and pieces to cast darts and slings.

{6:52} Whereupon they also made engines against their engines, and held them battle a long season.

{6:53} Yet at the last, their vessels being without victuals, (for that it was the seventh year, and they in Judea that were delivered from the Gentiles, had eaten up the residue of the store;)

{6:54} There were but a few left in the sanctuary, because the famine did so prevail against them, that they were fain to disperse themselves, every man to his own place.

{6:55} At that time Lysias heard say, that Philip, whom Antiochus the king, whiles he lived, had appointed to bring up his son Antiochus, that he might be king,

{6:56} Was returned out of Persia and Media, and the king's host also that went with him, and that he sought to take unto him the ruling of the affairs.

{6:57} Wherefore he went in all haste, and said to the king and the captains of the host and the company, we decay daily, and our victuals are but small, and the place we lay siege unto is strong, and the affairs of the kingdom lie upon us:

{6:58} Now therefore let us be friends with these men, and make peace with them, and with all their nation;

{6:59} And covenant with them, that they shall live after their laws, as they did before: for they are therefore displeased, and have done all these things, because we abolished their laws.

{6:60} So the king and the princes were content: wherefore he sent unto them to make peace; and they accepted thereof.

{6:61} Also the king and the princes made an oath unto them: whereupon they went out of the strong hold.

{6:62} Then the king entered into mount Sion; but when he saw the strength of the place, he broke his oath that he had made, and gave commandment to pull down the wall round about.

{6:63} Afterward departed he in all haste, and returned unto Antiochia, where he found Philip to be master of the city: so he fought against him, and took the city by force.

{7:1} In the hundred and one and fiftieth year Demetrius the son of Seleucus departed from Rome, and came up with a few men unto a city of the sea coast, and reigned there.

{7:2} And as he entered into the palace of his ancestors, so it was, that his forces had taken Antiochus and Lysias, to bring them unto him.

{7:3} Wherefore, when he knew it, he said, let me not see their faces.

{7:4} So his host slew them. Now when Demetrius was set upon the throne of his kingdom,

{7:5} There came unto him all the wicked and ungodly men of Israel, having Alcimus, who was desirous to be high priest, for their captain:

{7:6} And they accused the people to the king, saying, Judas and his brethren have slain all thy friends, and driven us out of our own land.

{7.7} Now therefore send some man whom thou trustest, and let him go and see what havock he hath made among us, and in the king's land, and let him punish them with all them that aid them.

{7:8} Then the king chose Bacchides, a friend of the king, who ruled beyond the flood, and was a great man in the kingdom, and faithful to the king,

{7:9} And him he sent with that wicked Alcimus, whom he made high priest, and commanded that he should take vengeance of the children of Israel.

{7:10} So they departed, and came with a great power into the land of Judea, where they sent messengers to Judas and his brethren with peaceable words deceitfully.

{7:11} But they gave no heed to their words; for they saw that they were come with a great power.

{7:12} Then did there assemble unto Alcimus and Bacchides a company of scribes, to require justice.

{7:13} Now the Assideans were the first among the children of Israel that sought peace of them:

{7:14} For said they, one that is a priest of the seed of Aaron is come with this army, and he will do us no wrong.

{7:15} So he spake unto them, peaceably, and swore unto them, saying, we will procure the harm neither of you nor your friends.

{7:16} Whereupon they believed him: howbeit he took of them threescore men, and slew them in one day, according to the words which he wrote,

{7:17} The flesh of thy saints have they cast out, and their blood have they shed round about Jerusalem, and there was none to bury them.

{7:18} Wherefore the fear and dread of them fell upon all the people, who said, there is neither truth nor righteousness in them; for they have broken the covenant and oath that they made.

{7:19} After this, removed Bacchides from Jerusalem, and pitched his tents in Bezeth, where he sent and took many of the men that had forsaken him, and certain of the people also, and when he had slain them, he cast them into the great pit.

{7:20} Then committed he the country to Alcimus, and left with him a power to aid him: so Bacchides went to the king.

{7:21} But Alcimus contended for the high priesthood.

{7:22} And unto him resorted all such as troubled the people, who, after they had gotten the land of Juda into their power, did much hurt in Israel.

{7:23} Now when Judas saw all the mischief that Alcimus and his company had done among the Israelites, even above the heathen,

{7:24} He went out into all the coasts of Judea round about, and took vengeance of them that had revolted from him, so that they durst no more go forth into the country.

{7:25} On the other side, when Alcimus saw that Judas and his company had gotten the upper hand, and knew that he was not able to abide their force, he went again to the king, and said all the worst of them that he could.

{7:26} Then the king sent Nicanor, one of his honourable princes, a man that bare deadly hate unto Israel, with commandment to destroy the people.

{7:27} So Nicanor came to Jerusalem with a great force; and sent unto Judas and his brethren deceitfully with friendly words, saying,

{7:28} Let there be no battle between me and you; I will come with a few men, that I may see you in peace.

{7:29} He came therefore to Judas, and they saluted one another peaceably. Howbeit the enemies were prepared to take away Judas by violence.

{7:30} Which thing after it was known to Judas, to wit, that he came unto him with deceit, he was sore afraid of him, and would see his face no more.

{7:31} Nicanor also, when he saw that his counsel was discovered, went out to fight against Judas beside Capharsalama:

{7:32} Where there were slain of Nicanor's side about five thousand men, and the rest fled into the city of David.

{7:33} After this went Nicanor up to mount Sion, and there came out of the sanctuary certain of the priests and certain of the elders of the people, to salute him peaceably, and to shew him the burnt sacrifice that was offered for the king.

{7:34} But he mocked them, and laughed at them, and abused them shamefully, and spake proudly,

{7:35} And sware in his wrath, saying, Unless Judas and his host be now delivered into my hands, if ever I come again in safety, I will burn up this house: and with that he went out in a great rage.

{7:36} Then the priests entered in, and stood before the altar and the temple, weeping, and saying,

{7:37} Thou, O Lord, didst choose this house to be called by thy name, and to be a house of prayer and petition for thy people:

{7:38} Be avenged of this man and his host, and let them fall by the sword: remember their blasphemies, and suffer them not to continue any longer.

{7:39} So Nicanor went out of Jerusalem, and pitched his tents in Bethhoron, where an host out of Syria met him.

{7:40} But Judas pitched in Adasa with three thousand men, and there he prayed, saying,

{7:41} O Lord, when they that were sent from the king of the Assyrians blasphemed, thine angel went out, and smote an hundred fourscore and five thousand of them.

{7:42} Even so destroy thou this host before us this day, that the rest may know that he hath spoken blasphemously against thy sanctuary, and judge thou him according to his wickedness.

{7:43} So the thirteenth day of the month Adar the hosts joined battle: but Nicanor's host was discomfited, and he himself was first slain in the battle.

{7:44} Now when Nicanor's host saw that he was slain, they cast away their weapons, and fled.

{7:45} Then they pursued after them a day's journey, from Adasa unto Gazera, sounding an alarm after them with their trumpets.

{7:46} Whereupon they came forth out of all the towns of Judea round about, and closed them in; so that they, turning back upon them that pursued them, were all slain with the sword, and not one of them was left.

{7:47} Afterwards they took the spoils, and the prey, and smote off Nicanors head, and his right hand, which he stretched out so proudly, and brought them away, and hanged them up toward Jerusalem.

{7:48} For this cause the people rejoiced greatly, and they kept that day a day of great gladness.

{7:49} Moreover they ordained to keep yearly this day, being the thirteenth of Adar.

{7:50} Thus the land of Juda was in rest a little while.

{8:1} Now Judas had heard of the the Romans, that they were mighty and valiant men, and such as would lovingly accept all that joined themselves unto them, and make a league of amity with all that came unto them;

{8:2} And that they were men of great valour. It was told him also of their wars and noble acts which they had done among the Galatians, and how they had conquered them, and brought them under tribute;

{8:3} And what they had done in the country of Spain, for the winning of the mines of the silver and gold which is there;

{8:4} And that by their policy and patience they had conquered all the place, though it were very far from them; and the kings also that came against them from the uttermost part of the earth, till they had discomfited them, and given them a great overthrow, so that the rest did give them tribute every year:

{8:5} Beside this, how they had discomfited in battle Philip, and Perseus, king of the Citims, with others that lifted up themselves against them, and had overcome them:

{8:6} How also Antiochus the great king of Asia, that came against them in battle, having an hundred and twenty elephants, with horsemen, and chariots, and a very great army, was discomfited by them;

{8:7} And how they took him alive, and covenanted that he and such as reigned after him should pay a great tribute, and give hostages, and that which was agreed upon,

{8:8} And the country of India, and Media and Lydia and of the goodliest countries, which they took of him, and gave to king Eumenes:

{8:9} Moreover how the Grecians had determined to come and destroy them;

{8:10} And that they, having knowledge thereof sent against them a certain captain, and fighting with them slew many of them, and carried away captives their wives and their children, and spoiled them, and took possession of their lands, and pulled down their strong holds, and brought them to be their servants unto this day:

{8:11} It was told him besides, how they destroyed and brought under their dominion all other kingdoms and isles that at any time resisted them;

{8:12} But with their friends and such as relied upon them they kept amity: and that they had conquered kingdoms both far and nigh, insomuch as all that heard of their name were afraid of them:

{8:13} Also that, whom they would help to a kingdom, those reign; and whom again they would, they displace: finally, that they were greatly exalted:

{8:14} Yet for all this none of them wore a crown or was clothed in purple, to be magnified thereby:

{8:15} Moreover how they had made for themselves a senate house, wherein three hundred and twenty men sat in council daily, consulting alway for the people, to the end they might be well ordered:

{8:16} And that they committed their government to one man every year, who ruled over all their country, and that all were obedient to that one, and that there was neither envy nor emmulation among them.

{8:17} In consideration of these things, Judas chose Eupolemus the son of John, the son of Accos, and Jason the son of Eleazar, and sent them to Rome, to make a league of amity and confederacy with them,

{8:18} And to intreat them that they would take the yoke from them; for they saw that the kingdom of the Grecians did oppress Israel with servitude.

{8:19} They went therefore to Rome, which was a very great journey, and came into the senate, where they spake and said.

{8:20} Judas Maccabeus with his brethren, and the people of the Jews, have sent us unto you, to make a confederacy and peace with you, and that we might be registered your confederates and friends.

{8:21} So that matter pleased the Romans well.

{8:22} And this is the copy of the epistle which the senate wrote back again in tables of brass, and sent to Jerusalem, that there they might have by them a memorial of peace and confederacy:

{8:23} Good success be to the Romans, and to the people of the Jews, by sea and by land for ever: the sword also and enemy be far from them,

{8:24} If there come first any war upon the Romans or any of their confederates throughout all their dominion,

{8:25} The people of the Jews shall help them, as the time shall be appointed, with all their heart:

{0:26} Neither shall they give any thing unto them that make war upon them, or aid them with victuals, weapons, money, or ships, as it hath seemed good unto the Romans; but they shall keep their covenants without taking any thing therefore.

{8:27} In the same manner also, if war come first upon the nation of the Jews, the Romans shall help them with all their heart, according as the time shall be appointed them:

{8:28} Neither shall victuals be given to them that take part against them, or weapons, or money, or ships, as it hath seemed good to the Romans; but they shall keep their covenants, and that without deceit.

{8:29} According to these articles did the Romans make a covenant with the people of the Jews.

{8:30} Howbeit if hereafter the one party or the other shall think to meet to add or diminish any thing, they may do it at their pleasures, and whatsoever they shall add or take away shall be ratified.

{8:31} And as touching the evils that Demetrius doeth to the Jews, we have written unto him, saying, wherefore thou made thy yoke heavy upon our friends and confederates the Jews?

{8:32} If therefore they complain any more against thee, we will do them justice, and fight with thee by sea and by land.

{9:1} Furthermore, when Demetrius heard the Nicanor and his host were slain in battle, he sent Bacchides and Alcimus into the land of Judea the second time, and with them the chief strength of his host:

{9:2} Who went forth by the way that leadeth to Galgala, and pitched their tents before Masaloth, which is in Arbela, and after they had won it, they slew much people.

{9:3} Also the first month of the hundred fifty and second year they encamped before Jerusalem:

{9:4} From whence they removed, and went to Berea, with twenty thousand footmen and two thousand horsemen.

{9:5} Now Judas had pitched his tents at Eleasa, and three thousand chosen men with him:

{9:6} Who seeing the multitude of the other army to he so great were sore afraid; whereupon many conveyed themselves out of the host, insomuch as abode of them no more but eight hundred men.

{9:7} When Judas therefore saw that his host slipt away, and that the battle pressed upon him, he was sore troubled in mind, and much distressed, for that he had no time to gather them together.

{9:8} Nevertheless unto them that remained he said, Let us arise and go up against our enemies, if peradventure we may be able to fight with them.

{9:9} But they dehorted him, saying, we shall never be able: let us now rather save our lives, and hereafter we will return with our brethren, and fight against them: for we are but few.

{9:10} Then Judas said, God forbid that I should do this thing, and flee away from them: if our time be come, let us die manfully for our brethren, and let us not stain our honour.

{9:11} With that the host of Bacchides removed out of their tents, and stood over against them, their horsemen being divided into two troops, and their slingers and archers going before the host and they that marched in the foreward were all mighty men.

{9:12} As for Bacchides, he was in the right wing: so the host drew near on the two parts, and sounded their trumpets.

{9:13} They also of Judas' side, even they sounded their trumpets also, so that the earth shook at the noise of the armies, and the battle continued from morning till night.

{9:14} Now when Judas perceived that Bacchides and the strength of his army were on the right side, he took with him all the hardy men,

{9:15} Who discomfited the right wing, and pursued them unto the mount Azotus.

{9:16} But when they of the left wing saw that they of the right wing were discomfited, they followed upon Judas and those that were with him hard at the heels from behind:

{9:17} Whereupon there was a sore battle, insomuch as many were slain on both parts.

{9:18} Judas also was killed, and the remnant fled.

{9:19} THen Jonathan and Simon took Judas their brother, and buried him in the sepulchre of his fathers in Modin.

{9:20} Moreover they bewailed him, and all Israel made great lamentation for him, and mourned many days, saying,

{9:21} How is the valiant man fallen, that delivered Israel!

{9:22} As for the other things concerning Judas and his wars, and the noble acts which he did, and his greatness, they are not written:

for they were very many.

{9:23} Now after the death of Judas the wicked began to put forth their heads in all the coasts of Israel, and there arose up all such as wrought iniquity.

{9:24} In those days also was there a very great famine, by reason whereof the country revolted, and went with them.

{9:25} Then Bacchides chose the wicked men, and made them lords of the country.

{9:26} And they made enquiry and search for Judas' friends, and brought them unto Bacchides, who took vengeance of them, and used them despitefully.

{9:27} So was there a great affliction in Israel, the like whereof was not since the time that a prophet was not seen among them.

{9:28} For this cause all Judas' friends came together, and said unto Jonathan,

{9:29} Since thy brother Judas died, we have no man like him to go forth against our enemies, and Bacchides, and against them of our nation that are adversaries to us.

{9:30} Now therefore we have chosen thee this day to be our prince and captain in his stead, that thou mayest fight our battles.

{9:31} Upon this Jonathan took the governance upon him at that time, and rose up instead of his brother Judas.

{9:32} But when Bacchides gat knowledge thereof, he sought for to slay him

{9:33} Then Jonathan, and Simon his brother, and all that were with him, perceiving that, fled into the wilderness of Thecoe, and pitched their tents by the water of the pool Asphar.

{9:34} Which when Bacchides understood, he came near to Jordan with all his host upon the sabbath day.

{9:35} Now Jonathan had sent his brother John, a captain of the people, to pray his friends the Nabathites, that they might leave with them their carriage, which was much.

{9:36} But the children of Jambri came out of Medaba, and took John, and all that he had, and went their way with it.

{9:37} After this came word to Jonathan and Simon his brother, that the children of Jambri made a great marriage, and were bringing the bride from Nadabatha with a great train, as being the daughter of one of the great princes of Chanaan.

{9:38} Therefore they remembered John their brother, and went up, and hid themselves under the covert of the mountain:

{9:39} Where they lifted up their eyes, and looked, and, behold, there was much ado and great carriage: and the bridegroom came forth, and his friends and brethren, to meet them with drums, and instruments of musick, and many weapons.

{9:40} Then Jonathan and they that were with him rose up against them from the place where they lay in ambush, and made a slaughter of them in such sort, as many fell down dead, and the remnant fled into the mountain, and they took all their spoils.

{9:41} Thus was the marriage turned into mourning, and the noise of their melody into lamentation.

{9:42} So when they had avenged fully the blood of their brother, they turned again to the marsh of Jordan.

{9:43} Now when Bacchides heard hereof, he came on the sabbath day unto the banks of Jordan with a great power.

{9:44} Then Jonathan said to his company, let us go up now and fight for our lives, for it standeth not with us today, as in time past:

{9:45} For, behold, the battle is before us and behind us, and the water of Jordan on this side and that side, the marsh likewise and wood, neither is there place for us to turn aside.

{9:46} Wherefore cry ye now unto heaven, that ye may be delivered from the hand of your enemies.

{9:47} With that they joined battle, and Jonathan stretched forth his hand to smite Bacchides, but he turned back from him.

{9:48} Then Jonathan and they that were with him leapt into Jordan, and swam over unto the other bank: howbeit the other passed not over Jordan unto them.

{9:49} So there were slain of Bacchides' side that day about a thousand men.

{9:50} Afterward returned Bacchides to Jerusalem and repaired the strong cites in Judea; the fort in Jericho, and Emmaus, and Bethhoron, and Bethel, and Thamnatha, Pharathoni, and Taphon, these did he strengthen with high walls, with gates and with bars.

{9:51} And in them he set a garrison, that they might work malice upon Israel.

{9:52} He fortified also the city Bethsura, and Gazera, and the tower, and put forces in them, and provision of victuals.

{9:53} Besides, he took the chief men's sons in the country for hostages, and put them into the tower at Jerusalem to be kept.

{9:54} Moreover in the hundred fifty and third year, in the second month, Alcimus commanded that the wall of the inner court of the sanctuary should be pulled down; he pulled down also the works of the prophets

{9:55} And as he began to pull down, even at that time was Alcimus plagued, and his enterprizes hindered: for his mouth was stopped, and he was taken with a palsy, so that he could no more speak any thing, nor give order concerning his house.

{9:56} So Alcimus died at that time with great torment.

{9:57} Now when Bacchides saw that Alcimus was dead, he returned to the king: whereupon the land of Judea was in rest two years.

{9:58} Then all the ungodly men held a council, saying, Behold, Jonathan and his company are at ease, and dwell without care: now therefore we will bring Bacchides hither, who shall take them all in one night.

{9:59} So they went and consulted with him.

{9:60} Then removed he, and came with a great host, and sent letters privily to his adherents in Judea, that they should take Jonathan and those that were with him: howbeit they could not, because their counsel was known unto them.

{9:61} Wherefore they took of the men of the country, that were authors of that mischief, about fifty persons, and slew them.

{9:62} Afterward Jonathan, and Simon, and they that were with him, got them away to Bethbasi, which is in the wilderness, and they repaired the decays thereof, and made it strong.

{9:63} Which thing when Bacchides knew, he gathered together all his host, and sent word to them that were of Judea.

{9:64} Then went he and laid siege against Bethbasi; and they fought against it a long season and made engines of war.

{9:65} But Jonathan left his brother Simon in the city, and went forth himself into the country, and with a certain number went he forth.

{9:66} And he smote Odonarkes and his brethren, and the children of Phasiron in their tent.

{9:67} And when he began to smite them, and came up with his forces, Simon and his company went out of the city, and burned up the engines of war,

{9:68} And fought against Bacchides, who was discomfited by them, and they afflicted him sore: for his counsel and travail was in vain.

{9:69} Wherefore he was very wroth at the wicked men that gave him counsel to come into the country, inasmuch as he slew many of them, and purposed to return into his own country.

{9:70} Whereof when Jonathan had knowledge, he sent ambassadors unto him, to the end he should make peace with him, and deliver them the prisoners.

{9:71} Which thing he accepted, and did according to his demands, and sware unto him that he would never do him harm all the days of his life.

{9:72} When therefore he had restored unto him the prisoners that he had taken aforetime out of the land of Judea, he returned and went his way into his own land, neither came he any more into their borders.

{9:73} Thus the sword ceased from Israel: but Jonathan dwelt at Machmas, and began to govern the people; and he destroyed the ungodly men out of Israel.

{10:1} In the hundred and sixtieth year Alexander, the son of Antiochus surnamed Epiphanes, went up and took Ptolemais: for the people had received him, by means whereof he reigned there,

{10:2} Now when king Demetrius heard thereof, he gathered together an exceeding great host, and went forth against him to fight.

{10:3} Moreover Demetrius sent letters unto Jonathan with loving words, so as he magnified him.

{10:4} For said he, let us first make peace with him, before he join with Alexander against us:

{10:5} Else he will remember all the evils that we have done against him, and against his brethren and his people.

{10:6} Wherefore he gave him authority to gather together an host, and to provide weapons, that he might aid him in battle: he commanded also that the hostages that were in the tower should be delivered him.

{10:7} Then came Jonathan to Jerusalem, and read the letters in the audience of all the people, and of them that were in the tower:

{10:8} Who were sore afraid, when they heard that the king had given him authority to gather together an host.

{10:9} Whereupon they of the tower delivered their hostages unto Jonathan, and he delivered them unto their parents.

{10:10} This done, Jonathan settled himself in Jerusalem, and began to build and repair the city.

{10:11} And he commanded the workmen to build the walls and the mount Sion and about with square stones for fortification; and they did so.

{10:12} Then the strangers, that were in the fortresses which Bacchides had built, fled away;

{10:13} Insomuch as every man left his place, and went into his own country.

{10:14} Only at Bethsura certain of those that had forsaken the law and the commandments remained still: for it was their place of refuge.

{10:15} Now when king Alexander had heard what promises Demetrius had sent unto Jonathan: when also it was told him of the battles and noble acts which he and his brethren had done, and of the pains that they had endured,

{10:16} He said, shall we find such another man? now therefore we will make him our friend and confederate.

{10:17} Upon this he wrote a letter, and sent it unto him, according to these words, saying,

{10:18} King Alexander to his brother Jonathan sendeth greeting:

{10:19} We have heard of thee, that thou art a man of great power, and meet to be our friend.

{10:20} Wherefore now this day we ordain thee to be the high priest of thy nation, and to be called the king's friend; (and therewithal he sent him a purple robe and a crown of gold:) and require thee to take our part, and keep friendship with us.

{10:21} So in the seventh month of the hundred and sixtieth year, at the feast of the tabernacles, Jonathan put on the holy robe, and gathered together forces, and provided much armour.

{10:22} Whereof when Demetrius heard, he was very sorry, and said,

{10:23} What have we done, that Alexander hath prevented us in making amity with the Jews to strengthen himself?

{10:24} I also will write unto them words of encouragement, and promise them dignities and gifts, that I may have their aid.

{10:25} He sent unto them therefore to this effect: King Demetrius unto the people of the Jews sendeth greeting:

{10:26} Whereas ye have kept covenants with us, and continued in our friendship, not joining yourselves with our enemies, we have heard hereof, and are glad.

{10:27} Wherefore now continue ye still to be faithful unto us, and we will well recompense you for the things ye do in our behalf,

{10:28} And will grant you many immunities, and give you rewards.

{10:29} And now do I free you, and for your sake I release all the Jews, from tributes, and from the customs of salt, and from crown taxes,

{10:30} And from that which appertaineth unto me to receive for the third part or the seed, and the half of the fruit of the trees, I release it from this day forth, so that they shall not be taken of the land of Judea, nor of the three governments which are added thereunto out of the country of Samaria and Galilee, from this day forth for evermore.

{10:31} Let Jerusalem also be holy and free, with the borders thereof, both from tenths and tributes.

{10:32} And as for the tower which is at Jerusalem, I yield up authority over it, and give the high priest, that he may set in it such men as he shall choose to keep it.

{10:33} Moreover I freely set at liberty every one of the Jews, that were carried captives out of the land of Judea into any part of my kingdom, and I will that all my officers remit the tributes even of their cattle.

{10:34} Furthermore I will that all the feasts, and sabbaths, and new moons, and solemn days, and the three days before the feast, and the three days after the feast shall be all of immunity and freedom for all the Jews in my realm.

{10:35} Also no man shall have authority to meddle with or to molest any of them in any matter.

{10:36} I will further, that there be enrolled among the king's forces about thirty thousand men of the Jews, unto whom pay shall be given, as belongeth to all king's forces.

{10:37} And of them some shall be placed in the king's strong holds, of whom also some shall be set over the affairs of the kingdom, which are of trust: and I will that their overseers and governors be of themselves, and that they live after their own laws, even as the king hath commanded in the land of Judea.

{10:38} And concerning the three governments that are added to Judea from the country of Samaria, let them be joined with Judea, that they may be reckoned to be under one, nor bound to obey other authority than the high priest's.

{10:39} As for Ptolemais, and the land pertaining thereto, I give it as a free gift to the sanctuary at Jerusalem for the necessary expences of the sanctuary.

{10:40} Moreover I give every year fifteen thousand shekels of silver out of the king's accounts from the places appertaining.

{10:41} And all the overplus, which the officers payed not in as in former time, from henceforth shall be given toward the works of the temple.

{10:42} And beside this, the five thousand shekels of silver, which they took from the uses of the temple out of the accounts year by year, even those things shall be released, because they appertain to the priests that minister.

{10:43} And whosoever they be that flee unto the temple at Jerusalem, or be within the liberties hereof, being indebted unto the king, or for any other matter, let them be at liberty, and all that they have in my realm.

{10:44} For the building also and repairing of the works of the sanctuary expences shall be given of the king's accounts.

{10:45} Yea, and for the building of the walls of Jerusalem, and the fortifying thereof round about, expences shall be given out of the king's accounts, as also for the building of the walls in Judea.

{10:46} Now when Jonathan and the people heard these words, they gave no credit unto them, nor received them, because they remembered the great evil that he had done in Israel; for he had afflicted them very sore.

{10:47} But with Alexander they were well pleased, because he was the first that entreated of true peace with them, and they were confederate with him always.

{10:48} Then gathered king Alexander great forces, and camped over against Demetrius.

{10:49} And after the two kings had joined battle, Demetrius' host fled: but Alexander followed after him, and prevailed against them.

{10:50} And he continued the battle very sore until the sun went down: and that day was Demetrius slain.

{10:51} Afterward Alexander sent ambassadors to Ptolemee king of Egypt with a message to this effect:

{10:52} Forasmuch as I am come again to my realm, and am set in the throne of my progenitors, and have gotten the dominion, and overthrown Demetrius, and recovered our country;

{10:53} For after I had joined battle with him, both he and his host was discomfited by us, so that we sit in the throne of his kingdom:

{10:54} Now therefore let us make a league of amity together, and

give me now thy daughter to wife: and I will be thy son in law, and
will give both thee and her as according to thy dignity.

{10:55} Then Ptolemee the king gave answer, saying, Happy be the day
wherein thou didst return into the land of thy fathers, and satest in
the throne of their kingdom.

{10:56} And now will I do to thee, as thou hast written: meet me
therefore at Ptolemais, that we may see one another; for I will marry
my daughter to thee according to thy desire.

{10:57} So Ptolemee went out of Egypt with his daughter Cleopatra,
and they came unto Ptolemais in the hundred threescore and second year:

{10:58} Where king Alexander meeting him, he gave unto him his
daughter Cleopatra, and celebrated her marriage at Ptolemais with great
glory, as the manner of kings is.

{10:59} Now king Alexander had written unto Jonathan, that he should
come and meet him.

{10:60} Who thereupon went honourably to Ptolemais, where he met the
two kings, and gave them and their friends silver and gold, and many
presents, and found favour in their sight.

{10:61} At that time certain pestilent fellows of Israel, men of a wicked life, assembled themselves against him, to accuse him: but the king would not hear them.

{10:62} Yea more than that, the king commanded to take off his garments, and clothe him in purple: and they did so.

{10:63} And he made him sit by himself, and said into his princes, Go with him into the midst of the city, and make proclamation, that no man complain against him of any matter, and that no man trouble him for any manner of cause.

{10:64} Now when his accusers saw that he was honored according to the proclamation, and clothed in purple, they fled all away.

{10:65} So the king honoured him, and wrote him among his chief friends, and made him a duke, and partaker of his dominion.

{10:66} Afterward Jonathan returned to Jerusalem with peace and gladness.

{10:67} Furthermore in the; hundred threescore and fifth year came Demetrius son of Demetrius out of Crete into the land of his fathers:

{10:68} Whereof when king Alexander heard tell, he was right sorry, and returned into Antioch.

{10:69} Then Demetrius made Apollonius the governor of Celosyria his general, who gathered together a great host, and camped in Jamnia, and sent unto Jonathan the high priest, saying,

{10:70} Thou alone liftest up thyself against us, and I am laughed to scorn for thy sake, and reproached: and why dost thou vaunt thy power against us in the mountains?

{10:71} Now therefore, if thou trustest in thine own strength, come down to us into the plain field, and there let us try the matter together: for with me is the power of the cities.

{10:72} Ask and learn who I am, and the rest that take our part, and they shall tell thee that thy foot is not able to to flight in their own land.

{10:73} Wherefore now thou shalt not be able to abide the horsemen and so great a power in the plain, where is neither stone nor flint, nor place to flee unto.

{10:74} So when Jonathan heard these words of Apollonius, he was moved in his mind, and choosing ten thousand men he went out of Jerusalem, where Simon his brother met him for to help him.

{10:75} And he pitched his tents against Joppa: but; they of Joppa shut him out of the city, because Apollonius had a garrison there.

{10:76} Then Jonathan laid siege unto it: whereupon they of the city let him in for fear: and so Jonathan won Joppa.

{10:77} Whereof when Apollonius heard, he took three thousand horsemen, with a great host of footmen, and went to Azotus as one that journeyed, and therewithal drew him forth into the plain. because he had a great number of horsemen, in whom he put his trust.

{10:78} Then Jonathan followed after him to Azotus, where the armies joined battle.

{10:79} Now Apollonius had left a thousand horsemen in ambush.

{10:80} And Jonathan knew that there was an ambushment behind him; for they had compassed in his host, and cast darts at the people, from morning till evening.

{10:81} But the people stood still, as Jonathan had commanded them: and so the enemies' horses were tired.

{10:82} Then brought Simon forth his host, and set them against the footmen, (for the horsemen were spent) who were discomfited by him, and fled.

{10:83} The horsemen also, being scattered in the field, fled to Azotus, and went into Bethdagon, their idol's temple, for safety.

{10:84} But Jonathan set fire on Azotus, and the cities round about it, and took their spoils; and the temple of Dagon, with them that were fled into it, he burned with fire.

{10:85} Thus there were burned and slain with the sword well nigh eight thousand men.

{10:86} And from thence Jonathan removed his host, and camped against Ascalon, where the men of the city came forth, and met him with great pomp.

{10:87} After this returned Jonathan and his host unto Jerusalem, having any spoils.

{10:88} Now when king Alexander heard these things, he honoured Jonathan yet more.

{10:89} And sent him a buckle of gold, as the use is to be given to such as are of the king's blood: he gave him also Accaron with the borders thereof in possession.

{11:1} And the king of Egypt gathered together a great host, like the sand that lieth upon the sea shore, and many ships, and went about through deceit to get Alexander's kingdom, and join it to his own.

{11:2} Whereupon he took his journey into Spain in peaceable manner, so as they of the cities opened unto him, and met him: for king Alexander had commanded them so to do, because he was his brother in law.

{11:3} Now as Ptolemee entered into the cities, he set in every one of them a garrison of soldiers to keep it.

{11:4} And when he came near to Azotus, they shewed him the temple of Dagon that was burnt, and Azotus and the suburbs thereof that were destroyed, and the bodies that were cast abroad and them that he had burnt in the battle; for they had made heaps of them by the way where he should pass.

{11:5} Also they told the king whatsoever Jonathan had done, to the intent he might blame him: but the king held his peace.

{11:6} Then Jonathan met the king with great pomp at Joppa, where they saluted one another, and lodged.

{11:7} Afterward Jonathan, when he had gone with the king to the river called Eleutherus, returned again to Jerusalem.

{11:8} King Ptolemee therefore, having gotten the dominion of the cities by the sea unto Seleucia upon the sea coast, imagined wicked counsels against Alexander.

{11:9} Whereupon he sent ambasadors unto king Demetrius, saying, Come, let us make a league betwixt us, and I will give thee my daughter whom Alexander hath, and thou shalt reign in thy father's kingdom:

{11:10} For I repent that I gave my daughter unto him, for he sought to slay me.

{11:11} Thus did he slander him, because he was desirous of his kingdom.

{11:12} Wherefore he took his daughter from him, and gave her to Demetrius, and forsook Alexander, so that their hatred was openly known.

{11:13} Then Ptolemee entered into Antioch, where he set two crowns upon his head, the crown of Asia, and of Egypt.

{11:14} In the mean season was king Alexander in Cilicia, because those that dwelt in those parts had revolted from him.

{11:15} But when Alexander heard of this, he came to war against him: whereupon king Ptolemee brought forth his host, and met him with a mighty power, and put him to flight.

{11:16} So Alexander fled into Arabia there to be defended; but king Ptolemee was exalted:

{11:17} For Zabdiel the Arabian took off Alexander's head, and sent it unto Ptolemee.

{11:18} King Ptolemee also died the third day after, and they that were in the strong holds were slain one of another.

{11:19} By this means Demetrius reigned in the hundred threescore and seventh year.

{11:20} At the same time Jonathan gathered together them that were in Judea to take the tower that was in Jerusalem: and he made many engines of war against it.

{11:21} Then came ungodly persons, who hated their own people, went unto the king, and told him that Jonathan besieged the tower,

{11:22} Whereof when he heard, he was angry, and immediately removing, he came to Ptolemais, and wrote unto Jonathan, that he should not lay siege to the tower, but come and speak with him at Ptolemais in great haste.

{11:23} Nevertheless Jonathan, when he heard this, commanded to besiege it still: and he chose certain of the elders of Israel and the priests, and put himself in peril;

{11:24} And took silver and gold, and raiment, and divers presents besides, and went to Ptolemais unto the king, where he found favour in his sight.

{11:25} And though certain ungodly men of the people had made complaints against him,

{11:26} Yet the king entreated him as his predecessors had done before, and promoted him in the sight of all his friends,

{11:27} And confirmed him in the high priesthood, and in all the honours that he had before, and gave him preeminence among his chief friends.

{11:28} Then Jonathan desired the king, that he would make Judea free from tribute, as also the three governments, with the country of

Samaria; and he promised him three hundred talents.

{11:29} So the king consented, and wrote letters unto Jonathan of all these things after this manner:

{11:30} King Demetrius unto his brother Jonathan, and unto the nation of the Jews, sendeth greeting:

{11:31} We send you here a copy of the letter which we did write unto our cousin Lasthenes concerning you, that ye might see it.

{11:32} King Demetrius unto his father Lasthenes sendeth greeting:

{11:33} We are determined to do good to the people of the Jews, who are our friends, and keep covenants with us, because of their good will toward us.

{11:34} Wherefore we have ratified unto them the borders of Judea, with the three governments of Apherema and Lydda and Ramathem, that are added unto Judea from the country of Samaria, and all things appertaining unto them, for all such as do sacrifice in Jerusalem, instead of the payments which the king received of them yearly aforetime out of the fruits of the earth and of trees.

{11:35} And as for other things that belong unto us, of the tithes and customs pertaining unto us, as also the saltpits, and the crown taxes, which are due unto us, we discharge them of them all for their relief.

{11:36} And nothing hereof shall be revoked from this time forth for ever.

{11:37} Now therefore see that thou make a copy of these things, and let it be delivered unto Jonathan, and set upon the holy mount in a conspicuous place.

{11:38} After this, when king Demetrius saw that the land was quiet before him, and that no resistance was made against him, he sent away all his forces, every one to his own place, except certain bands of strangers, whom he had gathered from the isles of the heathen: wherefore all the forces of his fathers hated him.

{11:39} Moreover there was one Tryphon, that had been of Alexander's part afore, who, seeing that all the host murmured against Demetrius, went to Simalcue the Arabian that brought up Antiochus the young son of Alexander,

{11:40} And lay sore upon him to deliver him this young Antiochus, that he might reign in his father's stead: he told him therefore all that Demetrius had done, and how his men of war were at enmity with him, and there he remained a long season.

{11:41} In the mean time Jonathan sent unto king Demetrius, that he would cast those of the tower out of Jerusalem, and those also in the fortresses: for they fought against Israel.

{11:42} So Demetrius sent unto Jonathan, saying, I will not only do this for thee and thy people, but I will greatly honour thee and thy nation, if opportunity serve.

{11:43} Now therefore thou shalt do well, if thou send me men to help me; for all my forces are gone from me.

{11:44} Upon this Jonathan sent him three thousand strong men unto Antioch: and when they came to the king, the king was very glad of their coming.

{11:45} Howbeit they that were of the city gathered themselves together into the midst of the city, to the number of an hundred and twenty thousand men, and would have slain the king.

{11:46} Wherefore the king fled into the court, but they of the city kept the passages of the city, and began to fight.

{11:47} Then the king called to the Jews for help, who came unto him all at once, and dispersing themselves through the city slew that day in the city to the number of an hundred thousand.

{11:48} Also they set fire on the city, and gat many spoils that day, and delivered the king.

{11:49} So when they of the city saw that the Jews had got the city as they would, their courage was abated: wherefore they made supplication to the king, and cried, saying,

{11:50} Grant us peace, and let the Jews cease from assaulting us and the city.

{11:51} With that they cast away their weapons, and made peace; and the Jews were honoured in the sight of the king, and in the sight of all that were in his realm; and they returned to Jerusalem, having great spoils.

{11:52} So king Demetrius sat on the throne of his kingdom, and the land was quiet before him.

{11:53} Nevertheless he dissembled in all that ever he spake, and estranged himself from Jonathan, neither rewarded he him according to the benefits which he had received of him, but troubled him very sore.

{11:54} After this returned Tryphon, and with him the young child Antiochus, who reigned, and was crowned.

{11:55} Then there gathered unto him all the men of war, whom Demetrius had put away, and they fought against Demetrius, who turned his back and fled.

{11:56} Moreover Tryphon took the elephants, and won Antioch.

{11:57} At that time young Antiochus wrote unto Jonathan, saying, I confirm thee in the high priesthood, and appoint thee ruler over the four governments, and to be one of the king's friends.

{11:58} Upon this he sent him golden vessels to be served in, and gave him leave to drink in gold, and to be clothed in purple, and to wear a golden buckle.

{11:59} His brother Simon also he made captain from the place called The ladder of Tyrus unto the borders of Egypt.

{11:60} Then Jonathan went forth, and passed through the cities beyond the water, and all the forces of Syria gathered themselves unto him for to help him: and when he came to Ascalon, they of the city met him honourably.

{11:61} From whence he went to Gaza, but they of Gaza shut him out; wherefore he laid siege unto it, and burned the suburbs thereof with fire, and spoiled them.

{11:62} Afterward, when they of Gaza made supplication unto Jonathan, he made peace with them, and took the sons of their chief men for hostages, and sent them to Jerusalem, and passed through the country unto Damascus.

{11:63} Now when Jonathan heard that Demetrius' princes were come to Cades, which is in Galilee, with a great power, purposing to remove him out of the country,

{11:64} He went to meet them, and left Simon his brother in the country.

{11:65} Then Simon encamped against Bethsura and fought against it a long season, and shut it up:

{11:66} But they desired to have peace with him, which he granted them, and then put them out from thence, and took the city, and set a garrison in it.

{11:67} As for Jonathan and his host, they pitched at the water of Gennesar, from whence betimes in the morning they gat them to the plain of Nasor.

{11:68} And, behold, the host of strangers met them in the plain, who, having laid men in ambush for him in the mountains, came themselves over against him.

{11:69} So when they that lay in ambush rose out of their places and joined battle, all that were of Jonathan's side fled;

{11:70} Insomuch as there was not one of them left, except Mattathias the son of Absalom, and Judas the son of Calphi, the captains of the host.

{11:71} Then Jonathan rent his clothes, and cast earth upon his head, and prayed.

{11:72} Afterwards turning again to battle, he put them to flight, and so they ran away.

{11:73} Now when his own men that were fled saw this, they turned again unto him, and with him pursued them to Cades, even unto their own tents, and there they camped.

{11:74} So there were slain of the heathen that day about three thousand men: but Jonathan returned to Jerusalem.

{12:1} Now when Jonathan saw that time served him, he chose certain men, and sent them to Rome, for to confirm and renew the friendship that they had with them.

{12:2} He sent letters also to the Lacedemonians, and to other places, for the same purpose.

{12:3} So they went unto Rome, and entered into the senate, and said, Jonathan the high priest, and the people of the Jews, sent us unto you, to the end ye should renew the friendship, which ye had with them, and league, as in former time.

{12:4} Upon this the Romans gave them letters unto the governors of every place that they should bring them into the land of Judea peaceably.

{12:5} And this is the copy of the letters which Jonathan wrote to the Lacedemonians:

{12:6} Jonathan the high priest, and the elders of the nation, and the priests, and the other of the Jews, unto the Lacedemonians their brethren send greeting:

{12:7} There were letters sent in times past unto Onias the high priest from Darius, who reigned then among you, to signify that ye are our brethren, as the copy here underwritten doth specify.

{12:8} At which time Onias entreated the ambassador that was sent honourably, and received the letters, wherein declaration was made of the league and friendship.

{12:9} Therefore we also, albeit we need none of these things, that we have the holy books of scripture in our hands to comfort us,

{12:10} Have nevertheless attempted to send unto you for the renewing of brotherhood and friendship, lest we should become strangers unto you altogether: for there is a long time passed since ye sent unto us.

{12:11} We therefore at all times without ceasing, both in our feasts, and other convenient days, do remember you in the sacrifices which we offer, and in our prayers, as reason is, and as it becometh us to think upon our brethren:

{12:12} And we are right glad of your honour.

{12:13} As for ourselves, we have had great troubles and wars on every side, forsomuch as the kings that are round about us have fought against us.

{12:14} Howbeit we would not be troublesome unto you, nor to others of our confederates and friends, in these wars:

{12:15} For we have help from heaven that succoureth us, so as we are delivered from our enemies, and our enemies are brought under foot.

{12:16} For this cause we chose Numenius the son of Antiochus, and Antipater he son of Jason, and sent them unto the Romans, to renew the amity that we had with them, and the former league.

{12:17} We commanded them also to go unto you, and to salute and to deliver you our letters concerning the renewing of our brotherhood.

{12:18} Wherefore now ye shall do well to give us an answer thereto.

{12:19} And this is the copy of the letters which Oniares sent.

{12:20} Areus king of the Lacedemonians to Onias the high priest, greeting:

{12:21} It is found in writing, that the Lacedemonians and Jews are brethren, and that they are of the stock of Abraham:

{12:22} Now therefore, since this is come to our knowledge, ye shall do well to write unto us of your prosperity.

{12:23} We do write back again to you, that your cattle and goods are our's, and our's are your's We do command therefore our ambassadors to make report unto you on this wise.

{12:24} Now when Jonathan heard that Demebius' princes were come to fight against him with a greater host than afore,

{12:25} He removed from Jerusalem, and met them in the land of Amathis: for he gave them no respite to enter his country.

{12:26} He sent spies also unto their tents, who came again, and told him that they were appointed to come upon them in the night season.

{12:27} Wherefore so soon as the sun was down, Jonathan commanded his men to watch, and to be in arms, that all the night long they might be ready to fight: also he sent forth centinels round about the host.

{12:28} But when the adversaries heard that Jonathan and his men were ready for battle, they feared, and trembled in their hearts, and they kindled fires in their camp.

{12:29} Howbeit Jonathan and his company knew it not till the morning: for they saw the lights burning.

{12:30} Then Jonathan pursued after them, but overtook them not: for they were gone over the river Eleutherus.

{12:31} Wherefore Jonathan turned to the Arabians, who were called Zabadeans, and smote them, and took their spoils.

{12:32} And removing thence, he came to Damascus, and so passed through all the country,

{12:33} Simon also went forth, and passed through the country unto Ascalon, and the holds there adjoining, from whence he turned aside to Joppa, and won it.

{12:34} For he had heard that they would deliver the hold unto them that took Demetrius' part; wherefore he set a garrison there to keep it.

{12:35} After this came Jonathan home again, and calling the elders of the people together, he consulted with them about building strong holds in Judea,

{12:36} And making the walls of Jerusalem higher, and raising a great mount between the tower and the city, for to separate it from the city, that so it might be alone, that men might neither sell nor buy in it.

{12:37} Upon this they came together to build up the city, forasmuch as part of the wall toward the brook on the east side was fallen down, and they repaired that which was called Caphenatha.

{12:38} Simon also set up Adida in Sephela, and made it strong with gates and bars.

{12:39} Now Tryphon went about to get the kingdom of Asia, and to kill Antiochus the king, that he might set the crown upon his own head.

{12:40} Howbeit he was afraid that Jonathan would not suffer him, and that he would fight against him; wherefore he sought a way how to take Jonathan, that he might kill him. So he removed, and came to Bethsan.

{12:41} Then Jonathan went out to meet him with forty thousand men chosen for the battle, and came to Bethsan.

{12:42} Now when Tryphon saw Jonathan came with so great a force, he durst not stretch his hand against him;

{12:43} But received him honourably, and commended him unto all his friends, and gave him gifts, and commanded his men of war to be as obedient unto him, as to himself.

{12:44} Unto Jonathan also he said, why hast thou brought all this people to so great trouble, seeing there is no war betwixt us?

{12:45} Therefore send them now home again, and choose a few men to wait on thee, and come thou with me to Ptolemais, for I will give it thee, and the rest of the strong holds and forces, and all that have any charge: as for me, I will return and depart: for this is the cause of my coming.

{12:46} So Jonathan believing him did as he bade him, and sent away his host, who went into the land of Judea.

{12:47} And with himself he retained but three thousand men, of whom he sent two thousand into Galilee, and one thousand went with him.

{12:48} Now as soon as Jonathan entered into Ptolemais, they of Ptolemais shut the gates and took him, and all them that came with him they slew with the sword.

{12:49} Then sent Tryphon an host of footmen and horsemen into Galilee, and into the great plain, to destroy all Jonathan's company.

{12:50} But when they knew that Jonathan and they that were with him were taken and slain, they encouraged one another; and went close together, prepared to fight.

{12:51} They therefore that followed upon them, perceiving that they were ready to fight for their lives, turned back again.

{12:52} Whereupon they all came into the land of Judea peaceably, and there they bewailed Jonathan, and them that were with him, and they were sore afraid; wherefore all Israel made great lamentation.

{12:53} Then all the heathen that were round about then sought to destroy them: for said they, they have no captain, nor any to help them: now therefore let us make war upon them, and take away their memorial from among men.

{13:1} Now when Simon heard that Tryphon had gathered together a great host to invade the land of Judea, and destroy it,

{13:2} And saw that the people was in great trembling and fear, he went up to Jerusalem, and gathered the people together,

{13:3} And gave them exhortation, saying, Ye yourselves know what great things I, and my brethren, and my father's house, have done for the laws and the sanctuary, the battles also and troubles which we have seen.

{13:4} By reason whereof all my brethren are slain for Israel's sake, and I am left alone.

{13:5} Now therefore be it far from me, that I should spare mine own life in any time of trouble: for I am no better than my brethren.

{13:6} Doubtless I will avenge my nation, and the sanctuary, and our wives, and our children: for all the heathen are gathered to destroy us of very malice.

{13:7} Now as soon as the people heard these words, their spirit revived.

{13:8} And they answered with a loud voice, saying, thou shalt be our leader instead of Judas and Jonathan thy brother.

{13:9} Fight thou our battles, and whatsoever, thou commandest us, that will we do.

{13:10} So then he gathered together all the men of war, and made haste to finish the walls of Jerusalem, and he fortified it round about.

{13:11} Also he sent Jonathan the son of Absolom, and with him a great power, to Joppa. who casting out them that were therein remained there in it.

{13:12} So Tryphon removed from Ptolemaus with a great power to invade the land of Judea, and Jonathan was with him in ward.

{13:13} But Simon pitched his tents at Adida, over against the plain.

{13:14} Now when Tryphon knew that Simon was risen up instead of his brother Jonathan, and meant to join battle with him, he sent messengers unto him, saying,

{13:15} Whereas we have Jonathan thy brother in hold, it is for money that he is owing unto the king's treasure, concerning the business that was committed unto him.

{13:16} Wherefore now send an hundred talents of silver, and two of his sons for hostages, that when he is at liberty he may not revolt from us, and we will let him go.

{13:17} Hereupon Simon, albeit he perceived that they spake deceitfully unto him yet sent he the money and the children, lest peradventure he should procure to himself great hatred of the people:

{13:18} Who might have said, Because I sent him not the money and the children, therefore is Jonathan dead.

{13:19} So he sent them the children and the hundred talents: howbeit Tryphon dissembled neither would he let Jonathan go.

{13:20} And after this came Tryphon to invade the land, and destroy it, going round about by the way that leadeth unto Adora: but Simon and his host marched against him in every place, wheresoever he went.

{13:21} Now they that were in the tower sent messengers unto Tryphon, to the end that he should hasten his coming unto them by the wilderness, and send them victuals.

{13:22} Wherefore Tryphon made ready all his horsemen to come that night: but there fell a very great snow, by reason whereof he came not. So he departed, and came into the country of Galaad.

{13:23} And when he came near to Bascama he slew Jonathan, who was buried there.

{13:24} Afterward Tryphon returned and went into his own land.

{13:25} Then sent Simon, and took the bones of Jonathan his brother, and buried them in Modin, the city of his fathers.

{13:26} And all Israel made great lamentation for him, and bewailed him many days.

{13:27} Simon also built a monument upon the sepulchre of his father and his brethren, and raised it aloft to the sight, with hewn stone behind and before.

{13:28} Moreover he set up seven pyramids, one against another, for his father, and his mother, and his four brethren.

{13:29} And in these he made cunning devices, about the which he set great pillars, and upon the pillars he made all their armour for a perpetual memory, and by the armour ships carved, that they might be seen of all that sail on the sea.

{13:30} This is the sepulchre which he made at Modin, and it standeth yet unto this day.

{13:31} Now Tryphon dealt deceitfully with the young king Antiochus, and slew him.

{13:32} And he reigned in his stead, and crowned himself king of Asia, and brought a great calamity upon the land.

{13:33} Then Simon built up the strong holds in Judea, and fenced them about with high towers, and great walls, and gates, and bars, and laid up victuals therein.

{13:34} Moreover Simon chose men, and sent to king Demetrius, to the end he should give the land an immunity, because all that Tryphon did was to spoil.

{13:35} Unto whom king Demetrius answered and wrote after this manner:

{13:36} King Demetrius unto Simon the high priest, and friend of kings, as also unto the elders and nation of the Jews, sendeth greeting:

{13:37} The golden crown, and the scarlet robe, which ye sent unto us, we have received: and we are ready to make a stedfast peace with you, yea, and to write unto our officers, to confirm the immunities which we have granted.

{13:38} And whatsoever covenants we have made with you shall stand; and the strong holds, which ye have builded, shall be your own.

{13:39} As for any oversight or fault committed unto this day, we forgive it, and the crown tax also, which ye owe us: and if there were any other tribute paid in Jerusalem, it shall no more be paid.

{13:40} And look who are meet among you to be in our court, let then be enrolled, and let there be peace betwixt us.

{13:41} Thus the yoke of the heathen was taken away from Israel in the hundred and seventieth year.

{13:42} Then the people of Israel began to write in their instruments and contracts, In the first year of Simon the high priest, the governor and leader of the Jews.

{13:43} In those days Simon camped against Gaza and besieged it round about; he made also an engine of war, and set it by the city, and battered a certain tower, and took it.

{13:44} And they that were in the engine leaped into the city; whereupon there was a great uproar in the city:

{13:45} Insomuch as the people of the city rent their clothes, and climbed upon the walls with their wives and children, and cried with a loud voice, beseeching Simon to grant them peace.

{13:46} And they said, Deal not with us according to our wickedness, but according to thy mercy.

{13:47} So Simon was appeased toward them, and fought no more against them, but put them out of the city, and cleansed the houses wherein the idols were, and so entered into it with songs and thanksgiving.

{13:48} Yea, he put all uncleanness out of it, and placed such men there as would keep the law, and made it stronger than it was before, and built therein a dwellingplace for himself.

{13:49} They also of the tower in Jerusalem were kept so strait, that they could neither come forth, nor go into the country, nor buy, nor sell: wherefore they were in great distress for want of victuals, and a great number of them perished through famine.

{13:50} Then cried they to Simon, beseeching him to be at one with them: which thing he granted them; and when he had put them out from thence, he cleansed the tower from pollutions:

{13:51} And entered into it the three and twentieth day of the second month in the hundred seventy and first year, with thanksgiving, and branches of palm trees, and with harps, and cymbals, and with viols, and hymns, and songs: because there was destroyed a great enemy out of Israel.

{13:52} He ordained also that that day should be kept every year with gladness. Moreover the hill of the temple that was by the tower he made stronger than it was, and there he dwelt himself with his company.

{13:53} And when Simon saw that John his son was a valiant man, he made him captain of all the hosts; and he dwelt in Gazera.

{14:1} Now in the hundred threescore and twelfth year king Demetrius gathered his forces together, and went into Media to get him help to fight against Tryphone.

{14:2} But when Arsaces, the king of Persia and Media, heard that Demetrius was entered within his borders, he sent one of his princes to take him alive:

{14:3} Who went and smote the host of Demetrius, and took him, and brought him to Arsaces, by whom he was put in ward.

{14:4} As for the land of Judea, that was quiet all the days of Simon; for he sought the good of his nation in such wise, as that evermore his authority and honour pleased them well.

{14:5} And as he was honourable in all his acts, so in this, that he took Joppa for an haven, and made an entrance to the isles of the sea,

{14:6} And enlarged the bounds of his nation, and recovered the country,

{14:7} And gathered together a great number of captives, and had the dominion of Gazera, and Bethsura, and the tower, out of the which he took all uncleaness, neither was there any that resisted him.

{14:8} Then did they till their ground in peace, and the earth gave her increase, and the trees of the field their fruit.

{14:9} The ancient men sat all in the streets, communing together of good things, and the young men put on glorious and warlike apparel.

{14:10} He provided victuals for the cities, and set in them all manner of munition, so that his honourable name was renowned unto the end of the world.

{14:11} He made peace in the land, and Israel rejoiced with great joy:

{14:12} For every man sat under his vine and his fig tree, and there was none to fray them:

{14:13} Neither was there any left in the land to fight against them: yea, the kings themselves were overthrown in those days.

{14:14} Moreover he strengthened all those of his people that were brought low: the law he searched out; and every contemner of the law and wicked person he took away.

{14:15} He beautified the sanctuary, and multiplied vessels of the temple.

{14:16} Now when it was heard at Rome, and as far as Sparta, that Jonathan was dead, they were very sorry.

{14:17} But as soon as they heard that his brother Simon was made high priest in his stead, and ruled the country, and the cities therein:

{14:18} They wrote unto him in tables of brass, to renew the friendship and league which they had made with Judas and Jonathan his brethren:

{14:19} Which writings were read before the congregation at Jerusalem.

{14:20} And this is the copy of the letters that the Lacedemonians sent; The rulers of the Lacedemonians, with the city, unto Simon the high priest, and the elders, and priests, and residue of the people of the Jews, our brethren, send greeting:

{14:21} The ambassadors that were sent unto our people certified us of your glory and honour: wherefore we were glad of their coming,

{14:22} And did register the things that they spake in the council of the people in this manner; Numenius son of Antiochus, and Antipater son of Jason, the Jews' ambassadors, came unto us to renew the friendship they had with us.

{14:23} And it pleased the people to entertain the men honourably, and to put the copy of their ambassage in publick records, to the end the people of the Lacedemonians might have a memorial thereof: furthermore, we have written a copy thereof unto Simon the high priest.

{14:24} After this Simon sent Numenius to Rome with a great shield of gold of a thousand-pound weight to confirm the league with them.

{14:25} Whereof when the people heard, they said, What thanks shall we give to Simon and his sons?

{14:26} For he and his brethren and the house of his father have established Israel, and chased away in fight their enemies from them, and confirmed their liberty.

{14:27} So then they wrote it in tables of brass, which they set upon pillars in mount Sion: and this is the copy of the writing; The eighteenth day of the month Elul, in the hundred threescore and twelfth year, being the third year of Simon the high priest,

{14:28} At Saramel in the great congregation of the priests, and people, and rulers of the nation, and elders of the country, were these things notified unto us.

{14:29} Forasmuch as oftentimes there have been wars in the country, wherein for the maintenance of their sanctuary, and the law, Simon the son of Mattathias, of the posterity of Jarib, together with his brethren, put themselves in jeopardy, and resisting the enemies of their nation did their nation great honour:

{14:30} (For after that Jonathan, having gathered his nation together, and been their high priest, was added to his people,

{14:31} Their enemies prepared to invade their country, that they might destroy it, and lay hands on the sanctuary:

{14:32} At which time Simon rose up, and fought for his nation, and spent much of his own substance, and armed the valiant men of his nation and gave them wages,

{14:33} And fortified the cities of Judea, together with Bethsura, that lieth upon the borders of Judea, where the armour of the enemies had been before; but he set a garrison of Jews there:

{14:34} Moreover he fortified Joppa, which lieth upon the sea, and

Gazera, that bordereth upon Azotus, where the enemies had dwelt before: but he placed Jews there, and furnished them with all things convenient for the reparation thereof.)

{14:35} The people therefore sang the acts of Simon, and unto what glory he thought to bring his nation, made him their governor and chief priest, because he had done all these things, and for the justice and faith which he kept to his nation, and for that he sought by all means to exalt his people.

{14:36} For in his time things prospered in his hands, so that the heathen were taken out of their country, and they also that were in the city of David in Jerusalem, who had made themselves a tower, out of which they issued, and polluted all about the sanctuary, and did much hurt in the holy place:

{14:37} But he placed Jews therein. and fortified it for the safety of the country and the city, and raised up the walls of Jerusalem.

{14:38} King Demetrius also confirmed him in the high priesthood according to those things,

{14:39} And made him one of his friends, and honoured him with great honour.

{14:40} For he had heard say, that the Romans had called the Jews their friends and confederates and brethren; and that they had entertained the ambassadors of Simon honourably;

{14:41} Also that the Jews and priests were well pleased that Simon should be their governor and high priest for ever, until there should arise a faithful prophet;

{14:42} Moreover that he should be their captain, and should take charge of the sanctuary, to set them over their works, and over the country, and over the armour, and over the fortresses, that, I say, he should take charge of the sanctuary;

{14:43} Beside this, that he should be obeyed of every man, and that all the writings in the country should be made in his name, and that he should be clothed in purple, and wear gold:

{14:44} Also that it should be lawful for none of the people or priests to break any of these things, or to gainsay his words, or to gather an assembly in the country without him, or to be clothed in purple, or wear a buckle of gold;

{14:45} And whosoever should do otherwise, or break any of these things, he should be punished.

{14:46} Thus it liked all the people to deal with Simon, and to do as hath been said.

{14:47} Then Simon accepted hereof, and was well pleased to be high priest, and captain and governor of the Jews and priests, and to defend them all.

{14:48} So they commanded that this writing should be put in tables of brass, and that they should be set up within the compass of the sanctuary in a conspicuous place;

{14:49} Also that the copies thereof should be laid up in the treasury, to the end that Simon and his sons might have them.

{15:1} Moreover Antiochus son of Demetrius the king sent letters from the isles of the sea unto Simon the priest and prince of the Jews, and to all the people;

{15:2} The contents whereof were these: King Antiochus to Simon the high priest and prince of his nation, and to the people of the Jews, greeting:

{15:3} Forasmuch as certain pestilent men have usurped the kingdom of our fathers, and my purpose is to challenge it again, that I may restore it to the old estate, and to that end have gathered a multitude of foreign soldiers together, and prepared ships of war;

{15:4} My meaning also being to go through the country, that I may be avenged of them that have destroyed it, and made many cities in the kingdom desolate:

{15:5} Now therefore I confirm unto thee all the oblations which the kings before me granted thee, and whatsoever gifts besides they granted.

{15:6} I give thee leave also to coin money for thy country with thine own stamp.

{15:7} And as concerning Jerusalem and the sanctuary, let them be free; and all the armour that thou hast made, and fortresses that thou hast built, and keepest in thine hands, let them remain unto thee.

{15:8} And if anything be, or shall be, owing to the king, let it be forgiven thee from this time forth for evermore.

{15:9} Furthermore, when we have obtained our kingdom, we will honour thee, and thy nation, and thy temple, with great honour, so that your honour shall be known throughout the world.

{15:10} In the hundred threescore and fourteenth year went Antiochus into the land of his fathers: at which time all the forces came together unto him, so that few were left with Tryphon.

{15:11} Wherefore being pursued by king Antiochus, he fled unto Dora, which lieth by the sea side:

{15:12} For he saw that troubles came upon him all at once, and that his forces had forsaken him.

{15:13} Then camped Antiochus against Dora, having with him an hundred and twenty thousand men of war, and eight thousand horsemen.

{15:14} And when he had compassed the city round about, and joined ships close to the town on the sea side, he vexed the city by land and by sea, neither suffered he any to go out or in.

{15:15} In the mean season came Numenius and his company from Rome,
having letters to the kings and countries; wherein were written these things:

{15:16} Lucius, consul of the Romans unto king Ptolemee, greeting:

{15:17} The Jews' ambassadors, our friends and confederates, came unto us to renew the old friendship and league, being sent from Simon the high priest, and from the people of the Jews:

{15:18} And they brought a shield of gold of a thousand pound.

{15:19} We thought it good therefore to write unto the kings and countries, that they should do them no harm, nor fight against them, their cities, or countries, nor yet aid their enemies against them.

{15:20} It seemed also good to us to receive the shield of them.

{15:21} If therefore there be any pestilent fellows, that have fled from their country unto you, deliver them unto Simon the high priest, that he may punish them according to their own law.

{15:22} The same things wrote he likewise unto Demetrius the king, and Attalus, to Ariarathes, and Arsaces,

{15:23} And to all the countries and to Sampsames, and the Lacedemonians, and to Delus, and Myndus, and Sicyon, and Caria, and Samos, and Pamphylia, and Lycia, and Halicarnassus, and Rhodus, and Aradus, and Cos, and Side, and Aradus, and Gortyna, and Cnidus, and Cyprus, and Cyrene.

{15:24} And the copy hereof they wrote to Simon the high priest.

{15:25} So Antiochus the king camped against Dora the second day, assaulting it continually, and making engines, by which means he shut up Tryphon, that he could neither go out nor in.

{15:26} At that time Simon sent him two thousand chosen men to aid him; silver also, and gold, and much armour.

{15:27} Nevertheless he would not receive them, but brake all the covenants which he had made with him afore, and became strange unto him.

{15:28} Furthermore he sent unto him Athenobius, one of his friends, to commune with him, and say, Ye withhold Joppa and Gazera; with the tower that is in Jerusalem, which are cities of my realm.

{15:29} The borders thereof ye have wasted, and done great hurt in the land, and got the dominion of many places within my kingdom.

{15:30} Now therefore deliver the cities which ye have taken, and the tributes of the places, whereof ye have gotten dominion without the borders of Judea:

{15:31} Or else give me for them five hundred talents of silver; and for the harm that ye have done, and the tributes of the cities, other five hundred talents: if not, we will come and fight against you

{15:32} So Athenobius the king's friend came to Jerusalem: and when he saw the glory of Simon, and the cupboard of gold and silver plate, and his great attendance, he was astonished, and told him the king's message.

{15:33} Then answered Simon, and said unto him, We have neither taken other men's land, nor holden that which appertaineth to others, but the inheritance of our fathers, which our enemies had wrongfully in possession a certain time.

{15:34} Wherefore we, having opportunity, hold the inheritance of our fathers.

{15:35} And whereas thou demandest Joppa and Gazera, albeit they did great harm unto the people in our country, yet will we give thee an hundred talents for them. Hereunto Athenobius answered him not a word;

{15:36} But returned in a rage to the king, and made report unto him of these speeches, and of the glory of Simon, and of all that he had seen: whereupon the king was exceeding wroth.

{15:37} In the mean time fled Tryphon by ship unto Orthosias.

{15:38} Then the king made Cendebeus captain of the sea coast, and gave him an host of footmen and horsemen,

{15:39} And commanded him to remove his host toward Judea; also he commanded him to build up Cedron, and to fortify the gates, and to war against the people; but as for the king himself, he pursued Tryphon.

{15:40} So Cendebeus came to Jamnia and began to provoke the people and to invade Judea, and to take the people prisoners, and slay them.

{15:41} And when he had built up Cedrou, he set horsemen there, and an host of footmen, to the end that issuing out they might make outroads upon the ways of Judea, as the king had commanded him.

{16:1} Then came up John from Gazera, and told Simon his father what Cendebeus had done.

{16:2} Wherefore Simon called his two eldest sons, Judas and John, and said unto them, I, and my brethren, and my father's house, have ever from my youth unto this day fought against the enemies of Israel; and things have prospered so well in our hands, that we have delivered Israel oftentimes.

{16:3} But now I am old, and ye, by God's mercy, are of a sufficient age: be ye instead of me and my brother, and go and fight for our nation, and the help from heaven be with you.

{16:4} So he chose out of the country twenty thousand men of war with horsemen, who went out against Cendebeus, and rested that night at

Modin.

{16:5} And when as they rose in the morning, and went into the plain, behold, a mighty great host both of footmen and horsemen came against them: howbeit there was a water brook betwixt them.

{16:6} So he and his people pitched over against them: and when he saw that the people were afraid to go over the water brook, he went first over himself, and then the men seeing him passed through after him.

{16:7} That done, he divided his men, and set the horsemen in the midst of the footmen: for the enemies' horsemen were very many.

{16:8} Then sounded they with the holy trumpets: whereupon Cendebeus and his host were put to flight, so that many of them were slain, and the remnant gat them to the strong hold.

{16:9} At that time was Judas John's brother wounded; but John still followed after them, until he came to Cedron, which Cendebeus had built.

{16:10} So they fled even unto the towers in the fields of Azotus; wherefore he burned it with fire: so that there were slain of them about two thousand men. Afterward he returned into the land of Judea in peace.

{16:11} Moreover in the plain of Jericho was Ptolemeus the son of Abubus made captain, and he had abundance of silver and gold:

{16:12} For he was the high priest's son in law.

{16:13} Wherefore his heart being lifted up, he thought to get the country to himself, and thereupon consulted deceitfully against Simon and his sons to destroy them.

{16:14} Now Simon was visiting the cities that were in the country, and taking care for the good ordering of them; at which time he came down himself to Jericho with his sons, Mattathias and Judas, in the hundred threescore and seventeenth year, in the eleventh month, called Sabat:

{16:15} Where the son of Abubus receiving them deceitfully into a little hold, called Docus, which he had built, made them a great banquet: howbeit he had hid men there.

{16:16} So when Simon and his sons had drunk largely, Ptolemee and his men rose up, and took their weapons, and came upon Simon into the banqueting place, and slew him, and his two sons, and certain of his servants.

{16:17} In which doing he committed a great treachery, and recompensed evil for good.

{16:18} Then Ptolemee wrote these things, and sent to the king, that he should send him an host to aid him, and he would deliver him the country and cities.

{16:19} He sent others also to Gazera to kill John: and unto the tribunes he sent letters to come unto him, that he might give them silver, and gold, and rewards.

{16:20} And others he sent to take Jerusalem, and the mountain of the temple.

{16:21} Now one had run afore to Gazera and told John that his father and brethren were slain, and, quoth he, Ptolemee hath sent to slay thee also.

{16:22} Hereof when he heard, he was sore astonished: so he laid hands on them that were come to destroy him, and slew them; for he knew that they sought to make him away.

{16:23} As concerning the rest of the acts of John, and his wars, and worthy deeds which he did, and the building of the walls which he made, and his doings,

{16:24} Behold, these are written in the chronicles of his priesthood, from the time he was made high priest after his father.

The Second Book of the Maccabees

{1:1} The brethren, the Jews that be at Jerusalem and in the land of Judea, wish unto the brethren, the Jews that are throughout Egypt health and peace:

{1:2} God be gracious unto you, and remember his covenant that he made with Abraham, Isaac, and Jacob, his faithful servants;

{1:3} And give you all an heart to serve him, and to do his will, with a good courage and a willing mind;

{1:4} And open your hearts in his law and commandments, and send you peace,

{1:5} And hear your prayers, and be at one with you, and never forsake you in time of trouble.

{1:6} And now we be here praying for you.

{1:7} What time as Demetrius reigned, in the hundred threescore and ninth year, we the Jews wrote unto you in the extremity of trouble that came upon us in those years, from the time that Jason and his company revolted from the holy land and kingdom,

{1:8} And burned the porch, and shed innocent blood: then we prayed unto the Lord, and were heard; we offered also sacrifices and fine flour, and lighted the lamps, and set forth the loaves.

{1:9} And now see that ye keep the feast of tabernacles in the month Casleu.

{1:10} In the hundred fourscore and eighth year, the people that were at Jerusalem and in Judea, and the council, and Judas, sent greeting and health unto Aristobulus, king Ptolemeus' master, who was of the stock of the anointed priests, and to the Jews that were in Egypt:

{1:11} Insomuch as God hath delivered us from great perils, we thank him highly, as having been in battle against a king.

{1:12} For he cast them out that fought within the holy city.

{1:13} For when the leader was come into Persia, and the army with him that seemed invincible, they were slain in the temple of Nanea by the deceit of Nanea's priests.

{1:14} For Antiochus, as though he would marry her, came into the place, and his friends that were with him, to receive money in name of a dowry.

{1:15} Which when the priests of Nanea had set forth, and he was entered with a small company into the compass of the temple, they shut the temple as soon as Antiochus was come in:

{1:16} And opening a privy door of the roof, they threw stones like thunderbolts, and struck down the captain, hewed them in pieces, smote off their heads and cast them to those that were without.

{1:17} Blessed be our God in all things, who hath delivered up the ungodly.

{1:18} Therefore whereas we are now purposed to keep the purification of the temple upon the five and twentieth day of the month Casleu, we thought it necessary to certify you thereof, that ye also might keep it, as the feast of the tabernacles, and of the fire, which was given us when Neemias offered sacrifice, after that he had builded the temple and the altar.

{1:19} For when our fathers were led into Persia, the priests that were then devout took the fire of the altar privily, and hid it in an hollow place of a pit without water, where they kept it sure, so that the place was unknown to all men.

{1:20} Now after many years, when it pleased God, Neemias, being sent from the king of Persia, did send of the posterity of those priests that had hid it to the fire: but when they told us they found no fire, but thick water;

{1:21} Then commanded he them to draw it up, and to bring it; and when the sacrifices were laid on, Neemias commanded the priests to sprinkle the wood and the things laid thereupon with the water.

{1:22} When this was done, and the time came that the sun shone, which afore was hid in the cloud, there was a great fire kindled, so that every man marveled.

{1:23} And the priests made a prayer whilst the sacrifice was consuming, I say, both the priests, and all the rest, Jonathan beginning, and the rest answering thereunto, as Neemias did.

{1:24} And the prayer was after this manner; O Lord, Lord God, Creator of all things, who art fearful and strong, and righteous, and merciful, and the only and gracious King,

{1:25} The only giver of all things, the only just, almighty, and everlasting, thou that deliverest Israel from all trouble, and didst choose the fathers, and sanctify them:

{1:26} Receive the sacrifice for thy whole people Israel, and preserve thine own portion, and sanctify it.

{1:27} Gather those together that are scattered from us, deliver them that serve among the heathen, look upon them that are despised and abhorred, and let the heathen know that thou art our God.

{1:28} Punish them that oppress us, and with pride do us wrong.

{1:29} Plant thy people again in thy holy place, as Moses hath spoken.

{1:30} And the priests sung psalms of thanksgiving.

{1:31} Now when the sacrifice was consumed, Neemias commanded the water that was left to be poured on the great stones.

{1:32} When this was done, there was kindled a flame: but it was consumed by the light that shined from the altar.

{1:33} So when this matter was known, it was told the king of Persia, that in the place, where the priests that were led away had hid the fire, there appeared water, and that Neemias had purified the sacrifices therewith.

{1:34} Then the king, inclosing the place, made it holy, after he had tried the matter.

{1:35} And the king took many gifts, and bestowed thereof on those whom he would gratify.

{1:36} And Neemias called this thing Naphthar, which is as much as to say, a cleansing: but many men call it Nephi.

{2:1} It is also found in the records, that Jeremy the prophet commanded them that were carried away to take of the fire, as it hath been signified:

{2:2} And how that the prophet, having given them the law, charged them not to forget the commandments of the Lord, and that they should not err in their minds, when they see images of silver and gold, with their ornaments.

{2:3} And with other such speeches exhorted he them, that the law should not depart from their hearts.

{2:4} It was also contained in the same writing, that the prophet, being warned of God, commanded the tabernacle and the ark to go with him, as he went forth into the mountain, where Moses climbed up, and saw the heritage of God.

{2:5} And when Jeremy came thither, he found an hollow cave, wherein he laid the tabernacle, and the ark, and the altar of incense, and so stopped the door.

{2:6} And some of those that followed him came to mark the way, but they could not find it.

{2:7} Which when Jeremy perceived, he blamed them, saying, As for that place, it shall be unknown until the time that God gather his people again together, and receive them unto mercy.

{2:8} Then shall the Lord shew them these things, and the glory of the Lord shall appear, and the cloud also, as it was shewed under Moses, and as when Solomon desired that the place might be honourably sanctified.

{2:9} It was also declared, that he being wise offered the sacrifice of dedication, and of the finishing of the temple.

{2:10} And as when Moses prayed unto the Lord, the fire came down from heaven, and consumed the sacrifices: even so prayed Solomon also, and the fire came down from heaven, and consumed the burnt offerings.

{2:11} And Moses said, Because the sin offering was not to be eaten, it was consumed.

{2:12} So Solomon kept those eight days.

{2:13} The same things also were reported in the writings and commentaries of Neemias; and how he founding a library gathered together the acts of the kings, and the prophets, and of David, and the epistles of the kings concerning the holy gifts.

{2:14} In like manner also Judas gathered together all those things that were lost by reason of the war we had, and they remain with us,

{2:15} Wherefore if ye have need thereof, send some to fetch them unto you.

{2:16} Whereas we then are about to celebrate the purification, we have written unto you, and ye shall do well, if ye keep the same days.

{2:17} We hope also, that the God, that delivered all his people, and gave them all an heritage, and the kingdom, and the priesthood, and the sanctuary,

{2:18} As he promised in the law, will shortly have mercy upon us, and gather us together out of every land under heaven into the holy place: for he hath delivered us out of great troubles, and hath purified the place.

{2:19} Now as concerning Judas Maccabeus, and his brethren, and the purification of the great temple, and the dedication of the altar,

{2:20} And the wars against Antiochus Epiphanes, and Eupator his son,

{2:21} And the manifest signs that came from heaven unto those that behaved themselves manfully to their honour for Judaism: so that, being but a few, they overcame the whole country, and chased barbarous multitudes,

{2:22} And recovered again the temple renowned all the world over, and freed the city, and upheld the laws which were going down, the Lord being gracious unto them with all favour:

{2:23} All these things, I say, being declared by Jason of Cyrene in five books, we will assay to abridge in one volume.

{2:24} For considering the infinite number, and the difficulty which they find that desire to look into the narrations of the story, for the variety of the matter,

{2:25} We have been careful, that they that will read may have delight, and that they that are desirous to commit to memory might have ease, and that all into whose hands it comes might have profit.

{2:26} Therefore to us, that have taken upon us this painful labour of abridging, it was not easy, but a matter of sweat and watching;

{2:27} Even as it is no ease unto him that prepareth a banquet, and seeketh the benefit of others: yet for the pleasuring of many we will undertake gladly this great pains;

{2:28} Leaving to the author the exact handling of every particular, and labouring to follow the rules of an abridgement.

{2:29} For as the master builder of a new house must care for the whole building; but he that undertaketh to set it out, and paint it, must seek out fit things for the adorning thereof: even so I think it is with us.

{2:30} To stand upon every point, and go over things at large, and to be curious in particulars, belongeth to the first author of the story:

{2:31} But to use brevity, and avoid much labouring of the work, is to be granted to him that will make an abridgment.

{2:32} Here then will we begin the story: only adding thus much to that which hath been said, that it is a foolish thing to make a long prologue, and to be short in the story itself.

{3:1} Now when the holy city was inhabited with all peace, and the laws were kept very well, because of the godliness of Onias the high priest, and his hatred of wickedness,

{3:2} It came to pass that even the kings themselves did honour the place, and magnify the temple with their best gifts;

{3:3} Insomuch that Seleucus of Asia of his own revenues bare all the costs belonging to the service of the sacrifices.

{3:4} But one Simon of the tribe of Benjamin, who was made governor of the temple, fell out with the high priest about disorder in the city.

{3:5} And when he could not overcome Onias, he gat him to Apollonius the son of Thraseas, who then was governor of Celosyria and Phenice,

{3:6} And told him that the treasury in Jerusalem was full of infinite sums of money, so that the multitude of their riches, which did not pertain to the account of the sacrifices, was innumerable, and that it was possible to bring all into the king's hand.

{3:7} Now when Apollonius came to the king, and had shewed him of the money whereof he was told, the king chose out Heliodorus his treasurer, and sent him with a commandment to bring him the foresaid money.

{3:8} So forthwith Heliodorus took his journey; under a colour of visiting the cities of Celosyria and Phenice, but indeed to fulfil the king's purpose.

{3:9} And when he was come to Jerusalem, and had been courteously received of the high priest of the city, he told him what intelligence was given of the money, and declared wherefore he came, and asked if these things were so indeed.

{3:10} Then the high priest told him that there was such money laid up for the relief of widows and fatherless children:

{3:11} And that some of it belonged to Hircanus son of Tobias, a man of great dignity, and not as that wicked Simon had misinformed: the sum whereof in all was four hundred talents of silver, and two hundred of gold:

{3:12} And that it was altogether impossible that such wrongs should be done unto them, that had committed it to the holiness of the place, and to the majesty and inviolable sanctity of the temple, honoured over all the world.

{3:13} But Heliodorus, because of the king's commandment given him, said, That in any wise it must be brought into the king's treasury.

{3:14} So at the day which he appointed he entered in to order this matter: wherefore there was no small agony throughout the whole city.

{3:15} But the priests, prostrating themselves before the altar in their priests' vestments, called unto heaven upon him that made a law concerning things given to he kept, that they should safely be preserved for such as had committed them to be kept.

{3:16} Then whoso had looked the high priest in the face, it would have wounded his heart: for his countenance and the changing of his colour declared the inward agony of his mind.

{3:17} For the man was so compassed with fear and horror of the body, that it was manifest to them that looked upon him, what sorrow he had now in his heart.

{3:18} Others ran flocking out of their houses to the general supplication, because the place was like to come into contempt.

{3:19} And the women, girt with sackcloth under their breasts, abounded in the streets, and the virgins that were kept in ran, some to the gates, and some to the walls, and others looked out of the windows.

{3:20} And all, holding their hands toward heaven, made supplication.

{3:21} Then it would have pitied a man to see the falling down of the multitude of all sorts, and the fear of the high priest being in such an agony.

{3:22} They then called upon the Almighty Lord to keep the things committed of trust safe and sure for those that had committed them.

{3:23} Nevertheless Heliodorus executed that which was decreed.

{3:24} Now as he was there present himself with his guard about the treasury, the Lord of spirits, and the Prince of all power, caused a great apparition, so that all that presumed to come in with him were astonished at the power of God, and fainted, and were sore afraid.

{3:25} For there appeared unto them an horse with a terrible rider upon him, and adorned with a very fair covering, and he ran fiercely, and smote at Heliodorus with his forefeet, and it seemed that he that sat upon the horse had complete harness of gold.

{3:26} Moreover two other young men appeared before him, notable in strength, excellent in beauty, and comely in apparel, who stood by him on either side; and scourged him continually, and gave him many sore stripes.

{3:27} And Heliodorus fell suddenly unto the ground, and was compassed with great darkness: but they that were with him took him up, and put him into a litter.

{3:28} Thus him, that lately came with a great train and with all his guard into the said treasury, they carried out, being unable to help himself with his weapons: and manifestly they acknowledged the power of God.

{3:29} For he by the hand of God was cast down, and lay speechless without all hope of life.

{3:30} But they praised the Lord, that had miraculously honoured his own place: for the temple; which a little afore was full of fear and trouble, when the Almighty Lord appeared, was filled with joy and gladness.

{3:31} Then straightways certain of Heliodorus' friends prayed Onias, that he would call upon the most High to grant him his life, who lay ready to give up the ghost.

{3:32} So the high priest, suspecting lest the king should misconceive that some treachery had been done to Heliodorus by the

Jews, offered a sacrifice for the health of the man.

{3:33} Now as the high priest was making an atonement, the same young men in the same clothing appeared and stood beside Heliodorus, saying, Give Onias the high priest great thanks, insomuch as for his sake the Lord hath granted thee life:

{3:34} And seeing that thou hast been scourged from heaven, declare unto all men the mighty power of God. And when they had spoken these words, they appeared no more.

{3:35} So Heliodorus, after he had offered sacrifice unto the Lord, and made great vows unto him that had saved his life, and saluted Onias, returned with his host to the king.

{3:36} Then testified he to all men the works of the great God, which he had seen with his eyes.

{3:37} And when the king Heliodorus, who might be a fit man to be sent yet once again to Jerusalem, he said,

{3:38} If thou hast any enemy or traitor, send him thither, and thou shalt receive him well scourged, if he escapes with his life: for in that place, no doubt; there is an especial power of God.

{3:39} For he that dwelleth in heaven hath his eye on that place, and defendeth it; and he beateth and destroyeth them that come to hurt it.

{3:40} And the things concerning Heliodorus, and the keeping of the treasury, fell out on this sort.

{4:1} This Simon now, of whom we spake afore, having been a betrayer of the money, and of his country, slandered Onias, as if he ha terrified Heliodorus, and been the worker of these evils.

{4:2} Thus was he bold to call him a traitor, that had deserved well of the city, and tendered his own nation, and was so zealous of the laws.

{4:3} But when their hatred went so far, that by one of Simon's faction murders were committed,

{4:4} Onias seeing the danger of this contention, and that Apollonius, as being the governor of Celosyria and Phenice, did rage, and increase Simon's malice,

{4:5} He went to the king, not to be an accuser of his countrymen, but seeking the good of all, both publick and private.

{4:6} For he saw that it was impossible that the state should continue quiet, and Simon leave his folly, unless the king did look thereunto.

{4:7} But after the death of Seleucus, when Antiochus, called Epiphanes, took the kingdom, Jason the brother of Onias laboured underhand to be high priest,

{4:8} Promising unto the king by intercession three hundred and threescore talents of silver, and of another revenue eighty talents:

{4:9} Beside this, he promised to assign an hundred and fifty more, if he might have licence to set him up a place for exercise, and for the training up of youth in the fashions of the heathen, and to write them of Jerusalem by the name of Antiochians.

{4:10} Which when the king had granted, and he had gotten into his hand the rule he forthwith brought his own nation to Greekish fashion.

{4:11} And the royal privileges granted of special favour to the Jews by the means of John the father of Eupolemus, who went ambassador to Rome for amity and aid, he took away; and putting down the governments which were according to the law, he brought up new customs against the law:

{4:12} For he built gladly a place of exercise under the tower itself, and brought the chief young men under his subjection, and made them wear a hat.

{4:13} Now such was the height of Greek fashions, and increase of heathenish manners, through the exceeding profaneness of Jason, that ungodly wretch, and no high priest;

{4:14} That the priests had no courage to serve any more at the altar, but despising the temple, and neglecting the sacrifices, hastened to be partakers of the unlawful allowance in the place of exercise, after the game of Discus called them forth;

{4:15} Not setting by the honours of their fathers, but liking the glory of the Grecians best of all.

{4:16} By reason whereof sore calamity came upon them: for they had them to be their enemies and avengers, whose custom they followed so earnestly, and unto whom they desired to be like in all things.

{4:17} For it is not a light thing to do wickedly against the laws of God: but the time following shall declare these things.

{4:18} Now when the game that was used every fifth year was kept at Tyrus, the king being present,

{4:19} This ungracious Jason sent special messengers from Jerusalem, who were Antiochians, to carry three hundred drachms of silver to the sacrifice of Hercules, which even the bearers thereof thought fit not to bestow upon the sacrifice, because it was not convenient, but to be reserved for other charges.

{4:20} This money then, in regard of the sender, was appointed to Hercules' sacrifice; but because of the bearers thereof, it was employed to the making of gallies.

{4:21} Now when Apollonius the son of Menestheus was sent into Egypt for the coronation of king Ptolemeus Philometor, Antiochus, understanding him not to be well affected to his affairs, provided for his own safety: whereupon he came to Joppa, and from thence to Jerusalem:

{4:22} Where he was honourably received of Jason, and of the city, and was brought in with torch alight, and with great shoutings: and so afterward went with his host unto Phenice.

{4:23} Three years afterward Jason sent Menelaus, the aforesaid Simon's brother, to bear the money unto the king, and to put him in mind of certain necessary matters.

{4:24} But he being brought to the presence of the king, when he had magnified him for the glorious appearance of his power, got the priesthood to himself, offering more than Jason by three hundred talents of silver.

{4:25} So he came with the king's mandate, bringing nothing worthy the high priesthood, but having the fury of a cruel tyrant, and the rage of a savage beast.

{4:26} Then Jason, who had undermined his own brother, being undermined by another, was compelled to flee into the country of the Ammonites.

{4:27} So Menelaus got the principality: but as for the money that he had promised unto the king, he took no good order for it, albeit Sostratis the ruler of the castle required it:

{4:28} For unto him appertained the gathering of the customs. Wherefore they were both called before the king.

{4:29} Now Menelaus left his brother Lysimachus in his stead in the priesthood; and Sostratus left Crates, who was governor of the Cyprians.

{4:30} While those things were in doing, they of Tarsus and Mallos made insurrection, because they were given to the king's concubine, called Antiochus.

{4:31} Then came the king in all haste to appease matters, leaving Andronicus, a man in authority, for his deputy.

{4:32} Now Menelaus, supposing that he had gotten a convenient time, stole certain vessels of gold out of the temple, and gave some of them to Andronicus, and some he sold into Tyrus and the cities round about.

{4:33} Which when Onias knew of a surety, he reproved him, and withdrew himself into a sanctuary at Daphne, that lieth by Antiochia.

{4:34} Wherefore Menelaus, taking Andronicus apart, prayed, him to get Onias into his hands; who being persuaded thereunto, and coming to Onias in deceit, gave him his right hand with oaths; and though he were suspected by him, yet persuaded he him to come forth of the sanctuary: whom forthwith he shut up without regard of justice.

{4:35} For the which cause not only the Jews, but many also of other nations, took great indignation, and were much grieved for the unjust murder of the man.

{4:36} And when the king was come again from the places about Cilicia, the Jews that were in the city, and certain of the Greeks that abhorred the fact also, complained because Onias was slain without cause.

{4:37} Therefore Antiochus was heartily sorry, and moved to pity, and wept, because of the sober and modest behaviour of him that was dead.

{4:38} And being kindled with anger, forthwith he took away Andronicus his purple, and rent off his clothes, and leading him through the whole city unto that very place, where he had committed impiety against Onias, there slew he the cursed murderer. Thus the Lord rewarded him his punishment, as he had deserved.

{4:39} Now when many sacrileges had been committed in the city by Lysimachus with the consent of Menelaus, and the fruit thereof was spread abroad, the multitude gathered themselves together against Lysimachus, many vessels of gold being already carried away.

{4:40} Whereupon the common people rising, and being filled with rage, Lysimachus armed about three thousand men, and began first to offer violence; one Auranus being the leader, a man far gone in years, and no less in folly.

{4:41} They then seeing the attempt of Lysimachus, some of them caught stones, some clubs, others taking handfuls of dust, that was next at hand, cast them all together upon Lysimachus, and those that set upon them.

{4:42} Thus many of them they wounded, and some they struck to the ground, and all of them they forced to flee: but as for the churchrobber himself, him they killed beside the treasury.

{4:43} Of these matters therefore there was an accusation laid against Menelaus.

{4:44} Now when the king came to Tyrus, three men that were sent from the senate pleaded the cause before him:

{4:45} But Menelaus, being now convicted, promised Ptolemee the son of Dorymenes to give him much money, if he would pacify the king toward him.

{4:46} Whereupon Ptolemee taking the king aside into a certain gallery, as it were to take the air, brought him to be of another mind:

{4:47} Insomuch that he discharged Menelaus from the accusations, who notwithstanding was cause of all the mischief: and those poor men, who, if they had told their cause, yea, before the Scythians, should have been judged innocent, them he condemned to death.

{4:48} Thus they that followed the matter for the city, and for the people, and for the holy vessels, did soon suffer unjust punishment.

{4:49} Wherefore even they of Tyrus, moved with hatred of that wicked deed, caused them to be honourably buried.

{4:50} And so through the covetousness of them that were of power Menelaus remained still in authority, increasing in malice, and being a great traitor to the citizens.

{5:1} About the same time Antiochus prepared his second voyage into Egypt:

{5:2} And then it happened, that through all the city, for the space almost of forty days, there were seen horsemen running in the air, in cloth of gold, and armed with lances, like a band of soldiers,

{5:3} And troops of horsemen in array, encountering and running one against another, with shaking of shields, and multitude of pikes, and drawing of swords, and casting of darts, and glittering of golden ornaments, and harness of all sorts.

{5:4} Wherefore every man prayed that that apparition might turn to good.

{5:5} Now when there was gone forth a false rumour, as though

Antiochus had been dead, Jason took at the least a thousand men, and suddenly made an assault upon the city; and they that were upon the walls being put back, and the city at length taken, Menelaus fled into the castle:

{5:6} But Jason slew his own citizens without mercy, not considering that to get the day of them of his own nation would be a most unhappy day for him; but thinking they had been his enemies, and not his countrymen, whom he conquered.

{5:7} Howbeit for all this he obtained not the principality, but at the last received shame for the reward of his treason, and fled again into the country of the Ammonites.

{5:8} In the end therefore he had an unhappy return, being accused before Aretas the king of the Arabians, fleeing from city to city, pursued of all men, hated as a forsaker of the laws, and being had in abomination as an open enemy of his country and countrymen, he was cast out into Egypt.

{5:9} Thus he that had driven many out of their country perished in a strange land, retiring to the Lacedemonians, and thinking there to find succour by reason of his kindred:

{5:10} And he that had cast out many unburied had none to mourn for him, nor any solemn funerals at all, nor sepulchre with his fathers.

{5:11} Now when this that was done came to the king's car, he thought that Judea had revolted: whereupon removing out of Egypt in a furious mind, he took the city by force of arms,

{5:12} And commanded his men of war not to spare such as they met, and to slay such as went up upon the houses.

{5:13} Thus there was killing of young and old, making away of men, women, and children, slaying of virgins and infants.

{5:14} And there were destroyed within the space of three whole days fourscore thousand, whereof forty thousand were slain in the conflict; and no fewer sold than slain.

{5:15} Yet was he not content with this, but presumed to go into the most holy temple of all the world; Menelaus, that traitor to the laws, and to his own country, being his guide:

{5:16} And taking the holy vessels with polluted hands, and with profane hands pulling down the things that were dedicated by other kings to the augmentation and glory and honour of the place, he gave them away.

{5:17} And so haughty was Antiochus in mind, that he considered not that the Lord was angry for a while for the sins of them that dwelt in the city, and therefore his eye was not upon the place.

{5:18} For had they not been formerly wrapped in many sins, this man, as soon as he had come, had forthwith been scourged, and put back from his presumption, as Heliodorus was, whom Seleucus the king sent to view the treasury.

{5:19} Nevertheless God did not choose the people for the place's sake, but the place far the people's sake.

{5:20} And therefore the place itself, that was partaker with them of the adversity that happened to the nation, did afterward communicate in the benefits sent from the Lord: and as it was forsaken in the wrath of the Almighty, so again, the great Lord being reconciled, it was set up with all glory.

{5:21} So when Antiochus had carried out of the temple a thousand and eight hundred talents, he departed in all haste unto Antiochia, weening in his pride to make the land navigable, and the sea passable by foot: such was the haughtiness of his mind.

{5:22} And he left governors to vex the nation: at Jerusalem, Philip, for his country a Phrygian, and for manners more barbarous than he that set him there;

{5:23} And at Garizim, Andronicus; and besides, Menelaus, who worse than all the rest bare an heavy hand over the citizens, having a malicious mind against his countrymen the Jews.

{5:24} He sent also that detestable ringleader Apollonius with an army of two and twenty thousand, commanding him to slay all those that were in their best age, and to sell the women and the younger sort:

{5:25} Who coming to Jerusalem, and pretending peace, did forbear till the holy day of the sabbath, when taking the Jews keeping holy day, he commanded his men to arm themselves.

{5:26} And so he slew all them that were gone to the celebrating of the sabbath, and running through the city with weapons slew great multitudes.

{5:27} But Judas Maccabeus with nine others, or thereabout, withdrew himself into the wilderness, and lived in the mountains after the manner of beasts, with his company, who fed on herbs continually, lest they should be partakers of the pollution.

{6:1} Not long after this the king sent an old man of Athens to compel the Jews to depart from the laws of their fathers, and not to live after the laws of God:

{6:2} And to pollute also the temple in Jerusalem, and to call it the temple of Jupiter Olympius; and that in Garizim, of Jupiter the Defender of strangers, as they did desire that dwelt in the place.

{6:3} The coming in of this mischief was sore and grievous to the people:

{6:4} For the temple was filled with riot and revelling by the Gentiles, who dallied with harlots, and had to do with women within the circuit of the holy places, and besides that brought in things that were not lawful.

{6:5} The altar also was filled with profane things, which the law forbiddeth.

{6:6} Neither was it lawful for a man to keep sabbath days or ancient fasts, or to profess himself at all to be a Jew.

{6:7} And in the day of the king's birth every month they were brought by bitter constraint to eat of the sacrifices; and when the fast of Bacchus was kept, the Jews were compelled to go in procession to Bacchus, carrying ivy.

{6:8} Moreover there went out a decree to the neighbour cities of the heathen, by the suggestion of Ptolemee, against the Jews, that they should observe the same fashions, and be partakers of their sacrifices:

{6:9} And whoso would not conform themselves to the manners of the Gentiles should be put to death. Then might a man have seen the present misery.

{6:10} For there were two women brought, who had circumcised their children; whom when they had openly led round about the city, the babes handing at their breasts, they cast them down headlong from the wall.

{6:11} And others, that had run together into caves near by, to keep the sabbath day secretly, being discovered by Philip, were all burnt together, because they made a conscience to help themselves for the honour of the most sacred day.

{6:12} Now I beseech those that read this book, that they be not discouraged for these calamities, but that they judge those punishments not to be for destruction, but for a chastening of our nation.

{6:13} For it is a token of his great goodness, when wicked doers are not suffered any long time, but forthwith punished.

{6:14} For not as with other nations, whom the Lord patiently forbeareth to punish, till they be come to the fulness of their sins, so dealeth he with us,

{6:15} Lest that, being come to the height of sin, afterwards he should take vengeance of us.

{6:16} And therefore he never withdraweth his mercy from us: and though he punishes with adversity, yet doth he never forsake his people.

{6:17} But let this that we at spoken be for a warning unto us. And now will we come to the declaring of the matter in a few words.

{6:18} Eleazar, one of the principal scribes, an aged man, and of a well favoured countenance, was constrained to open his mouth, and to eat swine's flesh.

{6:19} But he, choosing rather to die gloriously, than to live stained with such an abomination, spit it forth, and came of his own accord to the torment,

{6:20} As it behoved them to come, that are resolute to stand out against such things, as are not lawful for love of life to be tasted.

{6:21} But they that had the charge of that wicked feast, for the old acquaintance they had with the man, taking him aside, besought him to bring flesh of his own provision, such as was lawful for him to use, and make as if he did eat of the flesh taken from the sacrifice commanded by the king;

{6:22} That in so doing he might be delivered from death, and for the old friendship with them find favour.

{6:23} But he began to consider discreetly, and as became his age, and the excellency of his ancient years, and the honour of his gray head, whereon was come, and his most honest education from a child, or rather the holy law made and given by God: therefore he answered accordingly, and willed them straightways to send him to the grave.

{6:24} For it becometh not our age, said he, in any wise to dissemble, whereby many young persons might think that Eleazar, being fourscore years old and ten, were now gone to a strange religion;

{6:25} And so they through mine hypocrisy, and desire to live a little time and a moment longer, should be deceived by me, and I get a stain to mine old age, and make it abominable.

{6:26} For though for the present time I should be delivered from the punishment of men: yet should I not escape the hand of the Almighty, neither alive, nor dead.

{6:27} Wherefore now, manfully changing this life, I will shew myself such an one as mine age requireth,

{6:28} And leave a notable example to such as be young to die willingly and courageously for the honourable and holy laws. And when he had said these words, immediately he went to the torment:

{6:29} They that led him changing the good will they bare him a little before into hatred, because the foresaid speeches proceeded, as they thought, from a desperate mind.

{6:30} But when he was ready to die with stripes, he groaned, and said, It is manifest unto the Lord, that hath the holy knowledge, that whereas I might have been delivered from death, I now endure sore pains in body by being beaten: but in soul am well content to suffer these things, because I fear him.

{6:31} And thus this man died, leaving his death for an example of a noble courage, and a memorial of virtue, not only unto young men, but unto all his nation.

{7:1} It came to pass also, that seven brethren with their mother were taken, and compelled by the king against the law to taste swine's flesh, and were tormented with scourges and whips.

{7:2} But one of them that spake first said thus, What wouldest thou ask or learn of us? we are ready to die, rather than to transgress the laws of our fathers.

{7:3} Then the king, being in a rage, commanded pans and caldrons to be made hot:

{7:4} Which forthwith being heated, he commanded to cut out the tongue of him that spake first, and to cut off the utmost parts of his body, the rest of his brethren and his mother looking on.

{7:5} Now when he was thus maimed in all his members, he commanded him being yet alive to be brought to the fire, and to be fried in the pan: and as the vapour of the pan was for a good space dispersed, they exhorted one another with the mother to die manfully, saying thus,

{7:6} The Lord God looketh upon us, and in truth hath comfort in us, as Moses in his song, which witnessed to their faces, declared, saying, And he shall be comforted in his servants.

{7:7} So when the first was dead after this number, they brought the second to make him a mocking stock: and when they had pulled off the skin of his head with the hair, they asked him, Wilt thou eat, before thou be punished throughout every member of thy body?

{7:8} But he answered in his own language, and said, No. Wherefore he also received the next torment in order, as the former did.

{7:9} And when he was at the last gasp, he said, Thou like a fury takest us out of this present life, but the King of the world shall raise us up, who have died for his laws, unto everlasting life.

{7:10} After him was the third made a mocking stock: and when he was required, he put out his tongue, and that right soon, holding forth his hands manfully.

{7:11} And said courageously, These I had from heaven; and for his laws I despise them; and from him I hope to receive them again.

{7:12} Insomuch that the king, and they that were with him, marvelled at the young man's courage, for that he nothing regarded the pains.

{7:13} Now when this man was dead also, they tormented and mangled the fourth in like manner.

{7:14} So when he was ready to die he said thus, It is good, being put to death by men, to look for hope from God to be raised up again by him: as for thee, thou shalt have no resurrection to life.

{7:15} Afterward they brought the fifth also, and mangled him.

{7:16} Then looked he unto the king, and said, Thou hast power over men, thou art corruptible, thou doest what thou wilt; yet think not that our nation is forsaken of God;

{7:17} But abide a while, and behold his great power, how he will torment thee and thy seed.

{7:18} After him also they brought the sixth, who being ready to die said, Be not deceived without cause: for we suffer these things for ourselves, having sinned against our God: therefore marvellous things are done unto us.

{7:19} But think not thou, that takest in hand to strive against God, that thou shalt escape unpunished.

{7:20} But the mother was marvellous above all, and worthy of honourable memory: for when she saw her seven sons slain within the space of one day, she bare it with a good courage, because of the hope that she had in the Lord.

{7:21} Yea, she exhorted every one of them in her own language, filled with courageous spirits; and stirring up her womanish thoughts with a manly stomach, she said unto them,

{7:22} I cannot tell how ye came into my womb: for I neither gave you breath nor life, neither was it I that formed the members of every one of you;

{7:23} But doubtless the Creator of the world, who formed the generation of man, and found out the beginning of all things, will also of his own mercy give you breath and life again, as ye now regard not your own selves for his laws' sake.

{7:24} Now Antiochus, thinking himself despised, and suspecting it to be a reproachful speech, whilst the youngest was yet alive, did not only exhort him by words, but also assured him with oaths, that he would make him both a rich and a happy man, if he would turn from the laws of his fathers; and that also he would take him for his friend, and trust him with affairs.

{7:25} But when the young man would in no case hearken unto him, the king called his mother, and exhorted her that she would counsel the young man to save his life.

{7:26} And when he had exhorted her with many words, she promised him that she would counsel her son.

{7:27} But she bowing herself toward him, laughing the cruel tyrant to scorn, spake in her country language on this manner; O my son, have pity upon me that bare thee nine months in my womb, and gave thee such three years, and nourished thee, and brought thee up unto this age, and endured the troubles of education.

{7:28} I beseech thee, my son, look upon the heaven and the earth, and all that is therein, and consider that God made them of things that were not; and so was mankind made likewise.

{7:29} Fear not this tormentor, but, being worthy of thy brethren, take thy death that I may receive thee again in mercy with thy brethren.

{7:30} Whiles she was yet speaking these words, the young man said, Whom wait ye for? I will not obey the king's commandment: but I will obey the commandment of the law that was given unto our fathers by Moses.

{7:31} And thou, that hast been the author of all mischief against the Hebrews, shalt not escape the hands of God.

{7:32} For we suffer because of our sins.

{7:33} And though the living Lord be angry with us a little while for our chastening and correction, yet shall he be at one again with his servants.

{7:34} But thou, O godless man, and of all other most wicked, be not lifted up without a cause, nor puffed up with uncertain hopes, lifting up thy hand against the servants of God:

{7:35} For thou hast not yet escaped the judgment of Almighty God, who seeth all things.

{7:36} For our brethren, who now have suffered a short pain, are dead under God's covenant of everlasting life: but thou, through the judgment of God, shalt receive just punishment for thy pride.

{7:37} But I, as my brethren, offer up my body and life for the laws of our fathers, beseeching God that he would speedily be merciful unto our nation; and that thou by torments and plagues mayest confess, that he alone is God;

{7:38} And that in me and my brethren the wrath of the Almighty, which is justly brought upon our nation, may cease.

{7:39} Than the king' being in a rage, handed him worse than all the rest, and took it grievously that he was mocked.

{7:40} So this man died undefiled, and put his whole trust in the Lord.

{7:41} Last of all after the sons the mother died.

{7:42} Let this be enough now to have spoken concerning the idolatrous feasts, and the extreme tortures.

{8:1} Then Judas Maccabeus, and they that were with him, went privily into the towns, and called their kinsfolks together, and took unto them all such as continued in the Jews' religion, and assembled about six thousand men.

{8:2} And they called upon the Lord, that he would look upon the people that was trodden down of all; and also pity the temple profaned of ungodly men;

{8:3} And that he would have compassion upon the city, sore defaced, and ready to be made even with the ground; and hear the blood that cried unto him,

{8:4} And remember the wicked slaughter of harmless infants, and the blasphemies committed against his name; and that he would shew his hatred against the wicked.

{8:5} Now when Maccabeus had his company about him, he could not be withstood by the heathen: for the wrath of the Lord was turned into mercy.

{8:6} Therefore he came at unawares, and burnt up towns and cities, and got into his hands the most commodious places, and overcame and put
to flight no small number of his enemies.

{8:7} But specially took he advantage of the night for such privy attempts, insomuch that the fruit of his holiness was spread every where.

{8:8} So when Philip saw that this man increased by little and little, and that things prospered with him still more and more, he wrote unto Ptolemeus, the governor of Celosyria and Phenice, to yield more aid to the king's affairs.

{8:9} Then forthwith choosing Nicanor the son of Patroclus, one of his special friends, he sent him with no fewer than twenty thousand of all nations under him, to root out the whole generation of the Jews; and with him he joined also Gorgias a captain, who in matters of war had great experience.

{8:10} So Nicanor undertook to make so much money of the captive Jews, as should defray the tribute of two thousand talents, which the king was to pay to the Romans.

{8:11} Wherefore immediately he sent to the cities upon the sea coast, proclaiming a sale of the captive Jews, and promising that they should have fourscore and ten bodies for one talent, not expecting the vengeance that was to follow upon him from the Almighty God.

{8:12} Now when word was brought unto Judas of Nicanor's coming, and he had imparted unto those that were with him that the army was at hand,

{8:13} They that were fearful, and distrusted the justice of God, fled, and conveyed themselves away.

{8:14} Others sold all that they had left, and withal besought the Lord to deliver them, sold by the wicked Nicanor before they met together:

{8:15} And if not for their own sakes, yet for the covenants he had made with their fathers, and for his holy and glorious name's sake, by which they were called.

{8:16} So Maccabeus called his men together unto the number of six thousand, and exhorted them not to be stricken with terror of the enemy, nor to fear the great multitude of the heathen, who came wrongly against them; but to fight manfully,

{8:17} And to set before their eyes the injury that they had unjustly done to the holy place, and the cruel handling of the city, whereof they made a mockery, and also the taking away of the government of their forefathers:

{8:18} For they, said he, trust in their weapons and boldness; but our confidence is in the Almighty who at a beck can cast down both them that come against us, and also all the world.

{8:19} Moreover, he recounted unto them what helps their forefathers had found, and how they were delivered, when under Sennacherib an hundred fourscore and five thousand perished.

{8:20} And he told them of the battle that they had in Babylon with the Galatians, how they came but eight thousand in all to the business, with four thousand Macedonians, and that the Macedonians being perplexed, the eight thousand destroyed an hundred and twenty thousand because of the help that they had from heaven, and so received a great booty.

{8:21} Thus when he had made them bold with these words, and ready to die for the law and the country, he divided his army into four parts;

{8:22} And joined with himself his own brethren, leaders of each band, to wit Simon, and Joseph, and Jonathan, giving each one fifteen hundred men.

{8:23} Also he appointed Eleazar to read the holy book: and when he had given them this watchword, the help of God; himself leading the first band,

{8:24} And by the help of the Almighty they slew above nine thousand of their enemies, and wounded and maimed the most part of Nicanor's host, and so put all to flight;

{8:25} And took their money that came to buy them, and pursued them far: but lacking time they returned:

{8:26} For it was the day before the sabbath, and therefore they would no longer pursue them.

{8:27} So when they had gathered their armour together, and spoiled their enemies, they occupied themselves about the sabbath, yielding exceeding praise and thanks to the Lord, who had preserved them unto that day, which was the beginning of mercy distilling upon them.

{8:28} And after the sabbath, when they had given part of the spoils to the maimed, and the widows, and orphans, the residue they divided among themselves and their servants.

{8:29} When this was done, and they had made a common supplication, they besought the merciful Lord to be reconciled with his servants for ever.

{8:30} Moreover of those that were with Timotheus and Bacchides, who fought against them, they slew above twenty thousand, and very easily got high and strong holds, and divided among themselves many spoils more, and made the maimed, orphans, widows, yea, and the aged also, equal in spoils with themselves.

{8:31} And when they had gathered their armour together, they laid them up all carefully in convenient places, and the remnant of the spoils they brought to Jerusalem.

{8:32} They slew also Philarches, that wicked person, who was with Timotheus, and had annoyed the Jews many ways.

{8:33} Furthermore at such time as they kept the feast for the victory in their country they burnt Callisthenes, that had set fire upon the holy gates, who had fled into a little house; and so he received a reward meet for his wickedness.

{8:34} As for that most ungracious Nicanor, who had brought a thousand merchants to buy the Jews,

{8:35} He was through the help of the Lord brought down by them, of whom he made least account; and putting off his glorious apparel, and discharging his company, he came like a fugitive servant through the midland unto Antioch having very great dishonour, for that his host was destroyed.

{8:36} Thus he, that took upon him to make good to the Romans their tribute by means of captives in Jerusalem, told abroad, that the Jews had God to fight for them, and therefore they could not be hurt, because they followed the laws that he gave them.

{9:1} About that time came Antiochus with dishonour out of the country of Persia

{9:2} For he had entered the city called Persepolis, and went about to rob the temple, and to hold the city; whereupon the multitude running to defend themselves with their weapons put them to flight; and so it happened, that Antiochus being put to flight of the inhabitants returned with shame.

{9:3} Now when he came to Ecbatane, news was brought him what had happened unto Nicanor and Timotheus.

{9:4} Then swelling with anger, he thought to avenge upon the Jews the disgrace done unto him by those that made him flee. Therefore commanded he his chariotman to drive without ceasing, and to dispatch the journey, the judgment of God now following him. For he had spoken proudly in this sort, that he would come to Jerusalem and make it a common burying place of the Jews.

{9:5} But the Lord Almighty, the God of Israel, smote him with an incurable and invisible plague: or as soon as he had spoken these words, a pain of the bowels that was remediless came upon him, and sore torments of the inner parts;

{9:6} And that most justly: for he had tormented other men's bowels with many and strange torments.

{9:7} Howbeit he nothing at all ceased from his bragging, but still was filled with pride, breathing out fire in his rage against the Jews, and commanding to haste the journey: but it came to pass that he fell down from his chariot, carried violently; so that having a sore fall, all the members of his body were much pained.

{9:8} And thus he that a little afore thought he might command the waves of the sea, (so proud was he beyond the condition of man) and weigh the high mountains in a balance, was now cast on the ground, and carried in an horselitter, shewing forth unto all the manifest power of God.

{9:9} So that the worms rose up out of the body of this wicked man, and whiles he lived in sorrow and pain, his flesh fell away, and the filthiness of his smell was noisome to all his army.

{9:10} And the man, that thought a little afore he could reach to the stars of heaven, no man could endure to carry for his intolerable stink.

{9:11} Here therefore, being plagued, he began to leave off his great pride, and to come to the knowledge of himself by the scourge of God, his pain increasing every moment.

{9:12} And when he himself could not abide his own smell, he said these words, It is meet to be subject unto God, and that a man that is mortal should not proudly think of himself if he were God.

{9:13} This wicked person vowed also unto the Lord, who now no more would have mercy upon him, saying thus,

{9:14} That the holy city (to the which he was going in haste to lay it even with the ground, and to make it a common buryingplace,) he would set at liberty:

{9:15} And as touching the Jews, whom he had judged not worthy so much as to be buried, but to be cast out with their children to be devoured of the fowls and wild beasts, he would make them all equals to the citizens of Athens:

{9:16} And the holy temple, which before he had spoiled, he would garnish with goodly gifts, and restore all the holy vessels with many more, and out of his own revenue defray the charges belonging to the sacrifices:

{9:17} Yea, and that also he would become a Jew himself, and go through all the world that was inhabited, and declare the power of God.

{9:18} But for all this his pains would not cease: for the just judgment of God was come upon him: therefore despairing of his health, he wrote unto the Jews the letter underwritten, containing the form of a supplication, after this manner:

{9:19} Antiochus, king and governor, to the good Jews his citizens wisheth much joy, health, and prosperity:

{9:20} If ye and your children fare well, and your affairs be to your contentment, I give very great thanks to God, having my hope in heaven.

{9:21} As for me, I was weak, or else I would have remembered kindly your honour and good will returning out of Persia, and being taken with a grievous disease, I thought it necessary to care for the common safety of all:

{9:22} Not distrusting mine health, but having great hope to escape this sickness.

{9:23} But considering that even my father, at what time he led an army into the high countries. appointed a successor,

{9:24} To the end that, if any thing fell out contrary to expectation, or if any tidings were brought that were grievous, they of the land, knowing to whom the state was left, might not be troubled:

{9:25} Again, considering how that the princes that are borderers and neighbours unto my kingdom wait for opportunities, and expect what shall be the event. I have appointed my son Antiochus king, whom I often committed and commended unto many of you, when I went up into the high provinces; to whom I have written as followeth:

{9:26} Therefore I pray and request you to remember the benefits that I have done unto you generally, and in special, and that every man will be still faithful to me and my son.

{9:27} For I am persuaded that he understanding my mind will favourably and graciously yield to your desires.

{9:28} Thus the murderer and blasphemer having suffered most grievously, as he entreated other men, so died he a miserable death in a strange country in the mountains.

{9:29} And Philip, that was brought up with him, carried away his body, who also fearing the son of Antiochus went into Egypt to Ptolemeus Philometor.

{10:1} Now Maccabeus and his company, the Lord guiding them, recovered the temple and the city:

{10:2} But the altars which the heathen had built in the open street, and also the chapels, they pulled down.

{10:3} And having cleansed the temple they made another altar, and striking stones they took fire out of them, and offered a sacrifice after two years, and set forth incense, and lights, and shewbread.

{10:4} When that was done, they fell flat down, and besought the Lord that they might come no more into such troubles; but if they sinned any more against him, that he himself would chasten them with mercy, and that they might not be delivered unto the blasphemous and barbarous nations.

{10:5} Now upon the same day that the strangers profaned the temple, on the very same day it was cleansed again, even the five and twentieth day of the same month, which is Casleu.

{10:6} And they kept the eight days with gladness, as in the feast of the tabernacles, remembering that not long afore they had held the feast of the tabernacles, when as they wandered in the mountains and dens like beasts.

{10:7} Therefore they bare branches, and fair boughs, and palms also, and sang psalms unto him that had given them good success in cleansing his place.

{10:8} They ordained also by a common statute and decree, That every year those days should be kept of the whole nation of the Jews.

{10:9} And this was the end of Antiochus, called Epiphanes.

{10:10} Now will we declare the acts of Antiochus Eupator, who was the son of this wicked man, gathering briefly the calamities of the wars.

{10:11} So when he was come to the crown, he set one Lysias over the affairs of his realm, and appointed him his chief governor of Celosyria and Phenice.

{10:12} For Ptolemeus, that was called Macron, choosing rather to do justice unto the Jews for the wrong that had been done unto them, endeavoured to continue peace with them.

{10:13} Whereupon being accused of the king's friends before Eupator, and called traitor at every word because he had left Cyprus, that Philometor had committed unto him, and departed to Antiochus Epiphanes, and seeing that he was in no honourable place, he was so discouraged, that he poisoned himself and died.

{10:14} But when Gorgias was governor of the holds, he hired soldiers, and nourished war continually with the Jews:

{10:15} And therewithall the Idumeans, having gotten into their hands the most commodious holds, kept the Jews occupied, and receiving those that were banished from Jerusalem, they went about to nourish war.

{10:16} Then they that were with Maccabeus made supplication, and besought God that he would be their helper; and so they ran with violence upon the strong holds of the Idumeans,

{10:17} And assaulting them strongly, they won the holds, and kept off all that fought upon the wall, and slew all that fell into their hands, and killed no fewer than twenty thousand.

{10:18} And because certain, who were no less than nine thousand, were fled together into two very strong castles, having all manner of things convenient to sustain the siege,

{10:19} Maccabeus left Simon and Joseph, and Zaccheus also, and them that were with him, who were enough to besiege them, and departed himself unto those places which more needed his help.

{10:20} Now they that were with Simon, being led with covetousness, were persuaded for money through certain of those that were in the castle, and took seventy thousand drachms, and let some of them escape.

{10:21} But when it was told Maccabeus what was done, he called the governors of the people together, and accused those men, that they had sold their brethren for money, and set their enemies free to fight against them.

{10:22} So he slew those that were found traitors, and immediately took the two castles.

{10:23} And having good success with his weapons in all things he took in hand, he slew in the two holds more than twenty thousand.

{10:24} Now Timotheus, whom the Jews had overcome before, when he had gathered a great multitude of foreign forces, and horses out of Asia not a few, came as though he would take Jewry by force of arms.

{10:25} But when he drew near, they that were with Maccabeus turned themselves to pray unto God, and sprinkled earth upon their heads, and girded their loins with sackcloth,

{10:26} And fell down at the foot of the altar, and besought him to be merciful to them, and to be an enemy to their enemies, and an adversary to their adversaries, as the law declareth.

{10:27} So after the prayer they took their weapons, and went on further from the city: and when they drew near to their enemies, they kept by themselves.

{10:28} Now the sun being newly risen, they joined both together; the one part having together with their virtue their refuge also unto the Lord for a pledge of their success and victory: the other side making their rage leader of their battle

{10:29} But when the battle waxed strong, there appeared unto the enemies from heaven five comely men upon horses, with bridles of gold, and two of them led the Jews,

{10:30} And took Maccabeus betwixt them, and covered him on every side weapons, and kept him safe, but shot arrows and lightnings against the enemies: so that being confounded with blindness, and full of trouble, they were killed.

{10:31} And there were slain of footmen twenty thousand and five hundred, and six hundred horsemen.

{10:32} As for Timotheus himself, he fled into a very strong hold, called Gawra, where Chereas was governor.

{10:33} But they that were with Maccabeus laid siege against the fortress courageously four days.

{10:34} And they that were within, trusting to the strength of the place, blasphemed exceedingly, and uttered wicked words.

{10:35} Nevertheless upon the fifth day early twenty young men of Maccabeus' company, inflamed with anger because of the blasphemies, assaulted the wall manly, and with a fierce courage killed all that they met withal.

{10:36} Others likewise ascending after them, whiles they were busied with them that were within, burnt the towers, and kindling fires burnt the blasphemers alive; and others broke open the gates, and, having received in the rest of the army, took the city,

{10:37} And killed Timotheus, that was hid in a certain pit, and

Chereas his brother, with Apollophanes.

{10:38} When this was done, they praised the Lord with psalms and thanksgiving, who had done so great things for Israel, and given them the victory.

{11:1} Not long after the, Lysias the king's protector and cousin, who also managed the affairs, took sore displeasure for the things that were done.

{11:2} And when he had gathered about fourscore thousand with all the horsemen, he came against the Jews, thinking to make the city an habitation of the Gentiles,

{11:3} And to make a gain of the temple, as of the other chapels of the heathen, and to set the high priesthood to sale every year:

{11:4} Not at all considering the power of God but puffed up with his ten thousands of footmen, and his thousands of horsemen, and his fourscore elephants.

{11:5} So he came to Judea, and drew near to Bethsura, which was a strong town, but distant from Jerusalem about five furlongs, and he laid sore siege unto it.

{11:6} Now when they that were with Maccabeus heard that he besieged the holds, they and all the people with lamentation and tears besought the Lord that he would send a good angel to deliver Israel.

{11:7} Then Maccabeus himself first of all took weapons, exhorting the other that they would jeopard themselves together with him to help their brethren: so they went forth together with a willing mind.

{11:8} And as they were at Jerusalem, there appeared before them on horseback one in white clothing, shaking his armour of gold.

{11:9} Then they praised the merciful God all together, and took heart, insomuch that they were ready not only to fight with men, but with most cruel beasts, and to pierce through walls of iron.

{11:10} Thus they marched forward in their armour, having an helper from heaven: for the Lord was merciful unto them

{11:11} And giving a charge upon their enemies like lions, they slew eleven thousand footmen, and sixteen hundred horsemen, and put all the other to flight.

{11:12} Many of them also being wounded escaped naked; and Lysias himself fled away shamefully, and so escaped.

{11:13} Who, as he was a man of understanding, casting with himself what loss he had had, and considering that the Hebrews could not be overcome, because the Almighty God helped them, he sent unto them,

{11:14} And persuaded them to agree to all reasonable conditions, and promised that he would persuade the king that he must needs be a friend unto them.

{11:15} Then Maccabeus consented to all that Lysias desired, being careful of the common good; and whatsoever Maccabeus wrote unto Lysias concerning the Jews, the king granted it.

{11:16} For there were letters written unto the Jews from Lysias to this effect: Lysias unto the people of the Jews sendeth greeting:

{11:17} John and Absolom, who were sent from you, delivered me the petition subscribed, and made request for the performance of the contents thereof.

{11:18} Therefore what things soever were meet to be reported to the king, I have declared them, and he hath granted as much as might be.

{11:19} And if then ye will keep yourselves loyal to the state, hereafter also will I endeavour to be a means of your good.

{11:20} But of the particulars I have given order both to these and the other that came from me, to commune with you.

{11:21} Fare ye well. The hundred and eight and fortieth year, the four and twentieth day of the month Dioscorinthius.

{11:22} Now the king's letter contained these words: King Antiochus unto his brother Lysias sendeth greeting:

{11:23} Since our father is translated unto the gods, our will is, that they that are in our realm live quietly, that every one may attend upon his own affairs.

{11:24} We understand also that the Jews would not consent to our father, for to be brought unto the custom of the Gentiles, but had rather keep their own manner of living: for the which cause they require of us, that we should suffer them to live after their own laws.

{11:25} Wherefore our mind is, that this nation shall be in rest, and we have determined to restore them their temple, that they may live according to the customs of their forefathers.

{11:26} Thou shalt do well therefore to send unto them, and grant them peace, that when they are certified of our mind, they may be of good comfort, and ever go cheerfully about their own affairs.

{11:27} And the letter of the king unto the nation of the Jews was after this manner: King Antiochus sendeth greeting unto the council, and the rest of the Jews:

{11:28} If ye fare well, we have our desire; we are also in good health.

{11:29} Menelaus declared unto us, that your desire was to return home, and to follow your own business:

{11:30} Wherefore they that will depart shall have safe conduct till the thirtieth day of Xanthicus with security.

{11:31} And the Jews shall use their own kind of meats and laws, as before; and none of them any manner of ways shall be molested for things ignorantly done.

{11:32} I have sent also Menelaus, that he may comfort you.

{11:33} Fare ye well. In the hundred forty and eighth year, and the fifteenth day of the month Xanthicus.

{11:34} The Romans also sent unto them a letter containing these words: Quintus Memmius and Titus Manlius, ambassadors of the Romans, send greeting unto the people of the Jews.

{11:35} Whatsoever Lysias the king's cousin hath granted, therewith we also are well pleased.

{11:36} But touching such things as he judged to be referred to the king, after ye have advised thereof, send one forthwith, that we may declare as it is convenient for you: for we are now going to Antioch.

{11:37} Therefore send some with speed, that we may know what is your mind.

{11:38} Farewell. This hundred and eight and fortieth year, the fifteenth day of the month Xanthicus.

{12:1} When these covenants were made, Lysias went unto the king, and the Jews were about their husbandry.

{12:2} But of the governours of several places, Timotheus, and Apollonius the son of Genneus, also Hieronymus, and Demophon, and beside them Nicanor the governor of Cyprus, would not suffer them to be quiet and live in peace.

{12:3} The men of Joppa also did such an ungodly deed: they prayed the Jews that dwelt among them to go with their wives and children into the boats which they had prepared, as though they had meant them no hurt.

{12:4} Who accepted of it according to the common decree of the city, as being desirous to live in peace, and suspecting nothing: but when they were gone forth into the deep, they drowned no less than two hundred of them.

{12:5} When Judas heard of this cruelty done unto his countrymen, he commanded those that were with him to make them ready.

{12:6} And calling upon God the righteous Judge, he came against those murderers of his brethren, and burnt the haven by night, and set the boats on fire, and those that fled thither he slew.

{12:7} And when the town was shut up, he went backward, as if he would return to root out all them of the city of Joppa.

{12:8} But when he heard that the Jamnites were minded to do in like manner unto the Jews that dwelt among them,

{12:9} He came upon the Jamnites also by night, and set fire on the haven and the navy, so that the light of the fire was seen at Jerusalem two hundred and forty furlongs off.

{12:10} Now when they were gone from thence nine furlongs in their journey toward Timotheus, no fewer than five thousand men on foot and five hundred horsemen of the Arabians set upon him.

{12:11} Whereupon there was a very sore battle; but Judas' side by the help of God got the victory; so that the Nomades of Arabia, being overcome, besought Judas for peace, promising both to give him cattle, and to pleasure him otherwise.

{12:12} Then Judas, thinking indeed that they would be profitable in many things, granted them peace: whereupon they shook hands, and so they departed to their tents.

{12:13} He went also about to make a bridge to a certain strong city, which was fenced about with walls, and inhabited by people of divers countries; and the name of it was Caspis.

{12:14} But they that were within it put such trust in the strength of the walls and provision of victuals, that they behaved themselves rudely toward them that were with Judas, railing and blaspheming, and uttering such words as were not to be spoken.

{12:15} Wherefore Judas with his company, calling upon the great Lord of the world, who without rams or engines of war did cast down Jericho in the time of Joshua, gave a fierce assault against the walls,

{12:16} And took the city by the will of God, and made unspeakable slaughters, insomuch that a lake two furlongs broad near adjoining thereunto, being filled full, was seen running with blood.

{12:17} Then departed they from thence seven hundred and fifty furlongs, and came to Characa unto the Jews that are called Tubieni.

{12:18} But as for Timotheus, they found him not in the places: for before he had dispatched any thing, he departed from thence, having left a very strong garrison in a certain hold.

{12:19} Howbeit Dositheus and Sosipater, who were of Maccabeus' captains, went forth, and slew those that Timotheus had left in the fortress, above ten thousand men.

{12:20} And Maccabeus ranged his army by bands, and set them over the bands, and went against Timotheus, who had about him an hundred and twenty thousand men of foot, and two thousand and five hundred horsemen.

{12:21} Now when Timotheus had knowledge of Judas' coming, he sent the women and children and the other baggage unto a fortress called Carnion: for the town was hard to besiege, and uneasy to come unto, by reason of the straitness of all the places.

{12:22} But when Judas his first band came in sight, the enemies, being smitten with fear and terror through the appearing of him who seeth all things, fled again, one running into this way, another that way, so as that they were often hurt of their own men, and wounded with the points of their own swords.

{12:23} Judas also was very earnest in pursuing them, killing those wicked wretches, of whom he slew about thirty thousand men.

{12:24} Moreover Timotheus himself fell into the hands of Dositheus and Sosipater, whom he besought with much craft to let him go with his life, because he had many of the Jews' parents, and the brethren of some of them, who, if they put him to death, should not be regarded.

{12:25} So when he had assured them with many words that he would restore them without hurt, according to the agreement, they let him go for the saving of their brethren.

{12:26} Then Maccabeus marched forth to Carnion, and to the temple of Atargatis, and there he slew five and twenty thousand persons.

{12:27} And after he had put to flight and destroyed them, Judas removed the host toward Ephron, a strong city, wherein Lysias abode, and a great multitude of divers nations, and the strong young men kept the walls, and defended them mightily: wherein also was great provision of engines and darts.

{12:28} But when Judas and his company had called upon Almighty God, who with his power breaketh the strength of his enemies, they won the city, and slew twenty and five thousand of them that were within,

{12:29} From thence they departed to Scythopolis, which lieth six hundred furlongs from Jerusalem,

{12:30} But when the Jews that dwelt there had testified that the Scythopolitans dealt lovingly with them, and entreated them kindly in the time of their adversity;

{12:31} They gave them thanks, desiring them to be friendly still unto them: and so they came to Jerusalem, the feast of the weeks approaching.

{12:32} And after the feast, called Pentecost, they went forth against Gorgias the governor of Idumea,

{12:33} Who came out with three thousand men of foot and four hundred horsemen.

{12:34} And it happened that in their fighting together a few of the Jews were slain.

{12:35} At which time Dositheus, one of Bacenor's company, who was on horseback, and a strong man, was still upon Gorgias, and taking hold of his coat drew him by force; and when he would have taken that cursed man alive, a horseman of Thracia coming upon him smote off his shoulder, so that Gorgias fled unto Marisa.

{12:36} Now when they that were with Gorgias had fought long, and were weary, Judas called upon the Lord, that he would shew himself to be their helper and leader of the battle.

{12:37} And with that he began in his own language, and sung psalms with a loud voice, and rushing unawares upon Gorgias' men, he put them to flight.

{12:38} So Judas gathered his host, and came into the city of Odollam, And when the seventh day came, they purified themselves, as the custom was, and kept the sabbath in the same place.

{12:39} And upon the day following, as the use had been, Judas and his company came to take up the bodies of them that were slain, and to bury them with their kinsmen in their fathers' graves.

{12:40} Now under the coats of every one that was slain they found things consecrated to the idols of the Jamnites, which is forbidden the Jews by the law. Then every man saw that this was the cause wherefore they were slain.

{12:41} All men therefore praising the Lord, the righteous Judge, who had opened the things that were hid,

{12:42} Betook themselves unto prayer, and besought him that the sin committed might wholly be put out of remembrance. Besides, that noble Judas exhorted the people to keep themselves from sin, forsomuch as they saw before their eyes the things that came to pass for the sins of those that were slain.

{12:43} And when he had made a gathering throughout the company to the sum of two thousand drachms of silver, he sent it to Jerusalem to offer a sin offering, doing therein very well and honestly, in that he was mindful of the resurrection:

{12:44} For if he had not hoped that they that were slain should have risen again, it had been superfluous and vain to pray for the dead.

{12:45} And also in that he perceived that there was great favour laid up for those that died godly, it was an holy and good thought. Whereupon he made a reconciliation for the dead, that they might be delivered from sin.

{13:1} In the hundred forty and ninth year it was told Judas, that

Antiochus Eupator was coming with a great power into Judea,

{13:2} And with him Lysias his protector, and ruler of his affairs, having either of them a Grecian power of footmen, an hundred and ten thousand, and horsemen five thousand and three hundred, and elephants two and twenty, and three hundred chariots armed with hooks.

{13:3} Menelaus also joined himself with them, and with great dissimulation encouraged Antiochus, not for the safeguard of the country, but because he thought to have been made governor.

{13:4} But the King of kings moved Antiochus' mind against this wicked wretch, and Lysias informed the king that this man was the cause of all mischief, so that the king commanded to bring him unto Berea, and to put him to death, as the manner is in that place.

{13:5} Now there was in that place a tower of fifty cubits high, full of ashes, and it had a round instrument which on every side hanged down into the ashes.

{13:6} And whosoever was condemned of sacrilege, or had committed any other grievous crime, there did all men thrust him unto death.

{13:7} Such a death it happened that wicked man to die, not having so much as burial in the earth; and that most justly:

{13:8} For inasmuch as he had committed many sins about the altar, whose fire and ashes were holy, he received his death in ashes.

{13:9} Now the king came with a barbarous and haughty mind to do far worse to the Jews, than had been done in his father's time.

{13:10} Which things when Judas perceived, he commanded the multitude to call upon the Lord night and day, that if ever at any other time, he would now also help them, being at the point to be put from their law, from their country, and from the holy temple:

{13:11} And that he would not suffer the people, that had even now been but a little refreshed, to be in subjection to the blasphemous nations.

{13:12} So when they had all done this together, and besought the merciful Lord with weeping and fasting, and lying flat upon the ground three days long, Judas, having exhorted them, commanded they should be in a readiness.

{13:13} And Judas, being apart with the elders, determined, before the king's host should enter into Judea, and get the city, to go forth and try the matter in fight by the help of the Lord.

{13:14} So when he had committed all to the Creator of the world, and exhorted his soldiers to fight manfully, even unto death, for the laws, the temple, the city, the country, and the commonwealth, he camped by Modin:

{13:15} And having given the watchword to them that were about him, Victory is of God; with the most valiant and choice young men he went in into the king's tent by night, and slew in the camp about four thousand men, and the chiefest of the elephants, with all that were upon him.

{13:16} And at last they filled the camp with fear and tumult, and departed with good success.

{13:17} This was done in the break of the day, because the protection of the Lord did help him.

{13:18} Now when the king had taken a taste of the manliness of the Jews, he went about to take the holds by policy,

{13:19} And marched toward Bethsura, which was a strong hold of the Jews: but he was put to flight, failed, and lost of his men:

{13:20} For Judas had conveyed unto them that were in it such things as were necessary.

{13:21} But Rhodocus, who was in the Jews' host, disclosed the secrets to the enemies; therefore he was sought out, and when they had gotten him, they put him in prison.

{13:22} The king treated with them in Bethsum the second time, gave his hand, took theirs, departed, fought with Judas, was overcome;

{13:23} Heard that Philip, who was left over the affairs in Antioch, was desperately bent, confounded, intreated the Jews, submitted himself, and swore to all equal conditions, agreed with them, and offered sacrifice, honoured the temple, and dealt kindly with the place,

{13:24} And accepted well of Maccabeus, made him principal governor from Ptolemais unto the Gerrhenians;

{13:25} Came to Ptolemais: the people there were grieved for the covenants; for they stormed, because they would make their covenants void:

{13:26} Lysias went up to the judgment seat, said as much as could be in defence of the cause, persuaded, pacified, made them well affected, returned to Antioch. Thus it went touching the king's coming and departing.

{14:1} After three years was Judas informed, that Demetrius the son of Seleucus, having entered by the haven of Tripolis with a great power and navy,

{14:2} Had taken the country, and killed Antiochus, and Lysias his protector.

{14:3} Now one Alcimus, who had been high priest, and had defiled himself wilfully in the times of their mingling with the Gentiles, seeing that by no means he could save himself, nor have any more access to the holy altar,

{14:4} Came to king Demetrius in the hundred and one and fiftieth year, presenting unto him a crown of gold, and a palm, and also of the boughs which were used solemnly in the temple: and so that day he held his peace.

{14:5} Howbeit having gotten opportunity to further his foolish enterprize, and being called into counsel by Demetrius, and asked how the Jews stood affected, and what they intended, he answered thereunto:

{14:6} Those of the Jews that he called Assideans, whose captain is Judas Maccabeus, nourish war and are seditious, and will not let the rest be in peace.

{14:7} Therefore I, being deprived of mine ancestors' honour, I mean the high priesthood, am now come hither:

{14:8} First, verily for the unfeigned care I have of things pertaining to the king; and secondly, even for that I intend the good of mine own countrymen: for all our nation is in no small misery through the unadvised dealing of them aforersaid.

{14:9} Wherefore, O king, seeing knowest all these things, be careful for the country, and our nation, which is pressed on every side, according to the clemency that thou readily shewest unto all.

{14:10} For as long as Judas liveth, it is not possible that the state should be quiet.

{14:11} This was no sooner spoken of him, but others of the king's friends, being maliciously set against Judas, did more incense Demetrius.

{14:12} And forthwith calling Nicanor, who had been master of the elephants, and making him governor over Judea, he sent him forth,

{14:13} Commanding him to slay Judas, and to scatter them that were with him, and to make Alcimus high priest of the great temple.

{14:14} Then the heathen, that had fled out of Judea from Judas, came to Nicanor by flocks, thinking the harm and calamities ot the Jews to be their welfare.

{14:15} Now when the Jews heard of Nicanor's coming, and that the heathen were up against them, they cast earth upon their heads, and made supplication to him that had established his people for ever, and who always helpeth his portion with manifestation of his presence.

{14:16} So at the commandment of the captain they removed straightways from thence, and came near unto them at the town of Dessau.

{14:17} Now Simon, Judas' brother, had joined battle with Nicanor, but was somewhat discomfited through the sudden silence of his enemies.

{14:18} Nevertheless Nicanor, hearing of the manliness of them that were with Judas, and the courageousness that they had to fight for their country, durst not try the matter by the sword.

{14:19} Wherefore he sent Posidonius, and Theodotus, and Mattathias, to make peace.

{14:20} So when they had taken long advisement thereupon, and the captain had made the multitude acquainted therewith, and it appeared that they were all of one mind, they consented to the covenants,

{14:21} And appointed a day to meet in together by themselves: and when the day came, and stools were set for either of them,

{14:22} Ludas placed armed men ready in convenient places, lest some treachery should be suddenly practised by the enemies: so they made a peaceable conference.

{14:23} Now Nicanor abode in Jerusalem, and did no hurt, but sent away the people that came flocking unto him.

{14:24} And he would not willingly have Judas out of his sight: for he love the man from his heart

{14:25} He prayed him also to take a wife, and to beget children: so he married, was quiet, and took part of this life.

{14:26} But Alcimus, perceiving the love that was betwixt them, and considering the covenants that were made, came to Demetrius, and told him that Nicanor was not well affected toward the state; for that he had ordained Judas, a traitor to his realm, to be the king's successor.

{14:27} Then the king being in a rage, and provoked with the accusations of the most wicked man, wrote to Nicanor, signifying that he was much displeased with the covenants, and commanding him that he should send Maccabeus prisoner in all haste unto Antioch.

{14:28} When this came to Nicanor's hearing, he was much confounded in himself, and took it grievously that he should make void the articles which were agreed upon, the man being in no fault.

{14:29} But because there was no dealing against the king, he watched his time to accomplish this thing by policy.

{14:30} Notwithstanding, when Maccabeus saw that Nicanor began to be churlish unto him, and that he entreated him more roughly than he was wont, perceiving that such sour behaviour came not of good, he gathered together not a few of his men, and withdrew himself from Nicanor.

{14:31} But the other, knowing that he was notably prevented by Judas' policy, came into the great and holy temple, and commanded the priests, that were offering their usual sacrifices, to deliver him the man.

{14:32} And when they sware that they could not tell where the man was whom he sought,

{14:33} He stretched out his right hand toward the temple, and made an oath in this manner: If ye will not deliver me Judas as a prisoner, I will lay this temple of God even with the ground, and I will break down the altar, and erect a notable temple unto Bacchus.

{14:34} After these words he departed. Then the priests lifted up their hands toward heaven, and besought him that was ever a defender of their nation, saying in this manner;

{14:35} Thou, O Lord of all things, who hast need of nothing, wast pleased that the temple of thine habitation should be among us:

{14:36} Therefore now, O holy Lord of all holiness, keep this house ever undefiled, which lately was cleansed, and stop every unrighteous mouth.

{14:37} Now was there accused unto Nicanor one Razis, one of the elders of Jerusalem, a lover of his countrymen, and a man of very good report, who for his kindness was called a father of the Jews.

{14:38} For in the former times, when they mingled not themselves with the Gentiles, he had been accused of Judaism, and did boldly jeopard his body and life with all vehemency for the religion of the Jews.

{14:39} So Nicanor, willing to declare the hate that he bare unto the Jews, sent above five hundred men of war to take him:

{14:40} For he thought by taking him to do the Jews much hurt.

{14:41} Now when the multitude would have taken the tower, and violently broken into the outer door, and bade that fire should be brought to burn it, he being ready to be taken on every side fell upon his sword;

{14:42} Choosing rather to die manfully, than to come into the hands of the wicked, to be abused otherwise than beseemed his noble birth:

{14:43} But missing his stroke through haste, the multitude also rushing within the doors, he ran boldly up to the wall, and cast himself down manfully among the thickest of them.

{14:44} But they quickly giving back, and a space being made, he fell down into the midst of the void place.

{14:45} Nevertheless, while there was yet breath within him, being inflamed with anger, he rose up; and though his blood gushed out like spouts of water, and his wounds were grievous, yet he ran through the midst of the throng; and standing upon a steep rock,

{14:46} When as his blood was now quite gone, he plucked out his bowels, and taking them in both his hands, he cast them upon the throng, and calling upon the Lord of life and spirit to restore him those again, he thus died.

{15:1} But Nicanor, hearing that Judas and his company were in the strong places about Samaria, resolved without any danger to set upon them on the sabbath day.

{15:2} Nevertheless the Jews that were compelled to go with him said, O destroy not so cruelly and barbarously, but give honour to that day, which he, that seeth all things, hath honoured with holiness above all other days.

{15:3} Then the most ungracious wretch demanded, if there were a Mighty one in heaven, that had commanded the sabbath day to be kept.

{15:4} And when they said, There is in heaven a living Lord, and mighty, who commanded the seventh day to be kept:

{15:5} Then said the other, And I also am mighty upon earth, and I command to take arms, and to do the king's business. Yet he obtained not to have his wicked will done.

{15:6} So Nicanor in exceeding pride and haughtiness determined to set up a publick monument of his victory over Judas and them that were with him.

{15:7} But Maccabeus had ever sure confidence that the Lord would help him:

{15:8} Wherefore he exhorted his people not to fear the coming of the heathen against them, but to remember the help which in former times they had received from heaven, and now to expect the victory and aid, which should come unto them from the Almighty.

{15:9} And so comforting them out of the law and the prophets, and withal putting them in mind of the battles that they won afore, he made them more cheerful.

{15:10} And when he had stirred up their minds, he gave them their charge, shewing them therewithall the falsehood of the heathen, and the breach of oaths.

{15:11} Thus he armed every one of them, not so much with defence of shields and spears, as with comfortable and good words: and beside that, he told them a dream worthy to be believed, as if it had been so indeed, which did not a little rejoice them.

{15:12} And this was his vision: That Onias, who had been high priest, a virtuous and a good man, reverend in conversation, gentle in condition, well spoken also, and exercised from a child in all points of virtue, holding up his hands prayed for the whole body of the Jews.

{15:13} This done, in like manner there appeared a man with gray hairs, and exceeding glorious, who was of a wonderful and excellent majesty.

{15:14} Then Onias answered, saying, This is a lover of the brethren, who prayeth much for the people, and for the holy city, to wit, Jeremias the prophet of God.

{15:15} Whereupon Jeremias holding forth his right hand gave to Judas a sword of gold, and in giving it spake thus,

{15:16} Take this holy sword, a gift from God, with the which thou shalt wound the adversaries.

{15:17} Thus being well comforted by the words of Judas, which were very good, and able to stir them up to valour, and to encourage the hearts of the young men, they determined not to pitch camp, but courageously to set upon them, and manfully to try the matter by conflict, because the city and the sanctuary and the temple were in danger.

{15:18} For the care that they took for their wives, and their children, their brethren, and folks, was in least account with them: but the greatest and principal fear was for the holy temple.

{15:19} Also they that were in the city took not the least care, being troubled for the conflict abroad.

{15:20} And now, when as all looked what should be the trial, and the enemies were already come near, and the army was set in array, and the beasts conveniently placed, and the horsemen set in wings,

{15:21} Maccabeus seeing the coming of the multitude, and the divers preparations of armour, and the fierceness of the beasts, stretched out his hands toward heaven, and called upon the Lord that worketh wonders, knowing that victory cometh not by arms, but even as it seemeth good to him, he giveth it to such as are worthy:

{15:22} Therefore in his prayer he said after this manner; O Lord, thou didst send thine angel in the time of Ezekias king of Judea, and didst slay in the host of Sennacherib an hundred fourscore and five thousand:

{15:23} Wherefore now also, O Lord of heaven, send a good angel before us for a fear and dread unto them;

{15:24} And through the might of thine arm let those be stricken with terror, that come against thy holy people to blaspheme. And he ended thus.

{15:25} Then Nicanor and they that were with him came forward with trumpets and songs.

{15:26} But Judas and his company encountered the enemies with invocation and prayer.

{15:27} So that fighting with their hands, and praying unto God with their hearts, they slew no less than thirty and five thousand men: for through the appearance of God, they were greatly cheered.

{15:28} Now when the battle was done, returning again with joy, they knew that Nicanor lay dead in his harness.

{15:29} Then they made a great shout and a noise, praising the Almighty in their own language.

{15:30} And Judas, who was ever the chief defender of the citizens both in body and mind, and who continued his love toward his countrymen all his life, commanded to strike off Nicanor's head, and his hand with his shoulder, and bring them to Jerusalem.

{15:31} So when he was there, and called them of his nation together, and set the priests before the altar, he sent for them that were of the tower,

{15:32} And shewed them vile Nicanor's head, and the hand of that blasphemer, which with proud brags he had stretched out against the holy temple of the Almighty.

{15:33} And when he had cut out the tongue of that ungodly Nicanor, he commanded that they should give it by pieces unto the fowls, and hang up the reward of his madness before the temple.

{15:34} So every man praised toward the heaven the glorious Lord, saying, blessed be he that hath kept his own place undefiled.

{15:35} He hanged also Nicanor's head upon the tower, an evident and manifest sign unto all of the help of the Lord.

{15:36} And they ordained all with a common decree in no case to let that day pass without solemnity, but to celebrate the thirtieth day of the twelfth month, which in the Syrian tongue is called Adar, the day before Mardocheus' day.

{15:37} Thus went it with Nicanor: and from that time forth the Hebrews had the city in their power. And here will I make an end.

{15:38} And if I have done well, and as is fitting the story, it is that which I desired: but if slenderly and meanly, it is that which I could attain unto.

{15:39} For as it is hurtful to drink wine or water alone; and as wine mingled with water is pleasant, and delighteth the taste: even so speech finely framed delighteth the ears of them that read the story. And here shall be an end.

The Book of Baruch

{1:1} And these are the words of the book, which Baruch the son of Nerias, the son of Maasias, the son of Sedecias, the son of Asadias, the son of Chelcias, wrote in Babylon,

{1:2} In the fifth year, and in the seventh day of the month, what time as the Chaldeans took Jerusalem, and burnt it with fire.

{1:3} And Baruch did read the words of this book in the hearing of Jechonias the son of Joachim king of Juda, and in the ears of all the people that came to hear the book,

{1:4} And in the hearing of the nobles, and of the king's sons, and in the hearing of the elders, and of all the people, from the lowest unto the highest, even of all them that dwelt at Babylon by the river Sud.

{1:5} Whereupon they wept, fasted, and prayed before the Lord.

{1:6} They made also a collection of money according to every man's power:

{1:7} And they sent it to Jerusalem unto Joachim the high priest, the son of Chelcias, son of Salom, and to the priests, and to all the people which were found with him at Jerusalem,

{1:8} At the same time when he received the vessels of the house of the Lord, that were carried out of the temple, to return them into the land of Juda, the tenth day of the month Sivan, namely, silver vessels, which Sedecias the son of Josias king of Jada had made,

{1:9} After that Nabuchodonosor king of Babylon had carried away Jechonias, and the princes, and the captives, and the mighty men, and the people of the land, from Jerusalem, and brought them unto Babylon.

{1:10} And they said, Behold, we have sent you money to buy you burnt offerings, and sin offerings, and incense, and prepare ye manna, and offer upon the altar of the Lord our God;

{1:11} And pray for the life of Nabuchodonosor king of Babylon, and for the life of Balthasar his son, that their days may be upon earth as the days of heaven:

{1:12} And the Lord will give us strength, and lighten our eyes, and we shall live under the shadow of Nabuchodonosor king of Babylon, and under the shadow of Balthasar his son, and we shall serve them many days, and find favour in their sight.

{1:13} Pray for us also unto the Lord our God, for we have sinned against the Lord our God; and unto this day the fury of the Lord and his wrath is not turned from us.

{1:14} And ye shall read this book which we have sent unto you, to make confession in the house of the Lord, upon the feasts and solemn days.

{1:15} And ye shall say, To the Lord our God belongeth righteousness, but unto us the confusion of faces, as it is come to pass this day, unto them of Juda, and to the inhabitants of Jerusalem,

{1:16} And to our kings, and to our princes, and to our priests, and to our prophets, and to our fathers:

{1:17} For we have sinned before the Lord,

{1:18} And disobeyed him, and have not hearkened unto the voice of the Lord our God, to walk in the commandments that he gave us openly:

{1:19} Since the day that the Lord brought our forefathers out of the land of Egypt, unto this present day, we have been disobedient unto the Lord our God, and we have been negligent in not hearing his voice.

{1:20} Wherefore the evils cleaved unto us, and the curse, which the Lord appointed by Moses his servant at the time that he brought our fathers out of the land of Egypt, to give us a land that floweth with milk and honey, like as it is to see this day.

{1:21} Nevertheless we have not hearkened unto the voice of the Lord our God, according unto all the words of the prophets, whom he sent unto us:

{1:22} But every man followed the imagination of his own wicked heart, to serve strange gods, and to do evil in the sight of the Lord our God.

{2:1} Therefore the Lord hath made good his word, which he pronounced against us, and against our judges that judged Israel, and against our kings, and against our princes, and against the men of Israel and Juda,

{2:2} To bring upon us great plagues, such as never happened under the whole heaven, as it came to pass in Jerusalem, according to the things that were written in the law of Moses;

{2:3} That a man should eat the flesh of his own son, and the flesh of his own daughter.

{2:4} Moreover he hath delivered them to be in subjection to all the kingdoms that are round about us, to be as a reproach and desolation among all the people round about, where the Lord hath scattered them.

{2:5} Thus we were cast down, and not exalted, because we have sinned against the Lord our God, and have not been obedient unto his voice.

{2:6} To the Lord our God appertaineth righteousness: but unto us and to our fathers open shame, as appeareth this day.

{2:7} For all these plagues are come upon us, which the Lord hath pronounced against us

{2:8} Yet have we not prayed before the Lord, that we might turn every one from the imaginations of his wicked heart.

{2:9} Wherefore the Lord watched over us for evil, and the Lord hath brought it upon us: for the Lord is righteous in all his works which he hath commanded us.

{2:10} Yet we have not hearkened unto his voice, to walk in the commandments of the Lord, that he hath set before us.

{2:11} And now, O Lord God of Israel, that hast brought thy people out of the land of Egypt with a mighty hand, and high arm, and with signs, and with wonders, and with great power, and hast gotten thyself a name, as appeareth this day:

{2:12} O Lord our God, we have sinned, we have done ungodly, we have dealt unrighteously in all thine ordinances.

{2:13} Let thy wrath turn from us: for we are but a few left among the heathen, where thou hast scattered us.

{2:14} Hear our prayers, O Lord, and our petitions, and deliver us for thine own sake, and give us favour in the sight of them which have led us away:

{2:15} That all the earth may know that thou art the Lord our God, because Israel and his posterity is called by thy name.

{2:16} O Lord, look down from thine holy house, and consider us: bow down thine ear, O Lord, to hear us.

{2:17} Open thine eyes, and behold; for the dead that are in the graves, whose souls are taken from their bodies, will give unto the Lord neither praise nor righteousness:

{2:18} But the soul that is greatly vexed, which goeth stooping and feeble, and the eyes that fail, and the hungry soul, will give thee praise and righteousness, O Lord.

{2:19} Therefore we do not make our humble supplication before thee, O Lord our God, for the righteousness of our fathers, and of our kings.

{2:20} For thou hast sent out thy wrath and indignation upon us, as thou hast spoken by thy servants the prophets, saying,

{2:21} Thus saith the Lord, bow down your shoulders to serve the king of Babylon: so shall ye remain in the land that I gave unto your fathers.

{2:22} But if ye will not hear the voice of the Lord, to serve the king of Babylon,

{2:23} I will cause to cease out of the cites of Judah, and from without Jerusalem, the voice of mirth, and the voice of joy, the voice of the bridegroom, and the voice of the bride: and the whole land shall be desolate of inhabitants.

{2:24} But we would not hearken unto thy voice, to serve the king of Babylon: therefore hast thou made good the words that thou spakest by thy servants the prophets, namely, that the bones of our kings, and the bones of our fathers, should be taken out of their place.

{2:25} And, lo, they are cast out to the heat of the day, and to the frost of the night, and they died in great miseries by famine, by sword, and by pestilence.

{2:26} And the house which is called by thy name hast thou laid waste, as it is to be seen this day, for the wickedness of the house of Israel and the house of Juda.

{2:27} O Lord our God, thou hast dealt with us after all thy goodness, and according to all that great mercy of thine,

{2:28} As thou spakest by thy servant Moses in the day when thou didst command him to write the law before the children of Israel, saying,

{2:29} If ye will not hear my voice, surely this very great multitude shall be turned into a small number among the nations, where I will scatter them.

{2:30} For I knew that they would not hear me, because it is a stiffnecked people: but in the land of their captivities they shall remember themselves.

{2:31} And shall know that I am the Lord their God: for I will give them an heart, and ears to hear:

{2:32} And they shall praise me in the land of their captivity, and think upon my name,

{2:33} And return from their stiff neck, and from their wicked deeds: for they shall remember the way of their fathers, which sinned before the Lord.

{2:34} And I will bring them again into the land which I promised with an oath unto their fathers, Abraham, Isaac, and Jacob, and they shall be lords of it: and I will increase them, and they shall not be diminished.

{2:35} And I will make an everlasting covenant with them to be their God, and they shall be my people: and I will no more drive my people of Israel out of the land that I have given them.

{3:1} O Lord Almighty, God of Israel, the soul in anguish the troubled spirit, crieth unto thee.

{3:2} Hear, O Lord, and have mercy; ar thou art merciful: and have pity upon us, because we have sinned before thee.

{3:3} For thou endurest for ever, and we perish utterly.

{3:4} O Lord Almighty, thou God of Israel, hear now the prayers of the dead Israelites, and of their children, which have sinned before thee, and not hearkened unto the voice of thee their God: for the which cause these plagues cleave unto us.

{3:5} Remember not the iniquities of our forefathers: but think upon thy power and thy name now at this time.

{3:6} For thou art the Lord our God, and thee, O Lord, will we praise.

{3:7} And for this cause thou hast put thy fear in our hearts, to the intent that we should call upon thy name, and praise thee in our captivity: for we have called to mind all the iniquity of our forefathers, that sinned before thee.

{3:8} Behold, we are yet this day in our captivity, where thou hast scattered us, for a reproach and a curse, and to be subject to payments, according to all the iniquities of our fathers, which departed from the Lord our God.

{3:9} Hear, Israel, the commandments of life: give ear to understand wisdom.

{3:10} How happeneth it Israel, that thou art in thine enemies' land, that thou art waxen old in a strange country, that thou art defiled with the dead,

{3:11} That thou art counted with them that go down into the grave?

{3:12} Thou hast forsaken the fountain of wisdom.

{3:13} For if thou hadst walked in the way of God, thou shouldest have dwelled in peace for ever.

{3:14} Learn where is wisdom, where is strength, where is understanding; that thou mayest know also where is length of days, and life, where is the light of the eyes, and peace.

{3:15} Who hath found out her place? or who hath come into her treasures?

{3:16} Where are the princes of the heathen become, and such as ruled the beasts upon the earth;

{3:17} They that had their pastime with the fowls of the air, and they that hoarded up silver and gold, wherein men trust, and made no end of their getting?

{3:10} For they that wrought in silver, and were so careful, and whose works are unsearchable,

{3:19} They are vanished and gone down to the grave, and others are come up in their steads.

{3:20} Young men have seen light, and dwelt upon the earth: but the way of knowledge have they not known,

{3:21} Nor understood the paths thereof, nor laid hold of it: their children were far off from that way.

{3:22} It hath not been heard of in Chanaan, neither hath it been seen in Theman.

{3:23} The Agarenes that seek wisdom upon earth, the merchants of Meran and of Theman, the authors of fables, and searchers out of understanding; none of these have known the way of wisdom, or remember her paths.

{3:24} O Israel, how great is the house of God! and how large is the place of his possession!

{3:25} Great, and hath none end; high, and unmeasurable.

{3:26} There were the giants famous from the beginning, that were of so great stature, and so expert in war.

{3:27} Those did not the Lord choose, neither gave he the way of knowledge unto them:

{3:28} But they were destroyed, because they had no wisdom, and perished through their own foolishness.

{3:29} Who hath gone up into heaven, and taken her, and brought her down from the clouds?

{3:30} Who hath gone over the sea, and found her, and will bring her for pure gold?

{3:31} No man knoweth her way, nor thinketh of her path.

{3:32} But he that knoweth all things knoweth her, and hath found her out with his understanding: he that prepared the earth for evermore hath filled it with fourfooted beasts:

{3:33} He that sendeth forth light, and it goeth, calleth it again, and it obeyeth him with fear.

{3:34} The stars shined in their watches, and rejoiced: when he calleth them, they say, Here we be, and so with cheerfulness they shewed light unto him that made them.

{3:35} This is our God, and there shall none other be accounted of in comparison of him

{3:36} He hath found out all the way of knowledge, and hath given it unto Jacob his servant, and to Israel his beloved.

{3:37} Afterward did he shew himself upon earth, and conversed with men.

{4:1} This is the book of the commandments of God, and the law that endureth for ever: all they that keep it shall come to life; but such as leave it shall die.

{4:2} Turn thee, O Jacob, and take hold of it: walk in the presence of the light thereof, that thou mayest be illuminated.

{4:3} Give not thine honour to another, nor the things that are profitable unto thee to a strange nation.

{4:4} O Israel, happy are we: for things that are pleasing to God are made known unto us.

{4:5} Be of good cheer, my people, the memorial of Israel.

{4:6} Ye were sold to the nations, not for [your] destruction: but because ye moved God to wrath, ye were delivered unto the enemies.

{4:7} For ye provoked him that made you by sacrificing unto devils, and not to God.

{4:8} Ye have forgotten the everlasting God, that brought you up; and ye have grieved Jerusalem, that nursed you.

{4:9} For when she saw the wrath of God coming upon you, she said, Hearken, O ye that dwell about Sion: God hath brought upon me great mourning;

{4:10} For I saw the captivity of my sons and daughters, which the Everlasting brought upon them.

{4:11} With joy did I nourish them; but sent them away with weeping and mourning.

{4:12} Let no man rejoice over me, a widow, and forsaken of many, who for the sins of my children am left desolate; because they departed from the law of God.

{4:13} They knew not his statutes, nor walked in the ways of his commandments, nor trod in the paths of discipline in his righteousness.

{4:14} Let them that dwell about Sion come, and remember ye the captivity of my sons and daughters, which the Everlasting hath brought upon them.

{4:15} For he hath brought a nation upon them from far, a shameless nation, and of a strange language, who neither reverenced old man, nor pitied child.

{4:16} These have carried away the dear beloved children of the widow, and left her that was alone desolate without daughters.

{4:17} But what can I help you?

{4:18} For he that brought these plagues upon you will deliver you from the hands of your enemies.

{4:19} Go your way, O my children, go your way: for I am left desolate.

{4:20} I have put off the clothing of peace, and put upon me the sackcloth of my prayer: I will cry unto the Everlasting in my days.

{4:21} Be of good cheer, O my children, cry unto the Lord, and he will deliver you from the power and hand of the enemies.

{4:22} For my hope is in the Everlasting, that he will save you; and joy is come unto me from the Holy One, because of the mercy which shall soon come unto you from the Everlasting our Saviour.

{4:23} For I sent you out with mourning and weeping: but God will give you to me again with joy and gladness for ever.

{4:24} Like as now the neighbours of Sion have seen your captivity: so shall they see shortly your salvation from our God which shall come upon you with great glory, and brightness of the Everlasting.

{4:25} My children, suffer patiently the wrath that is come upon you from God: for thine enemy hath persecuted thee; but shortly thou shalt see his destruction, and shalt tread upon his neck.

{4:26} My delicate ones have gone rough ways, and were taken away as a flock caught of the enemies.

{4:27} Be of good comfort, O my children, and cry unto God: for ye shall be remembered of him that brought these things upon you.

{4:28} For as it was your mind to go astray from God: so, being returned, seek him ten times more.

{4:29} For he that hath brought these plagues upon you shall bring you everlasting joy with your salvation.

{4:30} Take a good heart, O Jerusalem: for he that gave thee that name will comfort thee.

{4:31} Miserable are they that afflicted thee, and rejoiced at thy fall.

{4:32} Miserable are the cities which thy children served: miserable is she that received thy sons.

{4:33} For as she rejoiced at thy ruin, and was glad of thy fall: so shall she be grieved for her own desolation.

{4:34} For I will take away the rejoicing of her great multitude, and her pride shall be turned into mourning.

{4:35} For fire shall come upon her from the Everlasting, long to endure; and she shall be inhabited of devils for a great time.

{4:36} O Jerusalem, look about thee toward the east, and behold the joy that cometh unto thee from God.

{4:37} Lo, thy sons come, whom thou sentest away, they come gathered together from the east to the west by the word of the Holy One, rejoicing in the glory of God.

{5:1} Put off, O Jerusalem, the garment of mourning and affliction, and put on the comeliness of the glory that cometh from God for ever.

{5:2} Cast about thee a double garment of the righteousness which cometh from God; and set a diadem on thine head of the glory of the Everlasting.

{5:3} For God will shew thy brightness unto every country under heaven.

{5:4} For thy name shall be called of God for ever The peace of righteousness, and The glory of God's worship.

{5:5} Arise, O Jerusalem, and stand on high, and look about toward the east, and behold thy children gathered from the west unto the east by the word of the Holy One, rejoicing in the remembrance of God.

{5:6} For they departed from thee on foot, and were led away of their enemies: but God bringeth them unto thee exalted with glory, as children of the kingdom.

{5:7} For God hath appointed that every high hill, and banks of long continuance, should be cast down, and valleys filled up, to make even the ground, that Israel may go safely in the glory of God,

{5:8} Moreover even the woods and every sweetsmelling tree shall overshadow Israel by the commandment of God.

{5:9} For God shall lead Israel with joy in the light of his glory with the mercy and righteousness that cometh from him.

The Book of Bel and the Dragon

The History of the Destruction of Bel and the Dragon, Cut off from the end of Daniel.

{1:1} And king Astyages was gathered to his fathers, and Cyrus of Persia received his kingdom.

{1:2} And Daniel conversed with the king, and was honoured above all his friends.

{1:3} Now the Babylons had an idol, called Bel, and there were spent upon him every day twelve great measures of fine flour, and forty sheep, and six vessels of wine.

{1:4} And the king worshipped it and went daily to adore it: but Daniel worshipped his own God. And the king said unto him, Why dost not thou worship Bel?

{1:5} Who answered and said, Because I may not worship idols made with hands, but the living God, who hath created the heaven and the earth, and hath sovereignty over all flesh.

{1:6} Then said the king unto him, Thinkest thou not that Bel is a living God? seest thou not how much he eateth and drinketh every day?

{1:7} Then Daniel smiled, and said, O king, be not deceived: for this is but clay within, and brass without, and did never eat or drink anything.

{1:8} So the king was wroth, and called for his priests, and said unto them, If ye tell me not who this is that devoureth these expences, ye shall die.

{1:9} But if ye can certify me that Bel devoureth them, then Daniel shall die: for he hath spoken blasphemy against Bel. And Daniel said unto the king, Let it be according to thy word.

{1:10} Now the priests of Bel were threescore and ten, beside their wives and children. And the king went with Daniel into the temple of Bel.

{1:11} So Bel's priests said, Lo, we go out: but thou, O king, set on the meat, and make ready the wine, and shut the door fast and seal it with thine own signet;

{1:12} And tomorrow when thou comest in, if thou findest not that Bel hath eaten up all, we will suffer death: or else Daniel, that speaketh falsely against us.

{1:13} And they little regarded it: for under the table they had made a privy entrance, whereby they entered in continually, and consumed those things.

{1:14} So when they were gone forth, the king set meats before Bel. Now Daniel had commanded his servants to bring ashes, and those they strewed throughout all the temple in the presence of the king alone: then went they out, and shut the door, and sealed it with the king's signet, and so departed.

{1:15} Now in the night came the priests with their wives and children, as they were wont to do, and did eat and drink up all.

{1:16} In the morning betime the king arose, and Daniel with him.

{1:17} And the king said, Daniel, are the seals whole? And he said, Yea, O king, they be whole.

{1:18} And as soon as he had opened the dour, the king looked upon the table, and cried with a loud voice, Great art thou, O Bel, and with thee is no deceit at all.

{1:19} Then laughed Daniel, and held the king that he should not go in, and said, Behold now the pavement, and mark well whose footsteps are these.

{1:20} And the king said, I see the footsteps of men, women, and children. And then the king was angry,

{1:21} And took the priests with their wives and children, who shewed him the privy doors, where they came in, and consumed such things as were upon the table.

{1:22} Therefore the king slew them, and delivered Bel into Daniel's power, who destroyed him and his temple.

{1:23} And in that same place there was a great dragon, which they of Babylon worshipped.

{1:24} And the king said unto Daniel, Wilt thou also say that this is of brass? lo, he liveth, he eateth and drinketh; thou canst not say that he is no living god: therefore worship him.

{1:25} Then said Daniel unto the king, I will worship the Lord my God: for he is the living God.

{1:26} But give me leave, O king, and I shall slay this dragon without sword or staff. The king said, I give thee leave.

{1:27} Then Daniel took pitch, and fat, and hair, and did seethe them together, and made lumps thereof: this he put in the dragon's mouth, and so the dragon burst in sunder : and Daniel said, Lo, these are the gods ye worship.

{1:28} When they of Babylon heard that, they took great indignation, and conspired against the king, saying, the king is become a Jew, and he hath destroyed Bel, he hath slain the dragon, and put the priests to death.

{1:29} So they came to the king, and said, Deliver us Daniel, or else we will destroy thee and thine house.

{1:30} Now when the king saw that they pressed him sore, being constrained, he delivered Daniel unto them:

{1:31} Who cast him into the lions' den: where he was six days.

{1:32} And in the den, there were seven lions, and they had given them every day two carcasses, and two sheep: which then were not given to them, to the intent they might devour Daniel.

{1:33} Now there was in Jewry a prophet, called Habbacuc, who had made pottage, and had broken bread in a bowl, and was going into the field, for to bring it to the reapers.

{1:34} But the angel of the Lord said unto Habbacuc, Go, carry the dinner that thou hast into Babylon unto Daniel, who is in the lions' den.

{1:35} And Habbacuc said, Lord, I never saw Babylon; neither do I know where the den is.

{1:36} Then the angel of the Lord took him by the crown, and bare him by the hair of his head, and through the vehemency of his spirit set him in Babylon over the den.

{1:37} And Habbacuc cried, saying, O Daniel, Daniel, take the dinner which God hath sent thee.

{1:38} And Daniel said, thou hast remembered me, O God: neither hast thou forsaken them that seek thee and love thee.

{1:39} So Daniel arose, and did eat: and the angel of the Lord set Habbacuc in his own place again immediately.

{1:40} Upon the seventh day the king went to bewail Daniel: and when he came to the den, he looked in, and behold, Daniel was sitting.

{1:41} Then cried the king with a loud voice, saying, Great art Lord God of Daniel, and there is none other beside thee.

{1:42} And he drew him out, and cast those that were the cause of his destruction into the den: and they were devoured in a moment before his face.

Ecclesiastes or the Preacher

{1:1} The words of the Preacher, the son of David, king in Jerusalem. {1:2} Vanity of vanities, saith the Preacher, vanity of vanities; all [is] vanity. {1:3} What profit hath a man of all his labour which he taketh under the sun? {1:4} [One] generation passeth away, and [another] generation cometh: but the earth abideth for ever. {1:5} The sun also ariseth, and the sun goeth down, and hasteth to his place where he arose. {1:6} The wind goeth toward the south, and turneth about unto the north; it whirleth about continually, and the wind returneth again according to his circuits. {1:7} All the rivers run into the sea; yet the sea [is] not full; unto the place from whence the rivers come, thither they return again. {1:8} All things [are] full of labour; man cannot utter [it:] the eye is not satisfied with seeing, nor the ear filled with hearing. {1:9} The thing that hath been, it [is that] which shall be; and that which is done [is] that which shall be done: and [there is] no new [thing] under the sun. {1:10} Is there [any] thing whereof it may be said, See, this [is] new? it hath been already of old time, which was before us. {1:11} [There is] no remembrance of former [things;] neither shall there be [any] remembrance of [things] that are to come with [those] that shall come after.

{1:12} I the Preacher was king over Israel in Jerusalem. {1:13} And I gave my heart to seek and search out by wisdom concerning all [things] that are done under heaven: this sore travail hath God given to the sons of man to be exercised therewith. {1:14} I have seen all the works that are done under the sun; and, behold, all [is] vanity and vexation of spirit. {1:15} [That which is] crooked cannot be made straight: and that which is wanting cannot be numbered. {1:16} I communed with mine own heart, saying, Lo, I am come to great estate, and have gotten more wisdom than all [they] that have been before me in Jerusalem: yea, my heart had great experience of wisdom and knowledge. {1:17} And I gave my heart to know wisdom, and to know madness and folly: I perceived that this also is vexation of spirit. {1:18} For in much wisdom [is] much grief: and he that increaseth knowledge increaseth sorrow.

{2:1} I said in mine heart, go to now, I will prove thee with mirth, therefore enjoy pleasure: and, behold, this also [is] vanity. {2:2} I said of laughter, [It is] mad: and of mirth, What doeth it? {2:3} I sought in mine heart to give myself unto wine, yet acquainting mine heart with wisdom; and to lay hold on folly, till I might see what [was] that good for the sons of men, which they should do under the heaven all the days of their life. {2:4} I made me great works; I builded me houses; I planted me vineyards: {2:5} I made me gardens and orchards, and I planted trees in them of all [kind of] fruits: {2:6} I made me pools of water, to water therewith the wood that bringeth forth trees: {2:7} I got [me] servants and maidens, and had servants born in my house; also I had great possessions of great and small cattle above all that were in Jerusalem before me: {2:8} I gathered me also silver and gold, and the peculiar treasure of kings and of the provinces: I gat me men singers and women singers, and the delights of the sons of men, [as] musical instruments, and that of all sorts. {2:9} So I was great, and increased more than all that were before me in Jerusalem: also my wisdom remained with me. {2:10} And whatsoever mine eyes desired I kept not from them, I withheld not my heart from any joy; for my heart rejoiced in all my labour: and this was my portion of all my labour. {2:11} Then I looked on all the works that my hands had wrought, and on the labour that I had laboured to do: and, behold, all [was] vanity and vexation of spirit, and [there was] no profit under the sun. {2:12} And I turned myself to behold wisdom, and madness, and folly: for what [can] the man [do] that cometh after the king? [even] that which hath been already done. {2:13} Then I saw that wisdom excelleth folly, as far as light excelleth darkness. {2:14} The wise man's eyes [are] in his head; but the fool walketh in darkness: and I myself perceived also that one event happeneth to them all. {2:15} Then said I in my heart, As it happeneth to the fool, so it happeneth even to me; and why was I then more wise? Then I said in my heart, that this also [is] vanity. {2:16} For [there is] no remembrance of the wise more than of the fool for ever; seeing that which now [is] in the days to come shall all be forgotten. And how dieth the wise [man?] as the fool. {2:17} Therefore I hated life; because the work that is wrought under the sun is grievous unto me: for all [is] vanity and vexation of spirit.

{2:18} Yea, I hated all my labour which I had taken under the sun: because I should leave it unto the man that shall be after me. {2:19} And who knoweth whether he shall be a wise [man] or a fool? yet shall he have rule over all my labour wherein I have laboured, and wherein I have shewed myself wise under the sun. This [is] also vanity. {2:20} Therefore I went about to cause my heart to despair of all the labour which I took under the sun. {2:21} For there is a man whose labour [is] in wisdom, and in knowledge, and in equity; yet to a man that hath not laboured therein shall he leave it [for] his portion. This also [is] vanity and a great evil. {2:22} For what hath man of all his labour, and of the vexation of his heart, wherein he hath laboured under the sun? {2:23} For all his days [are] sorrows, and his travail grief; yea, his heart taketh not rest in the night. This is also vanity.

{2:24} [There is] nothing better for a man, [than] that he should eat and drink, and [that] he should make his soul enjoy good in his labour. This also I saw, that it [was] from the hand of God. {2:25} For who can eat, or who else can hasten [hereunto,] more than I? {2:26} For [God] giveth to a man that [is] good in his sight wisdom, and knowledge, and joy: but to the sinner he giveth travail, to gather and to heap up, that he may give to [him that is] good before God. This also [is] vanity and vexation of spirit.

{3:1} To every [thing there is] a season, and a time to every purpose under the heaven: {3:2} A time to be born, and a time to die; a time to plant, and a time to pluck up [that which is] planted; {3:3} A time to kill, and a time to heal; a time to break down, and a time to build up; {3:4} A time to weep, and a time to laugh; a time to mourn, and a time to dance; {3:5} A time to cast away stones, and a time to gather stones together; a time to embrace, and a time to refrain from embracing; {3:6} A time to get, and a time to lose; a time to keep, and a time to cast away; {3:7} A time to rend, and a time to sew; a time to keep silence, and a time to speak; {3:8} A time to love, and a time to hate; a time of war, and a time of peace. {3:9} What profit hath he that worketh in that wherein he laboureth? {3:10} I have seen the travail, which God hath given to the sons of men to be exercised in it. {3:11} He hath made every [thing] beautiful in his time: also he hath set the world in their heart, so that no man can find out the work that God maketh from the beginning to the end. {3:12} I know that [there is] no good in them, but for [a man] to rejoice, and to do good in his life. {3:13} And also that every man should eat and drink, and enjoy the good of all his labour, it [is] the gift of God. {3:14} I know that, whatsoever God doeth, it shall be for ever: nothing can be put to it, nor any thing taken from it: and God doeth [it,] that [men] should fear before him. {3:15} That which hath been is now; and that which is to be hath already been; and God requireth that which is past.

{3:16} And moreover I saw under the sun the place of judgment, [that] wickedness [was] there; and the place of righteousness, [that] iniquity [was] there. {3:17} I said in mine heart, God shall judge the righteous and the wicked: for [there is] a time there for every purpose and for every work. {3:18} I said in mine heart concerning the estate of the sons of men, that God might manifest them, and that they might see that they themselves are beasts. {3:19} For that which befalleth the sons of men befalleth beasts; even one thing befalleth them: as the one dieth, so dieth the other; yea, they have all one breath; so that a man hath no preeminence above a beast: for all [is] vanity. {3:20} All go unto one place; all are of the dust, and all turn to dust again. {3:21} Who knoweth the spirit of man that goeth upward, and the spirit of the beast that goeth downward to the earth? {3:22} Wherefore I perceive that [there is] nothing better, than that a man should rejoice in his own works; for that [is] his portion: for who shall bring him to see what shall be after him?

{4:1} So I returned, and considered all the oppressions that are done under the sun: and behold the tears of [such as were] oppressed, and they had no comforter; and on the side of their oppressors [there was] power; but they had no comforter. {4:2} Wherefore I praised the dead which are already dead more than the living which are yet alive. {4:3} Yea, better [is he] than both they, which hath not yet been, who hath not seen the evil work that is done under the sun.

{4:4} Again, I considered all travail, and every right work, that for this a man is envied of his neighbour. This [is] also vanity and vexation of spirit. {4:5} The fool foldeth his hands together, and eateth his own flesh. {4:6} Better [is] an handful [with] quietness, than both the hands full [with] travail and vexation of spirit.

{4:7} Then I returned, and I saw vanity under the sun. {4:8} There is one [alone,] and [there is] not a second; yea, he hath neither child nor brother: yet [is there] no end of all his labour; neither is his eye satisfied with riches; neither [saith he,] For whom do I labour, and bereave my soul of good? This [is] also vanity, yea, it [is] a sore travail.

{4:9} Two [are] better than one; because they have a good reward for their labour. {4:10} For if they fall, the one will lift up his fellow: but woe to him [that is] alone when he falleth; for [he hath] not another to help him up. {4:11} Again, if two lie together, then they have heat: but how can one be warm [alone?]{4:12} And if one prevail against him, two shall withstand him; and a threefold cord is not quickly broken.

{4:13} Better [is] a poor and a wise child than an old and foolish king, who will no more be admonished. {4:14} For out of prison he cometh to reign; whereas also [he that is] born in his kingdom becometh poor. {4:15} I considered all the living which walk under the sun, with the second child that shall stand up in his stead. {4:16} [There is] no end of all the people, [even] of all that have been before them: they also that come after shall not rejoice in him. Surely this also [is] vanity and vexation of spirit.

{5:1} Keep thy foot when thou goest to the house of God, and be more ready to hear, than to give the sacrifice of fools: for they consider not that they do evil. {5:2} Be not rash with thy mouth, and let not thine heart be hasty to utter [any] thing before God: for God [is] in heaven, and thou upon earth: therefore let thy words be few. {5:3} For a dream cometh through the multitude of business; and a fool's voice [is known] by multitude of words. {5:4} When thou vowest a vow unto God, defer not to pay it; for [he hath] no pleasure in fools: pay that which thou hast vowed. {5:5} Better [is it] that thou shouldest not vow, than that thou shouldest vow and not pay. {5:6} Suffer not thy mouth to cause thy flesh to sin; neither say thou before the angel, that it [was] an error: wherefore should God be angry at thy voice, and destroy the work of thine hands? {5:7} For in the multitude of dreams and many words [there are] also [divers] vanities: but fear thou God.

{5:8} If thou seest the oppression of the poor, and violent perverting of judgment and justice in a province, marvel not at the matter: for [he that is] higher than the highest regardeth; and [there be] higher than they.

{5:9} Moreover the profit of the earth is for all: the king [himself] is served by the field. {5:10} He that loveth silver shall not be satisfied with silver; nor he that loveth abundance with increase: this [is] also vanity. {5:11} When goods increase, they are increased that eat them: and what good [is there] to the owners thereof, saving the beholding [of them] with their eyes? {5:12} The sleep of a labouring man [is] sweet, whether he eat little or much: but the abundance of the rich will not suffer him to sleep. {5:13} There is a sore evil [which] I have seen under the sun, [namely,] riches kept for the owners thereof to their hurt. {5:14} But those riches perish by evil travail: and he begetteth a son, and [there is] nothing in his hand. {5:15} As he came forth of his mother's womb, naked shall he return to go as he came, and shall take nothing of his labour, which he may carry away in his hand. {5:16} And this also [is] a sore evil, [that] in all points as he came, so shall he go: and what profit hath he that hath laboured for the wind? {5:17} All his days also he eateth in darkness, and [he hath] much sorrow and wrath with his sickness.

{5:18} Behold [that] which I have seen: [it is] good and comely [for one] to eat and to drink, and to enjoy the good of all his labour that he taketh under the sun all the days of his life, which God giveth him: for it [is] his portion. {5:19} Every man also to whom God hath given riches and wealth, and hath given him power to eat thereof, and to take his portion, and to rejoice in his labour; this [is] the gift of God. {5:20} For he shall not much remember the days of his life; because God answereth [him] in the joy of his heart.

{6:1} There is an evil which I have seen under the sun, and it [is] common among men: {6:2} A man to whom God hath given riches, wealth, and honour, so that he wanteth nothing for his soul of all that he desireth, yet God giveth him not power to eat thereof, but a stranger eateth it: this [is] vanity, and it [is] an evil disease.

{6:3} If a man beget an hundred [children,] and live many years, so that the days of his years be many, and his soul be not filled with good, and also [that] he have no burial; I say, [that] an untimely birth [is] better than he. {6:4} For he cometh in with vanity, and departeth in darkness, and his name shall be covered with darkness. {6:5} Moreover he hath not seen the sun, nor known [any thing:] this hath more rest than the other.

{6:6} Yea, though he live a thousand years twice [told,] yet hath he seen no good: do not all go to one place? {6:7} All the labour of man [is] for his mouth, and yet the appetite is not filled. {6:8} For what hath the wise more than the fool? what hath the poor, that knoweth to walk before the living?

{6:9} Better [is] the sight of the eyes than the wandering of the desire: this [is] also vanity and vexation of spirit. {6:10} That which hath been is named already, and it is known that it [is] man: neither may he contend with him that is mightier than he.

{6:11} Seeing there be many things that increase vanity, what [is] man the better? {6:12} For who knoweth what [is] good for man in [this] life, all the days of his vain life which he spendeth as a shadow? for who can tell a man what shall be after him under the sun?

{7:1} A good name [is] better than precious ointment; and the day of death than the day of one's birth.

{7:2} [It is] better to go to the house of mourning, than to go to the house of feasting: for that is the end of all men; and the living will lay [it] to his heart. {7:3} Sorrow [is] better than laughter: for by the sadness of the countenance the heart is made better. {7:4} The heart of the wise [is] in the house of mourning; but the heart of fools [is] in the house of mirth. {7:5} [It is] better to hear the rebuke of the wise, than for a man to hear the song of fools. {7:6} For as the crackling of thorns under a pot, so [is] the laughter of the fool: this also [is] vanity.

{7:7} Surely oppression maketh a wise man mad; and a gift destroyeth the heart. {7:8} Better [is] the end of a thing than the beginning thereof: [and] the patient in spirit [is] better than the proud in spirit. {7:9} Be not hasty in thy spirit to be angry: for anger resteth in the bosom of fools. {7:10} Say not thou, What is [the cause] that the former days were better than these? for thou dost not enquire wisely concerning this.

{7:11} Wisdom [is] good with an inheritance: and [by it there is] profit to them that see the sun. {7:12} For wisdom [is] a defence, [and] money [is] a defence: but the excellency of knowledge [is, that] wisdom giveth life to them that have it. {7:13} Consider the work of God: for who can make [that] straight, which he hath made crooked? {7:14} In the day of prosperity be joyful, but in the day of adversity consider: God also hath set the one over against the other, to the end that man should find nothing after him. {7:15} All [things] have I seen in the days of my vanity: there is a just [man] that perisheth in his righteousness, and there is a wicked [man] that prolongeth [his life] in his wickedness. {7:16} Be not righteous over much; neither make thyself over wise: why shouldest thou destroy thyself? {7:17} Be not over much wicked, neither be thou foolish: why shouldest thou die before thy time? {7:18} [It is] good that thou shouldest take hold of this; yea, also from this withdraw not thine hand: for he that feareth God shall come forth of them all. {7:19} Wisdom strengtheneth the wise more than ten mighty [men] which are in the city. {7:20} For [there is] not a just man upon earth, that doeth good, and sinneth not. {7:21} Also take no heed unto all words that are spoken; lest thou hear thy servant curse thee: {7:22} For oftentimes also thine own heart knoweth that thou thyself likewise hast cursed others.

{7:23} All this have I proved by wisdom: I said, I will be wise; but it [was] far from me. {7:24} That which is far off, and exceeding deep, who can find it out? {7:25} I applied mine heart to know, and to search, and to seek out wisdom, and the reason [of things,] and to know the wickedness of folly, even of foolishness [and] madness: {7:26} And I find more bitter than death the woman, whose heart [is] snares and nets, [and] her hands [as] bands: whoso pleaseth God shall escape from her; but the sinner shall be taken by her. {7:27} Behold, this have I found, saith the preacher, [counting] one by one, to find out the account: {7:28} Which yet my soul seeketh, but I find not: one man among a thousand have I found; but a woman among all those have I not found. {7:29} Lo, this only have I found, that God hath made man upright; but they have sought out many inventions.

{8:1} Who [is] as the wise [man?] and who knoweth the interpretation of a thing? a man's wisdom maketh his face to shine, and the boldness of his face shall be changed. {8:2} I [counsel thee] to keep the king's commandment, and [that] in regard of the oath of God. {8:3} Be not hasty to go out of his sight: stand not in an evil thing; for he doeth whatsoever pleaseth him. {8:4} Where the word of a king [is, there is] power: and who may say unto him, What doest thou? {8:5} Whoso keepeth the commandment shall feel no evil thing: and a wise man's heart discerneth both time and judgment.

{8:6} Because to every purpose there is time and judgment, therefore the misery of man [is] great upon him. {8:7} For he knoweth not that which shall be: for who can tell him when it shall be? {8:8} [There is] no man that hath power over the spirit to retain the spirit; neither [hath he] power in the day of death: and [there is] no discharge in [that] war; neither shall wickedness deliver those that are given to it. {8:9} All this have I seen, and applied my heart unto every work that is done under the sun: [there is] a time wherein one man ruleth over another to his own hurt. {8:10} And so I saw the wicked buried, who had come and gone from the place of the holy, and they were forgotten in the city where they had so done: this [is] also vanity. {8:11} Because sentence against an evil work is not executed speedily, therefore the heart of the sons of men is fully set in them to do evil.

{8:12} Though a sinner do evil an hundred times, and his [days] be prolonged, yet surely I know that it shall be well with them that fear God, which fear before him: {8:13} But it shall not be well with the wicked, neither shall he prolong [his] days, [which are] as a shadow; because he feareth not before God. {8:14} There is a vanity which is done upon the earth; that there be just [men,] unto whom it happeneth according to the work of the wicked; again, there be wicked [men,] to whom it happeneth according to the work of the righteous: I said that this also [is] vanity. {8:15} Then I commended mirth, because a man hath no better thing under the sun, than to eat, and to drink, and to be merry: for that shall abide with him of his labour the days of his life, which God giveth him under the sun.

{8:16} When I applied mine heart to know wisdom, and to see the business that is done upon the earth: (for also [there is that] neither day nor night seeth sleep with his eyes:) {8:17} Then I beheld all the work of God, that a man cannot find out the work that is done under the sun: because though a man labour to seek [it] out, yet he shall not find [it;] yea further; though a wise [man] think to know [it,] yet shall he not be able to find [it.]

{9:1} For all this I considered in my heart even to declare all this, that the righteous, and the wise, and their works, are in the hand of God: no man knoweth either love or hatred [by] all [that is] before them. {9:2} All [things come] alike to all: [there is] one event to the righteous, and to the wicked; to the good and to the clean, and to the unclean; to him that sacrificeth, and to him that sacrificeth not: as [is] the good, so [is] the sinner; [and] he that sweareth, as [he] that feareth an oath. {9:3} This [is] an evil among all [things] that are done under the sun, that [there is] one event unto all: yea, also the heart of the sons of men is full of evil, and madness is in their heart while they live, and after that [they go] to the dead.

{9:4} For to him that is joined to all the living there is hope: for a living dog is better than a dead lion. {9:5} For the living know that they shall die: but the dead know not any thing, neither have they any more a reward; for the memory of them is forgotten. {9:6} Also their love, and their hatred, and their envy, is now perished; neither have they any more a portion for ever in any [thing] that is done under the sun.

{9:7} Go thy way, eat thy bread with joy, and drink thy wine with a merry heart; for God now accepteth thy works. {9:8} Let thy garments be always white; and let thy head lack no ointment. {9:9} Live joyfully with the wife whom thou lovest all the days of the life of thy vanity, which he hath given thee under the sun, all the days of thy vanity: for that [is] thy portion in [this] life, and in thy labour which thou takest under the sun. {9:10} Whatsoever thy hand findeth to do, do [it] with thy might; for [there is] no work, nor device, nor knowledge, nor wisdom, in the grave, whither thou goest.

{9:11} I returned, and saw under the sun, that the race [is] not to the swift, nor the battle to the strong, neither yet bread to the wise, nor yet riches to men of understanding, nor yet favour to men of skill; but time and chance happeneth to them all. {9:12} For man also knoweth not his time: as the fishes that are taken in an evil net, and as the birds that are caught in the snare; so [are] the sons of men snared in an evil time, when it falleth suddenly upon them.

{9:13} This wisdom have I seen also under the sun, and it [seemed] great unto me: {9:14} [There was] a little city, and few men within it; and there came a great king against it, and besieged it, and built great bulwarks against it: {9:15} Now there was found in it a poor wise man, and he by his wisdom delivered the city; yet no man remembered that same poor man. {9:16} Then said I, Wisdom [is] better than strength: nevertheless the poor man's wisdom [is] despised, and his words are not heard. {9:17} The words of wise [men are] heard in quiet more than the cry of him that ruleth among fools. {9:18} Wisdom [is] better than weapons of war: but one sinner destroyeth much good.

{10:1} Dead flies cause the ointment of the apothecary to send forth a stinking savour: [so doth] a little folly him that is in reputation for wisdom [and] honour. {10:2} A wise man's heart [is] at his right hand; but a fool's heart at his left. {10:3} Yea also, when he that is a fool walketh by the way, his wisdom faileth [him,] and he saith to every one [that] he [is] a fool. {10:4} If the spirit of the ruler rise up against thee, leave not thy place; for yielding pacifieth great offences. {10:5} There is an evil [which] I have seen under the sun, as an error [which] proceedeth from the ruler: {10:6} Folly is set in great dignity, and the rich sit in low place. {10:7} I have seen servants upon horses, and princes walking as servants upon the earth. {10:8} He that diggeth a pit shall fall into it; and whoso breaketh an hedge, a serpent shall bite him. {10:9} Whoso removeth stones shall be hurt therewith; [and] he that cleaveth wood shall be endangered thereby. {10:10} If the iron be blunt, and he do not whet the edge, then must he put to more strength: but wisdom [is] profitable to direct. {10:11} Surely the serpent will bite without enchantment; and a babbler is no better. {10:12} The words of a wise man's mouth [are] gracious; but the lips of a fool will swallow up himself. {10:13} The beginning of the words of his mouth [is] foolishness: and the end of his talk [is] mischievous madness. {10:14} A fool also is full of words: a man cannot tell what shall be; and what shall be after him, who can tell him? {10:15} The labour of the foolish wearieth every one of them, because he knoweth not how to go to the city.

{10:16} Woe to thee, O land, when thy king [is] a child, and thy princes eat in the morning! {10:17} Blessed [art] thou, O land, when thy king [is] the son of nobles, and thy princes eat in due season, for strength, and not for drunkenness!

{10:18} By much slothfulness the building decayeth; and through idleness of the hands the house droppeth through.

{10:19} A feast is made for laughter, and wine maketh merry: but money answereth all [things.]

{10:20} Curse not the king, no not in thy thought; and curse not the rich in thy bedchamber: for a bird of the air shall carry the voice, and that which hath wings shall tell the matter.

{11:1} Cast thy bread upon the waters: for thou shalt find it after many days. {11:2} Give a portion to seven, and also to eight; for thou knowest not what evil shall be upon the earth. {11:3} If the clouds be full of rain, they empty [themselves] upon the earth: and if the tree fall toward the south, or toward the north, in the place where the tree falleth, there it shall be. {11:4} He that observeth the wind shall not sow; and he that regardeth the clouds shall not reap. {11:5} As thou knowest not what [is] the way of the spirit, [nor] how the bones [do grow] in the womb of her that is with child: even so thou knowest not the works of God who maketh all. {11:6} In the morning sow thy seed, and in the evening withhold not thine hand: for thou knowest not whether shall prosper, either this or that, or whether they both [shall be] alike good.

{11:7} Truly the light [is] sweet, and a pleasant [thing it is] for the eyes to behold the sun: {11:8} But if a man live many years, [and] rejoice in them all; yet let him remember the days of darkness; for they shall be many. All that cometh [is] vanity.

{11:9} Rejoice, O young man, in thy youth; and let thy heart cheer thee in the days of thy youth, and walk in the ways of thine heart, and in the sight of thine eyes: but know thou, that for all these [things] God will bring thee into judgment. {11:10} Therefore remove sorrow from thy heart, and put away evil from thy flesh: for childhood and youth [are] vanity.

{12:1} Remember now thy Creator in the days of thy youth, while the evil days come not, nor the years draw nigh, when thou shalt say, I have no pleasure in them; {12:2} While the sun, or the light, or the moon, or the stars, be not darkened, nor the clouds return after the rain: {12:3} In the day when the keepers of the house shall tremble, and the strong men shall bow themselves, and the grinders cease because they are few, and those that look out of the windows be darkened, {12:4} And the doors shall be shut in the streets, when the sound of the grinding is low, and he shall rise up at the voice of the bird, and all the daughters of music shall be brought low; {12:5} Also [when] they shall be afraid of [that which is] high, and fears [shall be] in the way, and the almond tree shall flourish, and the grasshopper shall be a burden, and desire shall fail: because man goeth to his long home, and the mourners go about the streets: {12:6} Or ever the silver cord be loosed, or the golden bowl be broken, or the pitcher be broken at the fountain, or the wheel broken at the cistern. {12:7} Then shall the dust return to the earth as it was: and the spirit shall return unto God who gave it.

{12:8} Vanity of vanities, saith the preacher; all [is] vanity. {12:9} And moreover, because the preacher was wise, he still taught the people knowledge; yea, he gave good heed, and sought out, [and] set in order many proverbs. {12:10} The preacher sought to find out acceptable words: and [that which was] written [was] upright, [even] words of truth. {12:11} The words of the wise [are] as goads, and as nails fastened by the masters of assemblies, [which] are given from one shepherd. {12:12} And further, by these, my son, be admonished: of making many books [there is] no end; and much study [is] a weariness of the flesh.

{12:13} Let us hear the conclusion of the whole matter: Fear God, and keep his commandments: for this [is] the whole [duty] of man. {12:14} For God shall bring every work into judgment, with every secret thing, whether [it be] good, or whether [it be] evil.

The Book of Esther

{1:1} Now it came to pass in the days of Ahasuerus, (this [is] Ahasuerus which reigned, from India even unto Ethiopia, [over] an hundred and seven and twenty provinces:) {1:2} [That] in those days, when the king Ahasuerus sat on the throne of his kingdom, which [was] in Shushan the palace, {1:3} In the third year of his reign, he made a feast unto all his princes and his servants; the power of Persia and Media, the nobles and princes of the provinces, [being] before him: {1:4} When he shewed the riches of his glorious kingdom and the honour of his excellent majesty many days, [even] an hundred and fourscore days. {1:5} And when these days were expired, the king made a feast unto all the people that were present in Shushan the palace, both unto great and small, seven days, in the court of the garden of the king's palace; {1:6} [Where were] white, green, and blue, [hangings,] fastened with cords of fine linen and purple to silver rings and pillars of marble: the beds [were of] gold and silver, upon a pavement of red, and blue, and white, and black, marble. {1:7} And they gave [them] drink in vessels of gold, (the vessels being diverse one from another,) and royal wine in abundance, according to the state of the king. {1:8} And the drinking [was] according to the law; none did compel: for so the king had appointed to all the officers of his house, that they should do according to every man's pleasure. {1:9} Also Vashti the queen made a feast for the women [in] the royal house which [belonged] to king Ahasuerus.

{1:10} On the seventh day, when the heart of the king was merry with wine, he commanded Mehuman, Biztha, Harbona, Bigtha, and Abagtha, Zethar, and Carcas, the seven chamberlains that served in the presence of Ahasuerus the king, {1:11} To bring Vashti the queen before the king with the crown royal, to shew the people and the princes her beauty: for she [was] fair to look on. {1:12} But the queen Vashti refused to come at the king's commandment by [his] chamberlains: therefore was the king very wroth, and his anger burned in him.

{1:13} Then the king said to the wise men, which knew the times, (for so [was] the king's manner toward all that knew law and judgment: {1:14} And the next unto him [was] Carshena, Shethar, Admatha, Tarshish, Meres, Marsena, [and] Memucan, the seven princes of Persia and Media, which saw the king's face, [and] which sat the first in the kingdom;) {1:15} What shall we do unto the queen Vashti according to law, because she hath not performed the commandment of the king Ahasuerus by the chamberlains? {1:16} And Memucan answered before the
king and the princes, Vashti the queen hath not done wrong to the king only, but also to all the princes, and to all the people that [are] in all the provinces of the king Ahasuerus. {1:17} For [this] deed of the queen shall come abroad unto all women, so that they shall despise their husbands in their eyes, when it shall be reported, The king Ahasuerus commanded Vashti the queen to be brought in before him, but she came not. {1:18} [Likewise] shall the ladies of Persia and Media

say this day unto all the king's princes, which have heard of the deed of the queen. Thus [shall there arise] too much contempt and wrath. {1:19} If it please the king, let there go a royal commandment from him, and let it be written among the laws of the Persians and the Medes, that it be not altered, That Vashti come no more before king Ahasuerus; and let the king give her royal estate unto another that is better than she. {1:20} And when the king's decree which he shall make shall be published throughout all his empire, (for it is great,) all the wives shall give to their husbands honour, both to great and small. {1:21} And the saying pleased the king and the princes; and the king did according to the word of Memucan: {1:22} For he sent letters into all the king's provinces, into every province according to the writing thereof, and to every people after their language, that every man should bear rule in his own house, and that [it] should be published according to the language of every people.

{2:1} After these things, when the wrath of king Ahasuerus was appeased, he remembered Vashti, and what she had done, and what was decreed against her. {2:2} Then said the king's servants that ministered unto him, let there be fair young virgins sought for the king: {2:3} And let the king appoint officers in all the provinces of his kingdom, that they may gather together all the fair young virgins unto Shushan the palace, to the house of the women unto the custody of Hege the king's chamberlain, keeper of the women; and let their things for purification be given [them:]{2:4} And let the maiden which pleaseth the king be queen instead of Vashti. And the thing pleased the king; and he did so.

{2:5} [Now] in Shushan the palace there was a certain Jew, whose name [was] Mordecai, the son of Jair, the son of Shimei, the son of Kish, a Benjamite; {2:6} Who had been carried away from Jerusalem with the captivity which had been carried away with Jeconiah king of Judah, whom Nebuchadnezzar the king of Babylon had carried away. {2:7} And he brought up Hadassah, that [is,] Esther, his uncle's daughter: for she had neither father nor mother, and the maid [was] fair and beautiful; whom Mordecai, when her father and mother were dead, took for his own daughter.

{2:8} So it came to pass, when the king's commandment and his decree was heard, and when many maidens were gathered together unto Shushan the palace, to the custody of Hegai, that Esther was brought also unto the king's house, to the custody of Hegai, keeper of the women. {2:9} And the maiden pleased him, and she obtained kindness of him; and he speedily gave her her things for purification, with such things as belonged to her, and seven maidens, [which were] meet to be given her, out of the king's house: and he preferred her and her maids unto the best [place] of the house of the women. {2:10} Esther had not shewed her people nor her kindred: for Mordecai had charged her that she should not shew [it.]{2:11} And Mordecai walked every day before the court of the women's house, to know how Esther did, and what should become of her.

{2:12} Now when every maid's turn was come to go in to king Ahasuerus, after that she had been twelve months, according to the manner of the women, (for so were the days of their purifications accomplished, [to wit,] six months with oil of myrrh, and six months with sweet odours, and with [other] things for the purifying of the women;) {2:13} Then thus came [every] maiden unto the king; whatsoever she desired was given her to go with her out of the house of the women unto the king's house. {2:14} In the evening she went, and on the morrow she returned into the second house of the women, to the custody of Shaashgaz, the king's chamberlain, which kept the concubines: she came in unto the king no more, except the king delighted in her, and that she were called by name.

{2:15} Now when the turn of Esther, the daughter of Abihail the uncle of Mordecai, who had taken her for his daughter, was come to go in unto the king, she required nothing but what Hegai the king's chamberlain, the keeper of the women, appointed. And Esther obtained favour in the sight of all them that looked upon her. {2:16} So Esther was taken unto king Ahasuerus into his house royal in the tenth month, which [is] the month Tebeth, in the seventh year of his reign. {2:17} And the king loved Esther above all the women, and she obtained grace and favour in his sight more than all the virgins; so that he set the royal crown upon her head, and made her queen instead of Vashti. {2:18}

Then the king made a great feast unto all his princes and his servants, [even] Esther's feast; and he made a release to the provinces, and gave gifts, according to the state of the king. {2:19} And when the virgins were gathered together the second time, then Mordecai sat in the king's gate. {2:20} Esther had not [yet] shewed her kindred nor her people; as Mordecai had charged her: for Esther did the commandment of Mordecai, like as when she was brought up with him.

{2:21} In those days, while Mordecai sat in the king's gate, two of the king's chamberlains, Bigthan and Teresh, of those which kept the door, were wroth, and sought to lay hand on the king Ahasuerus. {2:22} And the thing was known to Mordecai, who told it unto Esther the queen; and Esther certified the king [thereof] in Mordecai's name. {2:23} And when inquisition was made of the matter, it was found out; therefore they were both hanged on a tree: and it was written in the book of the chronicles before the king.

{3:1} After these things did king Ahasuerus promote Haman the son of Hammedatha the Agagite, and advanced him, and set his seat above all the princes that [were] with him. {3:2} And all the king's servants, that [were] in the king's gate, bowed, and reverenced Haman: for the king had so commanded concerning him. But Mordecai bowed not, nor did [him] reverence. {3:3} Then the king's servants, which [were] in the king's gate, said unto Mordecai, Why transgressest thou the king's commandment? {3:4} Now it came to pass, when they spake daily unto him, and he hearkened not unto them, that they told Haman, to see whether Mordecai's matters would stand: for he had told them that he [was] a Jew. {3:5} And when Haman saw that Mordecai bowed not, nor did him reverence, then was Haman full of wrath. {3:6} And he thought scorn to lay hands on Mordecai alone; for they had shewed him the people of Mordecai: wherefore Haman sought to destroy all the Jews that [were] throughout the whole kingdom of Ahasuerus, [even] the people of Mordecai.

{3:7} In the first month, that [is,] the month Nisan, in the twelfth year of king Ahasuerus, they cast Pur, that [is,] the lot, before Haman from day to day, and from month to month, [to] the twelfth [month,] that [is,] the month Adar.

{3:8} And Haman said unto king Ahasuerus, there is a certain people scattered abroad and dispersed among the people in all the provinces of thy kingdom; and their laws [are] diverse from all people; neither keep they the king's laws: therefore it [is] not for the king's profit to suffer them. {3:9} If it please the king, let it be written that they may be destroyed: and I will pay ten thousand talents of silver to the hands of those that have the charge of the business, to bring [it] into the king's treasuries. {3:10} And the king took his ring from his hand, and gave it unto Haman the son of Hammedatha the Agagite, the Jews' enemy. {3:11} And the king said unto Haman, the silver [is] given to thee, the people also, to do with them as it seemeth good to thee.

{3:12} Then were the king's scribes called on the thirteenth day of the first month, and there was written according to all that Haman had commanded unto the king's lieutenants, and to the governors that [were] over every province, and to the rulers of every people of every province according to the writing thereof, and [to] every people after their language; in the name of king Ahasuerus was it written, and sealed with the king's ring. {3:13} And the letters were sent by posts into all the king's provinces, to destroy, to kill, and to cause to perish, all Jews, both young and old, little children and women, in one day, [even] upon the thirteenth [day] of the twelfth month, which [is] the month Adar, and [to take] the spoil of them for a prey. {3:14} The copy of the writing for a commandment to be given in every province was published unto all people, that they should be ready against that day. {3:15} The posts went out, being hastened by the king's commandment, and the decree was given in Shushan the palace. And the king and Haman sat down to drink; but the city Shushan was perplexed.

{4:1} When Mordecai perceived all that was done, Mordecai rent his clothes, and put on sackcloth with ashes, and went out into the midst of the city, and cried with a loud and a bitter cry; {4:2} And came even before the king's gate: for none [might] enter into the king's gate clothed with sackcloth. {4:3} And in every province, whithersoever the king's commandment and his decree came, [there was] great mourning among the Jews, and fasting, and weeping, and wailing; and many lay in sackcloth and ashes.

{4:4} So Esther's maids and her chamberlains came and told [it] her. Then was the queen exceedingly grieved; and she sent raiment to clothe Mordecai, and to take away his sackcloth from him: but he received [it] not. {4:5} Then called Esther for Hatach, [one] of the king's chamberlains, whom he had appointed to attend upon her, and gave him a commandment to Mordecai, to know what it [was,] and why it [was.]{4:6} So Hatach went forth to Mordecai unto the street of the city, which [was] before the king's gate. {4:7} And Mordecai told him of all that had happened unto him, and of the sum of the money that Haman had promised to pay to the king's treasuries for the Jews, to destroy them. {4:8} Also he gave him the copy of the writing of the decree that was given at Shushan to destroy them, to shew [it] unto Esther, and to declare [it] unto her, and to charge her that she should go in unto the king, to make supplication unto him, and to make request before him for her people. {4:9} And Hatach came and told Esther the words of Mordecai.

{4:10} Again Esther spake unto Hatach, and gave him commandment unto
Mordecai; {4:11} All the king's servants, and the people of the king's provinces, do know, that whosoever, whether man or woman, shall come unto the king into the inner court, who is not called, [there is] one law of his to put [him] to death, except such to whom the king shall hold out the golden sceptre, that he may live: but I have not been called to come in unto the king these thirty days. {4:12} And they told to Mordecai Esther's words. {4:13} Then Mordecai commanded to answer

Esther, think not with thyself that thou shalt escape in the king's house, more than all the Jews. {4:14} For if thou altogether holdest thy peace at this time, [then] shall there enlargement and deliverance arise to the Jews from another place; but thou and thy father's house shall be destroyed: and who knoweth whether thou art come to the kingdom for [such] a time as this?

{4:15} Then Esther bade [them] return Mordecai [this answer,]{4:16} Go, gather together all the Jews that are present in Shushan, and fast ye for me, and neither eat nor drink three days, night or day: I also and my maidens will fast likewise; and so will I go in unto the king, which [is] not according to the law: and if I perish, I perish. {4:17} So Mordecai went his way, and did according to all that Esther had commanded him.

{5:1} Now it came to pass on the third day, that Esther put on [her] royal [apparel,] and stood in the inner court of the king's house, over against the king's house: and the king sat upon his royal throne in the royal house, over against the gate of the house. {5:2} And it was so, when the king saw Esther the queen standing in the court, [that] she obtained favour in his sight: and the king held out to Esther the golden sceptre that [was] in his hand. So Esther drew near, and touched the top of the sceptre. {5:3} Then said the king unto her, What wilt thou, queen Esther? and what [is] thy request? it shall be even given thee to the half of the kingdom. {5:4} And Esther answered, If [it seem] good unto the king, let the king and Haman come this day unto the banquet that I have prepared for him. {5:5} Then the king said, Cause Haman to make haste, that he may do as Esther hath said. So the king and Haman came to the banquet that Esther had prepared.

{5:6} And the king said unto Esther at the banquet of wine, What [is] thy petition? and it shall be granted thee: and what [is] thy request? even to the half of the kingdom it shall be performed. {5:7} Then answered Esther, and said, My petition and my request [is;]{5:8} If I have found favour in the sight of the king, and if it please the king to grant my petition, and to perform my request, let the king and Haman come to the banquet that I shall prepare for them, and I will do to morrow as the king hath said.

{5:9} Then went Haman forth that day joyful and with a glad heart: but when Haman saw Mordecai in the king's gate, that he stood not up, nor moved for him, he was full of indignation against Mordecai. {5:10} Nevertheless Haman refrained himself: and when he came home, he sent and called for his friends, and Zeresh his wife. {5:11} And Haman told them of the glory of his riches, and the multitude of his children, and all [the things] wherein the king had promoted him, and how he had advanced him above the princes and servants of the king. {5:12} Haman said moreover, Yea, Esther the queen did let no man come in with the king unto the banquet that she had prepared but myself; and to morrow am I invited unto her also with the king. {5:13} Yet all this availeth me nothing, so long as I see Mordecai the Jew sitting at the king's gate.

{5:14} Then said Zeresh his wife and all his friends unto him, Let a gallows be made of fifty cubits high, and to morrow speak thou unto the king that Mordecai may be hanged thereon: then go thou in merrily with the king unto the banquet. And the thing pleased Haman; and he caused the gallows to be made.

{6:1} On that night could not the king sleep, and he commanded to bring the book of records of the chronicles; and they were read before the king. {6:2} And it was found written, that Mordecai had told of Bigthana and Teresh, two of the king's chamberlains, the keepers of the door, who sought to lay hand on the king Ahasuerus. {6:3} And the king said, What honour and dignity hath been done to Mordecai for this? Then said the king's servants that ministered unto him, There is nothing done for him.

{6:4} And the king said, Who [is] in the court? Now Haman was come into the outward court of the king's house, to speak unto the king to hang Mordecai on the gallows that he had prepared for him. {6:5} And the king's servants said unto him, Behold, Haman standeth in the court. And the king said, let him come in. {6:6} So Haman came in. And the king said unto him, what shall be done unto the man whom the king delighteth to honour? Now Haman thought in his heart, To whom would the king delight to do honour more than to myself? {6:7} And Haman answered the king, For the man whom the king delighteth to honour, {6:8} Let the royal apparel be brought which the king [useth] to wear, and the horse that the king rideth upon, and the crown royal which is set upon his head: {6:9} And let this apparel and horse be delivered to the hand of one of the king's most noble princes, that they may array the man [withal] whom the king delighteth to honour, and bring him on horseback through the street of the city, and proclaim before him, Thus shall it be done to the man whom the king delighteth to honour. {6:10} Then the king said to Haman, Make haste, [and] take the apparel and the horse, as thou hast said, and do even so to Mordecai the Jew, that sitteth at the king's gate: let nothing fail of all that thou hast spoken. {6:11} Then took Haman the apparel and the horse, and arrayed Mordecai, and brought him on horseback through the street of the city, and proclaimed before him, Thus shall it be done unto the man whom the king delighteth to honour.

{6:12} And Mordecai came again to the king's gate. But Haman hasted to his house mourning, and having his head covered. {6:13} And Haman told Zeresh his wife and all his friends every [thing] that had befallen him. Then said his wise men and Zeresh his wife unto him, If Mordecai [be] of the seed of the Jews, before whom thou hast begun to fall, thou shalt not prevail against him, but shalt surely fall before him. {6:14} And while they [were] yet talking with him, came the king's chamberlains, and hasted to bring Haman unto the banquet that Esther had prepared.

{7:1} So the king and Haman came to banquet with Esther the queen. {7:2} And the king said again unto Esther on the second day at the banquet of wine, what [is] thy petition, queen Esther? and it shall be granted thee: and what [is] thy request? and it shall be performed, [even] to the half of the kingdom. {7:3} Then Esther the queen answered and said, If I have found favour in thy sight, O king, and if it please the king, let my life be given me at my petition, and my people at my request: {7:4} For we are sold, I and my people, to be destroyed, to be slain, and to perish. But if we had been sold for bondmen and bondwomen, I had held my tongue, although the enemy could not countervail the king's damage.

{7:5} Then the king Ahasuerus answered and said unto Esther the queen, Who is he, and where is he, that durst presume in his heart to do so? {7:6} And Esther said, the adversary and enemy [is] this wicked Haman. Then Haman was afraid before the king and the queen.

{7:7} And the king arising from the banquet of wine in his wrath [went] into the palace garden: and Haman stood up to make request for his life to Esther the queen; for he saw that there was evil determined against him by the king. {7:8} Then the king returned out of the palace garden into the place of the banquet of wine; and Haman was fallen upon the bed whereon Esther [was.] Then said the king, will he force the queen also before me in the house? As the word went out of the king's mouth, they covered Haman's face. {7:9} And Harbonah, one of the chamberlains, said before the king, Behold also, the gallows fifty cubits high, which Haman had made for Mordecai, who had spoken good for the king, standeth in the house of Haman. Then the king said, Hang him thereon. {7:10} So they hanged Haman on the gallows that he had prepared for Mordecai. Then was the king's wrath pacified.

{8:1} On that day did the king Ahasuerus give the house of Haman the Jews' enemy unto Esther the queen. And Mordecai came before the king; for Esther had told what he [was] unto her. {8:2} And the king took off his ring, which he had taken from Haman, and gave it unto Mordecai. And Esther set Mordecai over the house of Haman.

{8:3} And Esther spake yet again before the king, and fell down at his feet, and besought him with tears to put away the mischief of Haman the Agagite, and his device that he had devised against the Jews. {8:4} Then the king held out the golden sceptre toward Esther. So Esther arose, and stood before the king, {8:5} And said, If it please the king, and if I have found favour in his sight, and the thing [seem] right before the king, and I [be] pleasing in his eyes, let it be written to reverse the letters devised by Haman the son of Hammedatha the Agagite, which he wrote to destroy the Jews which [are] in all the king's provinces: {8:6} For how can I endure to see the evil that shall come unto my people? or how can I endure to see the destruction of my kindred?

{8:7} Then the king Ahasuerus said unto Esther the queen and to Mordecai the Jew, Behold, I have given Esther the house of Haman, and him they have hanged upon the gallows, because he laid his hand upon the Jews. {8:8} Write ye also for the Jews, as it liketh you, in the king's name, and seal [it] with the king's ring: for the writing which is written in the king's name, and sealed with the king's ring, may no man reverse. {8:9} Then were the king's scribes called at that time in the third month, that [is,] the month Sivan, on the three and twentieth [day] thereof; and it was written according to all that Mordecai commanded unto the Jews, and to the lieutenants, and the deputies and rulers of the provinces which [are] from India unto Ethiopia, an hundred twenty and seven provinces, unto every province according to the writing thereof, and unto every people after their language, and to the Jews according to their writing, and according to their language. {8:10} And he wrote in the king Ahasuerus' name, and sealed it with the king's ring, and sent letters by posts on horseback, [and] riders on mules, camels, [and] young dromedaries: {8:11} Wherein the king granted the Jews which [were] in every city to gather themselves together, and to stand for their life, to destroy, to slay, and to cause to perish, all the power of the people and province that would assault them, [both] little ones and women, and [to take] the spoil of them for a prey, {8:12} Upon one day in all the provinces of king Ahasuerus, [namely,] upon the thirteenth [day] of the twelfth month, which [is] the month Adar. {8:13} The copy of the writing for a commandment to be given in every province [was] published unto all people, and that the Jews should be ready against that day to avenge themselves on their enemies. {8:14} [So] the posts that rode upon mules [and] camels went out, being hastened and pressed on by the king's commandment. And the decree was given at Shushan the palace.

{8:15} And Mordecai went out from the presence of the king in royal apparel of blue and white, and with a great crown of gold, and with a garment of fine linen and purple: and the city of Shushan rejoiced and was glad. {8:16} The Jews had light, and gladness, and joy, and honour. {8:17} And in every province, and in every city, whithersoever the king's commandment and his decree came, the Jews had joy and gladness,
a feast and a good day. And many of the people of the land became Jews; for the fear of the Jews fell upon them.

{9:1} Now in the twelfth month, that [is,] the month Adar, on the thirteenth day of the same, when the king's commandment and his decree drew near to be put in execution, in the day that the enemies of the Jews hoped to have power over them, (though it was turned to the contrary, that the Jews had rule over them that hated them;) {9:2} The Jews gathered themselves together in their cities throughout all the provinces of the king Ahasuerus, to lay hand on such as sought their hurt: and no man could withstand them; for the fear of them fell upon all people. {9:3} And all the rulers of the provinces, and the lieutenants, and the deputies, and officers of the king, helped the Jews; because the fear of Mordecai fell upon them. {9:4} For Mordecai [was] great in the king's house, and his fame went out throughout all the provinces: for this man Mordecai waxed greater and greater. {9:5} Thus the Jews smote all their enemies with the stroke of the sword, and slaughter, and destruction, and did what they would unto those that hated them. {9:6} And in Shushan the palace the Jews slew and destroyed five hundred men. {9:7} And Parshandatha, and Dalphon, and Aspatha, {9:8} And Poratha, and Adalia, and Aridatha, {9:9} And Parmashta, and Arisai, and Aridai, and Vajezatha, {9:10} The ten sons of Haman the son of Hammedatha, the enemy of the Jews, slew they; but on the spoil laid they not their hand. {9:11} On that day the number of those that were slain in Shushan the palace was brought before the king.

{9:12} And the king said unto Esther the queen, The Jews have slain and destroyed five hundred men in Shushan the palace, and the ten sons of Haman; what have they done in the rest of the king's provinces? now what [is] thy petition? and it shall be granted thee: or what [is] thy request further? and it shall be done. {9:13} Then said Esther, If it please the king, let it be granted to the Jews which [are] in Shushan to do to morrow also according unto this day's decree, and let Haman's ten sons be hanged upon the gallows. {9:14} And the king commanded it so to be done: and the decree was given at Shushan; and they hanged Haman's ten sons. {9:15} For the Jews that [were] in Shushan gathered themselves together on the fourteenth day also of the month Adar, and slew three hundred men at Shushan; but on the prey they laid not their hand. {9:16} But the other Jews that [were] in the king's provinces gathered themselves together, and stood for their lives, and had rest from their enemies, and slew of their foes seventy and five thousand, but they laid not their hands on the prey, {9:17} On the thirteenth day of the month Adar; and on the fourteenth day of the same rested they, and made it a day of feasting and gladness. {9:18} But the Jews that [were] at Shushan assembled together on the thirteenth [day] thereof; and on the fourteenth thereof; and on the fifteenth [day] of the same they rested, and made it a day of feasting and gladness. {9:19} Therefore the Jews of the villages, that dwelt in the unwalled towns, made the fourteenth day of the month Adar [a day of] gladness and feasting, and a good day, and of sending portions one to another.

{9:20} And Mordecai wrote these things, and sent letters unto all the Jews that [were] in all the provinces of the king Ahasuerus, [both] nigh and far, {9:21} To stablish [this] among them, that they should keep the fourteenth day of the month Adar, and the fifteenth day of the same, yearly, {9:22} As the days wherein the Jews rested from their enemies, and the month which was turned unto them from sorrow to joy, and from mourning into a good day: that they should make them days of feasting and joy, and of sending portions one to another, and gifts to the poor. {9:23} And the Jews undertook to do as they had begun, and as Mordecai had written unto them; {9:24} Because Haman the son of Hammedatha, the Agagite, the enemy of all the Jews, had devised against the Jews to destroy them, and had cast Pur, that [is,] the lot, to consume them, and to destroy them; {9:25} But when [Esther] came before the king, he commanded by letters that his wicked device, which he devised against the Jews, should return upon his own head, and that he and his sons should be hanged on the gallows. {9:26} Wherefore they called these days Purim after the name of Pur. Therefore for all the words of this letter, and [of that] which they had seen concerning this matter, and which had come unto them, {9:27} The Jews ordained, and took upon them, and upon their seed, and upon all such as joined themselves unto them, so as it should not fail, that they would keep these two days according to their writing, and according to their [appointed] time every year; {9:28} And [that] these days [should be] remembered and kept throughout every generation, every family, every province, and every city; and [that] these days of Purim should not fail from among the Jews, nor the memorial of them perish from their seed. {9:29} Then Esther the queen, the daughter of Abihail, and Mordecai the Jew, wrote with all authority, to confirm this second letter of Purim. {9:30} And he sent the letters unto all the Jews, to the hundred twenty and seven provinces of the kingdom of Ahasuerus, [with] words of peace and truth, {9:31} To confirm these days of Purim in their times [appointed,] according as Mordecai the Jew and Esther the queen had enjoined them, and as they had decreed for themselves and for their seed, the matters of the fastings and their cry. {9:32} And the decree of Esther confirmed these matters of Purim; and it was written in the book.

{10:1} And the king Ahasuerus laid a tribute upon the land, and [upon] the isles of the sea. {10:2} And all the acts of his power and of his might, and the declaration of the greatness of Mordecai, whereunto the king advanced him, [are] they not written in the book of the chronicles of the kings of Media and Persia? {10:3} For Mordecai the Jew [was] next unto king Ahasuerus, and great among the Jews, and accepted of the multitude of his brethren, seeking the wealth of his people, and speaking peace to all his seed.

The Book of Judith

{1:1} In the twelfth year of the reign of Nabuchodonosor, who reigned in Nineve, the great city; in the days of Arphaxad, which reigned over the Medes in Ecbatane,

{1:2} And built in Ecbatane walls round about of stones hewn three cubits broad and six cubits long, and made the height of the wall seventy cubits, and the breadth thereof fifty cubits:

{1:3} And set the towers thereof upon the gates of it an hundred cubits high, and the breadth thereof in the foundation threescore cubits:

{1:4} And he made the gates thereof, even gates that were raised to the height of seventy cubits, and the breadth of them was forty cubits, for the going forth of his mighty armies, and for the setting in array of his footmen:

{1:5} Even in those days king Nabuchodonosor made war with king Arphaxad in the great plain, which is the plain in the borders of Ragau.

{1:6} And there came unto him all they that dwelt in the hill country, and all that dwelt by Euphrates, and Tigris and Hydaspes, and the plain of Arioch the king of the Elymeans, and very many nations of the sons of Chelod, assembled themselves to the battle.

{1:7} Then Nabuchodonosor king of the Assyrians sent unto all that dwelt in Persia, and to all that dwelt westward, and to those that dwelt in Cilicia, and Damascus, and Libanus, and Antilibanus, and to all that dwelt upon the sea coast,

{1:8} And to those among the nations that were of Carmel, and Galaad, and the higher Galilee, and the great plain of Esdrelom,

{1:9} And to all that were in Samaria and the cities thereof, and beyond Jordan unto Jerusalem, and Betane, and Chelus, and Kades, and the river of Egypt, and Taphnes, and Ramesse, and all the land of Gesem,

{1:10} Until ye come beyond Tanis and Memphis, and to all the inhabitants of Egypt, until ye come to the borders of Ethiopia.

{1:11} But all the inhabitants of the land made light of the commandment of Nabuchodonosor king of the Assyrians, neither went they with him to the battle; for they were not afraid of him: yea, he was before them as one man, and they sent away his ambassadors from them without effect, and with disgrace.

{1:12} Therefore Nabuchodonosor was very angry with all this country, and sware by his throne and kingdom, that he would surely be avenged upon all those coasts of Cilicia, and Damascus, and Syria, and that he would slay with the sword all the inhabitants of the land of Moab, and the children of Ammon, and all Judea, and all that were in Egypt, till ye come to the borders of the two seas.

{1:13} Then he marched in battle array with his power against king Arphaxad in the seventeenth year, and he prevailed in his battle: for he overthrew all the power of Arphaxad, and all his horsemen, and all his chariots,

{1:14} And became lord of his cities, and came unto Ecbatane, and took the towers, and spoiled the streets thereof, and turned the beauty thereof into shame.

{1:15} He took also Arphaxad in the mountains of Ragau, and smote him through with his darts, and destroyed him utterly that day.

{1:16} So he returned afterward to Nineve, both he and all his company of sundry nations being a very great multitude of men of war, and there he took his ease, and banqueted, both he and his army, an hundred and twenty days.

{2:1} And in the eighteenth year, the two and twentieth day of the first month, there was talk in the house of Nabuchodonosor king of the Assyrians that he should, as he said, avenge himself on all the earth.

{2:2} So he called unto him all his officers, and all his nobles, and communicated with them his secret counsel, and concluded the afflicting of the whole earth out of his own mouth.

{2:3} Then they decreed to destroy all flesh, that did not obey the commandment of his mouth.

{2:4} And when he had ended his counsel, Nabuchodonosor king of the Assyrians called Holofernes the chief captain of his army, which was next unto him, and said unto him.

{2:5} Thus saith the great king, the lord of the whole earth, Behold, thou shalt go forth from my presence, and take with thee men that trust in their own strength, of footmen an hundred and twenty thousand; and the number of horses with their riders twelve thousand.

{2:6} And thou shalt go against all the west country, because they disobeyed my commandment.

{2:7} And thou shalt declare unto that they prepare for me earth and water: for I will go forth in my wrath against them and will cover the whole face of the earth with the feet of mine army, and I will give thom for a cpoil unto thcm:

{2:8} So that their slain shall fill their valleys and brooks and the river shall be filled with their dead, till it overflow:

{2:9} And I will lead them captives to the utmost parts of all the earth.

{2:10} Thou therefore shalt go forth. and take beforehand for me all their coasts: and if they will yield themselves unto thee, thou shalt reserve them for me till the day of their punishment.

{2:11} But concerning them that rebel, let not thine eye spare them; but put them to the slaughter, and spoil them wheresoever thou goest.

{2:12} For as I live, and by the power of my kingdom, whatsoever I have spoken, that will I do by mine hand.

{2:13} And take thou heed that thou transgress none of the commandments of thy lord, but accomplish them fully, as I have commanded thee, and defer not to do them.

{2:14} Then Holofernes went forth from the presence of his lord, and called all the governors and captains, and the officers of the army of Assur;

{2:15} And he mustered the chosen men for the battle, as his lord had commanded him, unto an hundred and twenty thousand, and twelve thousand archers on horseback;

{2:16} And he ranged them, as a great army is ordered for the war.

{2:17} And he took camels and asses for their carriages, a very great number; and sheep and oxen and goats without number for their provision:

{2:18} And plenty of victual for every man of the army, and very much gold and silver out of the king's house.

{2:19} Then he went forth and all his power to go before king Nabuchodonosor in the voyage, and to cover all the face of the earth westward with their chariots, and horsemen, and their chosen footmen.

{2:20} A great number also sundry countries came with them like locusts, and like the sand of the earth: for the multitude was without number.

{2:21} And they went forth of Nineve three days' journey toward the plain of Bectileth, and pitched from Bectileth near the mountain which is at the left hand of the upper Cilicia.

{2:22} Then he took all his army, his footmen, and horsemen and chariots, and went from thence into the hill country;

{2:23} And destroyed Phud and Lud, and spoiled all the children of Rasses, and the children of Israel, which were toward the wilderness at the south of the land of the Chellians.

{2:24} Then he went over Euphrates, and went through Mesopotamia, and destroyed all the high cities that were upon the river Arbonai, till ye come to the sea.

{2:25} And he took the borders of Cilicia, and killed all that resisted him, and came to the borders of Japheth, which were toward the south, over against Arabia.

{2:26} He compassed also all the children of Madian, and burned up their tabernacles, and spoiled their sheepcotes.

{2:27} Then he went down into the plain of Damascus in the time of wheat harvest, and burnt up all their fields, and destroyed their flocks and herds, also he spoiled their cities, and utterly wasted their countries, and smote all their young men with the edge of the sword.

{2:28} Therefore the fear and dread of him fell upon all the inhabitants of the sea coasts, which were in Sidon and Tyrus, and them that dwelt in Sur and Ocina, and all that dwelt in Jemnaan; and they that dwelt in Azotus and Ascalon feared him greatly.

{3:1} So they sent ambassadors unto him to treat of peace, saying,

{3:2} Behold, we the servants of Nabuchodonosor the great king lie before thee; use us as shall be good in thy sight.

{3:3} Behold, our houses, and all our places, and all our fields of wheat, and flocks, and herds, and all the lodges of our tents lie before thy face; use them as it pleaseth thee.

{3:4} Behold, even our cities and the inhabitants thereof are thy servants; come and deal with them as seemeth good unto thee.

{3:5} So the men came to Holofernes, and declared unto him after this manner.

{3:6} Then came he down toward the sea coast, both he and his army, and set garrisons in the high cities, and took out of them chosen men for aid.

{3:7} So they and all the country round about received them with garlands, with dances, and with timbrels.

{3:8} Yet he did cast down their frontiers, and cut down their groves: for he had decreed to destroy all the gods of the land, that all nations should worship Nabuchodonosor only, and that all tongues and tribes should call upon him as god.

{3:9} Also he came over against Esdraelon near unto Judea, over against the great strait of Judea.

{3:10} And he pitched between Geba and Scythopolis, and there he tarried a whole month, that he might gather together all the carriages of his army.

{4:1} Now the children of Israel, that dwelt in Judea, heard all that Holofernes the chief captain of Nabuchodonosor king of the Assyrians had done to the nations, and after what manner he had spoiled all their temples, and brought them to nought.

{4:2} Therefore they were exceedingly afraid of him, and were troubled for Jerusalem, and for the temple of the Lord their God:

{4:3} For they were newly returned from the captivity, and all the people of Judea were lately gathered together: and the vessels, and the altar, and the house, were sanctified after the profanation.

{4:4} Therefore they sent into all the coasts of Samaria, and the villages and to Bethoron, and Belmen, and Jericho, and to Choba, and Esora, and to the valley of Salem:

{4:5} And possessed themselves beforehand of all the tops of the high mountains, and fortified the villages that were in them, and laid up victuals for the provision of war: for their fields were of late reaped.

{4:6} Also Joacim the high priest, which was in those days in Jerusalem, wrote to them that dwelt in Bethulia, and Betomestham, which is over against Esdraelon toward the open country, near to Dothaim,

{4:7} Charging them to keep the passages of the hill country: for by them there was an entrance into Judea, and it was easy to stop them that would come up, because the passage was straight, for two men at the most.

{4:8} And the children of Israel did as Joacim the high priest had commanded them, with the ancients of all the people of Israel, which dwelt at Jerusalem.

{4:9} Then every man of Israel cried to God with great fervency, and with great vehemency did they humble their souls:

{4:10} Both they, and their wives and their children, and their cattle, and every stranger and hireling, and their servants bought with money, put sackcloth upon their loins.

{4:11} Thus every man and women, and the little children, and the inhabitants of Jerusalem, fell before the temple, and cast ashes upon their heads, and spread out their sackcloth before the face of the Lord: also they put sackcloth about the altar,

{4:12} And cried to the God of Israel all with one consent earnestly, that he would not give their children for a prey, and their wives for a spoil, and the cities of their inheritance to destruction, and the sanctuary to profanation and reproach, and for the nations to rejoice at.

{4:13} So God heard their prayers, and looked upon their afflictions: for the people fasted many days in all Judea and Jerusalem before the sanctuary of the Lord Almighty.

{4:14} And Joacim the high priest, and all the priests that stood before the Lord, and they which ministered unto the Lord, had their loins girt with sackcloth, and offered the daily burnt offerings, with the vows and free gifts of the people,

{4:15} And had ashes on their mitres, and cried unto the Lord with all their power, that he would look upon all the house of Israel graciously.

{5:1} Then was it declared to Holofernes, the chief captain of the army of Assur, that the children of Israel had prepared for war, and had shut up the passages of the hill country, and had fortified all the tops of the high hills and had laid impediments in the champaign countries:

{5:2} Wherewith he was very angry, and called all the princes of Moab, and the captains of Ammon, and all the governors of the sea coast,

{5:3} And he said unto them, Tell me now, ye sons of Chanaan, who this people is, that dwelleth in the hill country, and what are the cities that they inhabit, and what is the multitude of their army, and wherein is their power and strength, and what king is set over them, or captain of their army;

{5:4} And why have they determined not to come and meet me, more than all the inhabitants of the west.

{5:5} Then said Achior, the captain of all the sons of Ammon, Let my lord now hear a word from the mouth of thy servant, and I will declare unto thee the truth concerning this people, which dwelleth near thee, and inhabiteth the hill countries. and there shall no lie come out of the mouth of thy servant.

{5:6} This people are descended of the Chaldeans:

{5:7} And they sojourned heretofore in Mesopotamia, because they would not follow the gods of their fathers, which were in the land of Chaldea.

{5:8} For they left the way of their ancestors, and worshipped the God of heaven, the God whom they knew: so they cast them out from the face of their gods, and they fled into Mesopotamia, and sojourned there many days.

{5:9} Then their God commanded them to depart from the place where they sojourned, and to go into the land of Chanaan: where they dwelt, and were increased with gold and silver, and with very much cattle.

{5:10} But when a famine covered all the land of Chanaan, they went down into Egypt, and sojourned there, while they were nourished, and became there a great multitude, so that one could not number their nation.

{5:11} Therefore the king of Egypt rose up against them, and dealt subtilly with them, and brought them low with labouring in brick, and made them slaves.

{5:12} Then they cried unto their God, and he smote all the land of Egypt with incurable plagues: so the Egyptians cast them out of their sight.

{5:13} And God dried the Red sea before them,

{5:14} And brought them to mount Sina, and Cades-Barne, and cast forth all that dwelt in the wilderness.

{5:15} So they dwelt in the land of the Amorites, and they destroyed by their strength all them of Esebon, and passing over Jordan they possessed all the hill country.

{5:16} And they cast forth before them the Chanaanite, the Pherezite, the Jebusite, and the Sychemite, and all the Gergesites, and they dwelt in that country many days.

{5:17} And whilst they sinned not before their God, they prospered, because the God that hateth iniquity was with them.

{5:18} But when they departed from the way which he appointed them, they were destroyed in many battles very sore, and were led captives into a land that was not their's, and the temple of their God was cast to tho ground, and thcir citics were taken by the enemies.

{5:19} But now are they returned to their God, and are come up from the places where they were scattered, and have possessed Jerusalem, where their sanctuary is, and are seated in the hill country; for it was desolate.

{5:20} Now therefore, my lord and governor, if there be any error against this people, and they sin against their God, let us consider that this shall be their ruin, and let us go up, and we shall overcome them.

{5:21} But if there be no iniquity in their nation, let my lord now pass by, lest their Lord defend them, and their God be for them, and we become a reproach before all the world.

{5:22} And when Achior had finished these sayings, all the people standing round about the tent murmured, and the chief men of Holofernes, and all that dwelt by the sea side, and in Moab, spake that he should kill him.

{5:23} For, say they, we will not be afraid of the face of the children of Israel: for, lo, it is a people that have no strength nor power for a strong battle

{5:24} Now therefore, lord Holofernes, we will go up, and they shall be a prey to be devoured of all thine army.

{6:1} And when the tumult of men that were about the council was ceased, Holofernes the chief captain of the army of Assur said unto Achior and all the Moabites before all the company of other nations,

{6:2} And who art thou, Achior, and the hirelings of Ephraim, that thou hast prophesied against us as to day, and hast said, that we should not make war with the people of Israel, because their God will defend them? and who is God but Nabuchodonosor?

{6:3} He will send his power, and will destroy them from the face of the earth, and their God shall not deliver them: but we his servants will destroy them as one man; for they are not able to sustain the power of our horses.

{6:4} For with them we will tread them under foot, and their mountains shall be drunken with their blood, and their fields shall be filled with their dead bodies, and their footsteps shall not be able to stand before us, for they shall utterly perish, saith king Nabuchodonosor, lord of all the earth: for he said, None of my words shall be in vain.

{6:5} And thou, Achior, an hireling of Ammon, which hast spoken these words in the day of thine iniquity, shall see my face no more from this day, until I take vengeance of this nation that came out of

Egypt.

{6:6} And then shall the sword of mine army, and the multitude of them that serve me, pass through thy sides, and thou shalt fall among their slain, when I return.

{6:7} Now therefore my servants shall bring thee back into the hill country, and shall set thee in one of the cities of the passages:

{6:8} And thou shalt not perish, till thou be destroyed with them.

{6:9} And if thou persuade thyself in thy mind that they shall be taken, let not thy countenance fall: I have spoken it, and none of my words shall be in vain.

{6:10} Then Holofernes commanded his servants, that waited in his tent, to take Achior, and bring him to Bethulia, and deliver him into the hands of the children of Israel.

{6:11} So his servants took him, and brought him out of the camp into the plain, and they went from the midst of the plain into the hill country, and came unto the fountains that were under Bethulia.

{6:12} And when the men of the city saw them, they took up their weapons, and went out of the city to the top of the hill: and every man that used a sling kept them from coming up by casting of stones against them.

{6:13} Nevertheless having gotten privily under the hill, they bound Achior, and cast him down, and left him at the foot of the hill, and returned to their lord.

{6:14} But the Israelites descended from their city, and came unto him, and loosed him, and brought him to Bethulia, and presented him to the governors of the city:

{6:15} Which were in those days Ozias the son of Micha, of the tribe of Simeon, and Chabris the son of Gothoniel, and Charmis the son of Melchiel.

{6:16} And they called together all the ancients of the city, and all their youth ran together, and their women, to the assembly, and they set Achior in the midst of all their people. Then Ozias asked him of that which was done.

{6:17} And he answered and declared unto them the words of the council of Holofernes, and all the words that he had spoken in the midst of the princes of Assur, and whatsoever Holofernes had spoken proudly against the house of Israel.

{6:18} Then the people fell down and worshipped God, and cried unto God. saying,

{6:19} O Lord God of heaven, behold their pride, and pity the low estate of our nation, and look upon the face of those that are sanctified unto thee this day.

{6:20} Then they comforted Achior, and praised him greatly.

{6:21} And Ozias took him out of the assembly unto his house, and made a feast to the elders; and they called on the God of Israel all that night for help.

{7:1} The next day Holofernes commanded all his army, and all his people which were come to take his part, that they should remove their camp against Bethulia, to take aforehand the ascents of the hill country, and to make war against the children of Israel.

{7:2} Then their strong men removed their camps in that day, and the army of the men of war was an hundred and seventy thousand footmen, and twelve thousand horsemen, beside the baggage, and other men that were afoot among them, a very great multitude.

{7:3} And they camped in the valley near unto Bethulia, by the fountain, and they spread themselves in breadth over Dothaim even to

Belmaim, and in length from Bethulia unto Cynamon, which is over against Esdraelon.

{7:4} Now the children of Israel, when they saw the multitude of them, were greatly troubled, and said every one to his neighbour, Now will these men lick up the face of the earth; for neither the high mountains, nor the valleys, nor the hills, are able to bear their weight.

{7:5} Then every man took up his weapons of war, and when they had kindled fires upon their towers, they remained and watched all that night.

{7:6} But in the second day Holofernes brought forth all his horsemen in the sight of the children of Israel which were in Bethulia,

{7:7} And viewed the passages up to the city, and came to the fountains of their waters, and took them, and set garrisons of men of war over them, and he himself removed toward his people.

{7:8} Then came unto him all the chief of the children of Esau, and all the governors of the people of Moab, and the captains of the sea coast, and said,

{7:9} Let our lord now hear a word, that there be not an overthrow in thine army.

{7:10} For this people of the children of Israel do not trust in their spears, but in the height of the mountains wherein they dwell, because it is not easy to come up to the tops of their mountains.

{7:11} Now therefore, my lord, fight not against them in battle array, and there shall not so much as one man of thy people perish.

{7:12} Remain in thy camp, and keep all the men of thine army, and let thy servants get into their hands the fountain of water, which issueth forth of the foot of the mountain:

{7:13} For all the inhabitants of Bethulia have their water thence; so shall thirst kill them, and they shall give up their city, and we and our people shall go up to the tops of the mountains that are near, and will camp upon them, to watch that none go out of the city.

{7:14} So they and their wives and their children shall be consumed with fire, and before the sword come against them, they shall be overthrown in the streets where they dwell.

{7:15} Thus shalt thou render them an evil reward; because they rebelled, and met not thy person peaceably.

{7:16} And these words pleased Holofernes and all his servants, and he appointed to do as they had spoken.

{7:17} So the camp of the children of Ammon departed, and with them five thousand of the Assyrians, and they pitched in the valley, and took the waters, and the fountains of the waters of the children of Israel.

{7:18} Then the children of Esau went up with the children of Ammon, and camped in the hill country over against Dothaim: and they sent some of them toward the south, and toward the east over against Ekrebel, which is near unto Chusi, that is upon the brook Mochmur; and the rest of the army of the Assyrians camped in the plain, and covered the face of the whole land; and their tents and carriages were pitched to a very great multitude.

{7:19} Then the children of Israel cried unto the Lord their God, because their heart failed, for all their enemies had compassed them round about, and there was no way to escape out from among them.

{7:20} Thus all the company of Assur remained about them, both their footmen, chariots, and horsemen, four and thirty days, so that all their vessels of water failed all the inhibitants of Bethulia.

{7:21} And the cisterns were emptied, and they had not water to drink their fill for one day; for they gave them drink by measure.

{7:22} Therefore their young children were out of heart, and their women and young men fainted for thirst, and fell down in the streets of the city, and by the passages of the gates, and there was no longer any strength in them.

{7:23} Then all the people assembled to Ozias, and to the chief of the city, both young men, and women, and children, and cried with a loud voice, and said before all the elders,

{7:24} God be judge between us and you: for ye have done us great injury, in that ye have not required peace of the children of Assur.

{7:25} For now we have no helper: but God hath sold us into their hands, that we should be thrown down before them with thirst and great destruction.

{7:26} Now therefore call them unto you, and deliver the whole city for a spoil to the people of Holofernes, and to all his army.

{7:27} For it is better for us to be made a spoil unto them, than to die for thirst: for we will be his servants, that our souls may live, and not see the death of our infants before our eyes, nor our wives nor our children to die.

{7:28} We take to witness against you the heaven and the earth, and our God and Lord of our fathers, which punisheth us according to our sins and the sins of our fathers, that he do not according as we have said this day.

{7:29} Then there was great weeping with one consent in the midst of the assembly; and they cried unto the Lord God with a loud voice.

{7:30} Then said Ozias to them, Brethren, be of good courage, let us yet endure five days, in the which space the Lord our God may turn his mercy toward us; for he will not forsake us utterly.

{7:31} And if these days pass, and there come no help unto us, I will do according to your word.

{7:32} And he dispersed the people, every one to their own charge; and they went unto the walls and towers of their city, and sent the women and children into their houses: and they were very low brought in the city.

{8:1} Now at that time Judith heard thereof, which was the daughter of Merari, the son of Ox, the son of Joseph, the son of Ozel, the son of Eloia, the son of Ananias, the son of Gedeon, the son of Raphaim, the son of Acitho, the son of Eliu, the son of Eliab, the son of

Nathanael, the son of Samael, the son of Salasadal, the son of Israel.

{8:2} And Manasses was her husband, of her tribe and kindred, who died in the barley harvest.

{8:3} For as he stood overseeing them that bound sheaves in the field, the heat came upon his head, and he fell on his bed, and died in the city of Bethulia: and they buried him with his fathers in the field between Dothaim and Balamo.

{8:4} So Judith was a widow in her house three years and four months.

{8:5} And she made her a tent upon the top of her house, and put on sackcloth upon her loins and ware her widow's apparel.

{8:6} And she fasted all the days of her widowhood, save the eves of the sabbaths, and the sabbaths, and the eves of the new moons, and the new moons and the feasts and solemn days of the house of Israel.

{8:7} She was also of a goodly countenance, and very beautiful to behold: and her husband Manasses had left her gold, and silver, and menservants and maidservants, and cattle, and lands; and she remained upon them.

{8:8} And there was none that gave her an ill word; as she feared

God greatly.

{8:9} Now when she heard the evil words of the people against the governor, that they fainted for lack of water; for Judith had heard all the words that Ozias had spoken unto them, and that he had sworn to deliver the city unto the Assyrians after five days;

{8:10} Then she sent her waitingwoman, that had the government of all things that she had, to call Ozias and Chabris and Charmis, the ancients of the city.

{8:11} And they came unto her, and she said unto them, Hear me now, O ye governors of the inhabitants of Bethulia: for your words that ye have spoken before the people this day are not right, touching this oath which ye made and pronounced between God and you, and have promised to deliver the city to our enemies, unless within these days the Lord turn to help you.

{8:12} And now who are ye that have tempted God this day, and stand instead of God among the children of men?

{8:13} And now try the Lord Almighty, but ye shall never know any thing.

{8:14} For ye cannot find the depth of the heart of man, neither can ye perceive the things that he thinketh: then how can ye search out God, that hath made all these things, and know his mind, or comprehend his purpose? Nay, my brethren, provoke not the Lord our God to anger.

{8:15} For if he will not help us within these five days, he hath power to defend us when he will, even every day, or to destroy us before our enemies.

{8:16} Do not bind the counsels of the Lord our God: for God is not as man, that he may be threatened; neither is he as the son of man, that he should be wavering.

{8:17} Therefore let us wait for salvation of him, and call upon him to help us, and he will hear our voice, if it please him.

{8:18} For there arose none in our age, neither is there any now in these days neither tribe, nor family, nor people, nor city among us, which worship gods made with hands, as hath been aforetime.

{8:19} For the which cause our fathers were given to the sword, and for a spoil, and had a great fall before our enemies.

{8:20} But we know none other god, therefore we trust that he will not despise us, nor any of our nation.

{8:21} For if we be taken so, all Judea shall lie waste, and our sanctuary shall be spoiled; and he will require the profanation thereof at our mouth.

{8:22} And the slaughter of our brethren, and the captivity of the country, and the desolation of our inheritance, will he turn upon our heads among the Gentiles, wheresoever we shall be in bondage; and we shall be an offence and a reproach to all them that possess us.

{8:23} For our servitude shall not be directed to favour: but the Lord our God shall turn it to dishonour.

{8:24} Now therefore, O brethren, let us shew an example to our brethren, because their hearts depend upon us, and the sanctuary, and the house, and the altar, rest upon us.

{8:25} Moreover let us give thanks to the Lord our God, which trieth us, even as he did our fathers.

{8:26} Remember what things he did to Abraham, and how he tried Isaac, and what happened to Jacob in Mesopotamia of Syria, when he kept the sheep of Laban his mother's brother.

{8:27} For he hath not tried us in the fire, as he did them, for the examination of their hearts, neither hath he taken vengeance on us: but the Lord doth scourge them that come near unto him, to admonish them.

{8:28} Then said Ozias to her, All that thou hast spoken hast thou spoken with a good heart, and there is none that may gainsay thy words.

{8:29} For this is not the first day wherein thy wisdom is manifested; but from the beginning of thy days all the people have known thy understanding, because the disposition of thine heart is good.

{8:30} But the people were very thirsty, and compelled us to do unto them as we have spoken, and to bring an oath upon ourselves, which we will not break.

{8:31} Therefore now pray thou for us, because thou art a godly woman, and the Lord will send us rain to fill our cisterns, and we shall faint no more.

{8:32} Then said Judith unto them, hear me, and I will do a thing, which shall go throughout all generations to the children of our nation.

{8:33} Ye shall stand this night in the gate, and I will go forth with my waiting woman: and within the days that ye have promised to deliver the city to our enemies the Lord will visit Israel by mine hand.

{8:34} But enquire not ye of mine act: for I will not declare it unto you, till the things be finished that I do.

{8:35} Then said Ozias and the princes unto her, Go in peace, and the Lord God be before thee, to take vengeance on our enemies.

{8:36} So they returned from the tent, and went to their wards.

{9:1} Judith fell upon her face, and put ashes upon her head, and uncovered the sackcloth wherewith she was clothed; and about the time that the incense of that evening was offered in Jerusalem in the house of the Lord Judith cried with a loud voice, and said,

{9:2} O Lord God of my father Simeon, to whom thou gavest a sword to take vengeance of the strangers, who loosened the girdle of a maid to defile her, and discovered the thigh to her shame, and polluted her virginity to her reproach; for thou saidst, It shall not be so; and yet they did so:

{9:3} Wherefore thou gavest their rulers to be slain, so that they dyed their bed in blood, being deceived, and smotest the servants with their lords, and the lords upon their thrones;

{9:4} And hast given their wives for a prey, and their daughters to be captives, and all their spoils to be divided among thy dear children; which were moved with thy zeal, and abhorred the pollution of their blood, and called upon thee for aid: O God, O my God, hear me also a widow.

{9:5} For thou hast wrought not only those things, but also the things which fell out before, and which ensued after; thou hast thought upon the things which are now, and which are to come.

{9:6} Yea, what things thou didst determine were ready at hand, and said, Lo, we are here: for all thy ways are prepared, and thy judgments are in thy foreknowledge.

{9:7} For, behold, the Assyrians are multiplied in their power; they are exalted with horse and man; they glory in the strength of their footmen; they trust in shield, and spear, and bow, and sling; and know not that thou art the Lord that breakest the battles: the Lord is thy name.

{9:8} Throw down their strength in thy power, and bring down their force in thy wrath: for they have purposed to defile thy sanctuary, and to pollute the tabernacle where thy glorious name resteth and to cast down with sword the horn of thy altar.

{9:9} Behold their pride, and send thy wrath upon their heads: give into mine hand, which am a widow, the power that I have conceived.

{9:10} Smite by the deceit of my lips the servant with the prince, and the prince with the servant: break down their stateliness by the hand of a woman.

{9:11} For thy power standeth not in multitude nor thy might in strong men: for thou art a God of the afflicted, an helper of the oppressed, an upholder of the weak, a protector of the forlorn, a saviour of them that are without hope.

{9:12} I pray thee, I pray thee, O God of my father, and God of the inheritance of Israel, Lord of the heavens and earth, Creator of the waters, king of every creature, hear thou my prayer:

{9:13} And make my speech and deceit to be their wound and stripe, who have purposed cruel things against thy covenant, and thy hallowed house, and against the top of Sion, and against the house of the possession of thy children.

{9:14} And make every nation and tribe to acknowledge that thou art the God of all power and might, and that there is none other that protecteth the people of Israel but thou.

{10:1} Now after that she had ceased to cry unto the God of Israel, and bad made an end of all these words.

{10:2} She rose where she had fallen down, and called her maid, and went down into the house in the which she abode in the sabbath days, and in her feast days,

{10:3} And pulled off the sackcloth which she had on, and put off the garments of her widowhood, and washed her body all over with water, and anointed herself with precious ointment, and braided the hair of her head, and put on a tire upon it, and put on her garments of gladness, wherewith she was clad during the life of Manasses her husband.

{10:4} And she took sandals upon her feet, and put about her her bracelets, and her chains, and her rings, and her earrings, and all her ornaments, and decked herself bravely, to allure the eyes of all men that should see her.

{10:5} Then she gave her maid a bottle of wine, and a cruse of oil, and filled a bag with parched corn, and lumps of figs, and with fine bread; so she folded all these things together, and laid them upon her.

{10:6} Thus they went forth to the gate of the city of Bethulia, and found standing there Ozias and the ancients of the city, Chabris and Charmis.

{10:7} And when they saw her, that her countenance was altered, and her apparel was changed, they wondered at her beauty very greatly, and said unto her.

{10:8} The God, the God of our fathers give thee favour, and accomplish thine enterprizes to the glory of the children of Israel, and to the exaltation of Jerusalem. Then they worshipped God.

{10:9} And she said unto them, Command the gates of the city to be opened unto me, that I may go forth to accomplish the things whereof ye have spoken with me. So they commanded the young men to open unto her, as she had spoken.

{10:10} And when they had done so, Judith went out, she, and her maid with her; and the men of the city looked after her, until she was gone down the mountain, and till she had passed the valley, and could see her no more.

{10:11} Thus they went straight forth in the valley: and the first watch of the Assyrians met her,

{10:12} And took her, and asked her, Of what people art thou? and whence comest thou? and whither goest thou? And she said, I am a woman
of the Hebrews, and am fled from them: for they shall be given you to be consumed:

{10:13} And I am coming before Holofernes the chief captain of your army, to declare words of truth; and I will shew him a way, whereby he shall go, and win all the hill country, without losing the body or life of any one of his men.

{10:14} Now when the men heard her words, and beheld her countenance, they wondered greatly at her beauty, and said unto her,

{10:15} Thou hast saved thy life, in that thou hast hasted to come down to the presence of our lord: now therefore come to his tent, and some of us shall conduct thee, until they have delivered thee to his hands.

{10:16} And when thou standest before him, be not afraid in thine heart, but shew unto him according to thy word; and he will entreat thee well.

{10:17} Then they chose out of them an hundred men to accompany her and her maid; and they brought her to the tent of Holofernes.

{10:18} Then was there a concourse throughout all the camp: for her coming was noised among the tents, and they came about her, as she stood without the tent of Holofernes, till they told him of her.

{10:19} And they wondered at her beauty, and admired the children of

Israel because of her, and every one said to his neighbour, Who would despise this people, that have among them such women? surely it is not good that one man of them be left who being let go might deceive the whole earth.

{10:20} And they that lay near Holofernes went out, and all his servants and they brought her into the tent.

{10:21} Now Holofernes rested upon his bed under a canopy, which was woven with purple, and gold, and emeralds, and precious stones.

{10:22} So they shewed him of her; and he came out before his tent with silver lamps going before him.

{10:23} And when Judith was come before him and his servants they all marvelled at the beauty of her countenance; and she fell down upon her face, and did reverence unto him: and his servants took her up.

{11:1} Then said Holofernes unto her, Woman, be of good comfort, fear not in thine heart: for I never hurt any that was willing to serve Nabuchodonosor, the king of all the earth.

{11:2} Now therefore, if thy people that dwelleth in the mountains had not set light by me, I would not have lifted up my spear against them: but they have done these things to themselves.

{11:3} But now tell me wherefore thou art fled from them, and art come unto us: for thou art come for safeguard; be of good comfort, thou shalt live this night, and hereafter:

{11:4} For none shall hurt thee, but entreat thee well, as they do the servants of king Nabuchodonosor my lord.

{11:5} Then Judith said unto him, Receive the words of thy servant, and suffer thine handmaid to speak in thy presence, and I will declare no lie to my lord this night.

{11:6} And if thou wilt follow the words of thine handmaid, God will bring the thing perfectly to pass by thee; and my lord shall not fail of his purposes.

{11:7} As Nabuchodonosor king of all the earth liveth, and as his power liveth, who hath sent thee for the upholding of every living thing: for not only men shall serve him by thee, but also the beasts of the field, and the cattle, and the fowls of the air, shall live by thy power under Nabuchodonosor and all his house.

{11:8} For we have heard of thy wisdom and thy policies, and it is reported in all the earth, that thou only art excellent in all the kingdom, and mighty in knowledge, and wonderful in feats of war.

{11:9} Now as concerning the matter, which Achior did speak in thy council, we have heard his words; for the men of Bethulia saved him, and he declared unto them all that he had spoken unto thee.

{11:10} Therefore, O lord and governor, respect not his word; but lay it up in thine heart, for it is true: for our nation shall not be punished, neither can sword prevail against them, except they sin against their God.

{11:11} And now, that my lord be not defeated and frustrate of his purpose, even death is now fallen upon them, and their sin hath overtaken them, wherewith they will provoke their God to anger whensoever they shall do that which is not fit to be done:

{11:12} For their victuals fail them, and all their water is scant, and they have determined to lay hands upon their cattle, and purposed to consume all those things, that God hath forbidden them to eat by his laws:

{11:13} And are resolved to spend the firstfruits of the the tenths of wine and oil, which they had sanctified, and reserved for the priests that serve in Jerusalem before the face of our God; the which things it is not lawful for any of the people so much as to touch with their hands.

{11:14} For they have sent some to Jerusalem, because they also that dwell there have done the like, to bring them a licence from the senate.

{11:15} Now when they shall bring them word, they will forthwith do it, and they shall be given to thee to be destroyed the same day.

{11:16} Wherefore I thine handmaid, knowing all this, am fled from their presence; and God hath sent me to work things with thee, whereat all the earth shall be astonished, and whosoever shall hear it.

{11:17} For thy servant is religious, and serveth the God of heaven day and night: now therefore, my lord, I will remain with thee, and thy servant will go out by night into the valley, and I will pray unto God, and he will tell me when they have committed their sins:

{11:18} And I will come and shew it unto thee: then thou shalt go forth with all thine army, and there shall be none of them that shall resist thee.

{11:19} And I will lead thee through the midst of Judea, until thou come before Jerusalem; and I will set thy throne in the midst thereof; and thou shalt drive them as sheep that have no shepherd, and a dog shall not so much as open his mouth at thee: for these things were told me according to my foreknowledge, and they were declared unto me, and I am sent to tell thee.

{11:20} Then her words pleased Holofernes and all his servants; and they marvelled at her wisdom, and said,

{11:21} There is not such a woman from one end of the earth to the other, both for beauty of face, and wisdom of words.

{11:22} Likewise Holofernes said unto her. God hath done well to send thee before the people, that strength might be in our hands and destruction upon them that lightly regard my lord.

{11:23} And now thou art both beautiful in thy countenance, and witty in thy words: surely if thou do as thou hast spoken thy God shall be my God, and thou shalt dwell in the house of king Nabuchodonosor, and shalt be renowned through the whole earth.

{12:1} Then he commanded to bring her in where his plate was set; and bade that they should prepare for her of his own meats, and that she should drink of his own wine.

{12:2} And Judith said, I will not eat thereof, lest there be an offence: but provision shall be made for me of the things that I have brought.

{12:3} Then Holofernes said unto her, If thy provision should fail, how should we give thee the like? for there be none with us of thy nation.

{12:4} Then said Judith unto him as thy soul liveth, my lord, thine handmaid shall not spend those things that I have, before the Lord work by mine hand the things that he hath determined.

{12:5} Then the servants of Holofernes brought her into the tent, and she slept till midnight, and she arose when it was toward the morning watch,

{12:6} And sent to Holofernes, saving, Let my lord now command that thine handmaid may go forth unto prayer.

{12:7} Then Holofernes commanded his guard that they should not stay her: thus she abode in the camp three days, and went out in the night into the valley of Bethulia, and washed herself in a fountain of water by the camp.

{12:8} And when she came out, she besought the Lord God of Israel to direct her way to the raising up of the children of her people.

{12:9} So she came in clean, and remained in the tent, until she did eat her meat at evening.

{12:10} And in the fourth day Holofernes made a feast to his own servants only, and called none of the officers to the banquet.

{12:11} Then said he to Bagoas the eunuch, who had charge over all that he had, go now, and persuade this Hebrew woman which is with thee, that she come unto us, and eat and drink with us.

{12:12} For, lo, it will be a shame for our person, if we shall let such a woman go, not having had her company; for if we draw her not unto us, she will laugh us to scorn.

{12:13} Then went Bagoas from the presence of Holofernes, and came to her, and he said, let not this fair damsel fear to come to my lord, and to be honoured in his presence, and drink wine, and be merry with us and be made this day as one of the daughters of the Assyrians, which serve in the house of Nabuchodonosor.

{12:14} Then said Judith unto him, who am I now, that I should gainsay my lord? surely whatsoever pleaseth him I will do speedily, and it shall be my joy unto the day of my death.

{12:15} So she arose, and decked herself with her apparel and all her woman's attire, and her maid went and laid soft skins on the ground for her over against Holofernes, which she had received of Bagoas far her daily use, that she might sit and eat upon them.

{12:16} Now when Judith came in and sat down, Holofernes his heart was ravished with her, and his mind was moved, and he desired greatly her company; for he waited a time to deceive her, from the day that he had seen her.

{12:17} Then said Holofernes unto her, Drink now, and be merry with us.

{12:18} So Judith said, I will drink now, my lord, because my life is magnified in me this day more than all the days since I was born.

{12:19} Then she took and ate and drank before him what her maid had prepared.

{12:20} And Holofernes took great delight in her, and drank more wine than he had drunk at any time in one day since he was born.

{13:1} Now when the evening was come, his servants made haste to depart, and Bagoas shut his tent without, and dismissed the waiters from the presence of his lord; and they went to their beds: for they were all weary, because the feast had been long.

{13:2} And Judith was left along in the tent, and Holofernes lying along upon his bed: for he was filled with wine.

{13:3} Now Judith had commanded her maid to stand without her bedchamber, and to wait for her. coming forth, as she did daily: for she said she would go forth to her prayers, and she spake to Bagoas according to the same purpose.

{13:4} So all went forth and none was left in the bedchamber, neither little nor great. Then Judith, standing by his bed, said in her heart, O Lord God of all power, look at this present upon the works of mine hands for the exaltation of Jerusalem.

{13:5} For now is the time to help thine inheritance, and to execute thine enterprizes to the destruction of the enemies which are risen against us.

{13:6} Then she came to the pillar of the bed, which was at Holofernes' head, and took down his fauchion from thence,

{13:7} And approached to his bed, and took hold of the hair of his head, and said, Strengthen me, O Lord God of Israel, this day.

{13:8} And she smote twice upon his neck with all her might, and she took away his head from him.

{13:9} And tumbled his body down from the bed, and pulled down the canopy from the pillars; and anon after she went forth, and gave Holofernes his head to her maid;

{13:10} And she put it in her bag of meat: so they twain went together according to their custom unto prayer: and when they passed the camp, they compassed the valley, and went up the mountain of Bethulia, and came to the gates thereof.

{13:11} Then said Judith afar off, to the watchmen at the gate, Open, open now the gate: God, even our God, is with us, to shew his power yet in Jerusalem, and his forces against the enemy, as he hath even done this day.

{13:12} Now when the men of her city heard her voice, they made haste to go down to the gate of their city, and they called the elders of the city.

{13:13} And then they ran all together, both small and great, for it was strange unto them that she was come: so they opened the gate, and received them, and made a fire for a light, and stood round about them.

{13:14} Then she said to them with a loud voice, Praise, praise God, praise God, I say, for he hath not taken away his mercy from the house of Israel, but hath destroyed our enemies by mine hands this night.

{13:15} So she took the head out of the bag, and shewed it, and said unto them, behold the head of Holofernes, the chief captain of the army of Assur, and behold the canopy, wherein he did lie in his drunkenness; and the Lord hath smitten him by the hand of a woman.

{13:16} As the Lord liveth, who hath kept me in my way that I went, my countenance hath deceived him to his destruction, and yet hath he not committed sin with me, to defile and shame me.

{13:17} Then all the people were wonderfully astonished, and bowed themselves and worshipped God, and said with one accord, Blessed be thou, O our God, which hast this day brought to nought the enemies of thy people.

{13:18} Then said Ozias unto her, O daughter, blessed art thou of the most high God above all the women upon the earth; and blessed be the Lord God, which hath created the heavens and the earth, which hath directed thee to the cutting off of the head of the chief of our enemies.

{13:19} For this thy confidence shall not depart from the heart of men, which remember the power of God for ever.

{13:20} And God turn these things to thee for a perpetual praise, to visit thee in good things because thou hast not spared thy life for the affliction of our nation, but hast revenged our ruin, walking a straight way before our God. And all the people said; So be it, so be it.

{14:1} Then said Judith unto them, Hear me now, my brethren, and take this head, and hang it upon the highest place of your walls.

{14:2} And so soon as the morning shall appear, and the sun shall come forth upon the earth, take ye everyone his weapons, and go forth every valiant man out of the city, and set ye a captain over them, as though ye would go down into the field toward the watch of the Assyrians; but go not down.

{14:3} Then they shall take their armour, and shall go into their camp, and raise up the captains of the army of Assur, and shall run to the tent of Holofernes, but shall not find him: then fear shall fall upon them, and they shall flee before your face.

{14:4} So ye, and all that inhabit the coast of Israel, shall pursue them, and overthrow them as they go.

{14:5} But before ye do these things, call me Achior the Ammonite, that he may see and know him that despised the house of Israel, and that sent him to us as it were to his death.

{14:6} Then they called Achior out of the house of Ozias; and when he was come, and saw the head of Holofernes in a man's hand in the assembly of the people, he fell down on his face, and his spirit failed.

{14:7} But when they had recovered him, he fell at Judith's feet, and reverenced her, and said, Blessed art thou in all the tabernacles of Juda, and in all nations, which hearing thy name shall be astonished.

{14:8} Now therefore tell me all the things that thou hast done in these days. Then Judith declared unto him in the midst of the people all that she had done, from the day that she went forth until that hour she spake unto them.

{14:9} And when she had left off speaking, the people shouted with a loud voice, and made a joyful noise in their city.

{14:10} And when Achior had seen all that the God of Israel had done, he believed in God greatly, and circumcised the flesh of his foreskin, and was joined unto the house of Israel unto this day.

{14:11} And as soon as the morning arose, they hanged the head of Holofernes upon the wall, and every man took his weapons, and they went forth by bands unto the straits of the mountain.

{14:12} But when the Assyrians saw them, they sent to their leaders, which came to their captains and tribunes, and to every one of their rulers.

{14:13} So they came to Holofernes' tent, and said to him that had the charge of all his things, waken now our lord: for the slaves have been bold to come down against us to battle, that they may be utterly destroyed.

{14:14} Then went in Bagoas, and knocked at the door of the tent; for he thought that he had slept with Judith.

{14:15} But because none answered, he opened it, and went into the bedchamber, and found him cast upon the floor dead, and his head was taken from him.

{14:16} Therefore he cried with a loud voice, with weeping, and sighing, and a mighty cry, and rent his garments.

{14:17} After he went into the tent where Judith lodged: and when he found her not, he leaped out to the people, and cried,

{14:18} These slaves have dealt treacherously; one woman of the Hebrews hath brought shame upon the house of king Nabuchodonosor: for, behold, Holofernes lieth upon the ground without a head.

{14:19} When the captains of the Assyrians' army heard these words, they rent their coats and their minds were wonderfully troubled, and there was a cry and a very great noise throughout the camp.

{15:1} And when they that were in the tents heard, they were astonished at the thing that was done.

{15:2} And fear and trembling fell upon them, so that there was no man that durst abide in the sight of his neighbour, but rushing out all together, they fled into every way of the plain, and of the hill country.

{15:3} They also that had camped in the mountains round about Bethulia fled away. Then the children of Israel, every one that was a warrior among them, rushed out upon them.

{15:4} Then sent Ozias to Betomasthem, and to Bebai, and Chobai, and Cola and to all the coasts of Israel, such as should tell the things that were done, and that all should rush forth upon their enemies to destroy them.

{15:5} Now when the children of Israel heard it, they all fell upon them with one consent, and slew them unto Chobai. likewise also they that came from Jerusalem, and from all the hill country, (for men had told them what things were done in the camp of their enemies) and they that were in Galaad, and in Galilee, chased them with a great slaughter, until they were past Damascus and the borders thereof.

{15:6} And the residue that dwelt at Bethulia, fell upon the camp of Assur, and spoiled them, and were greatly enriched.

{15:7} And the children of Israel that returned from the slaughter had that which remained; and the villages and the cities, that were in the mountains and in the plain, gat many spoils: for the multitude was very great.

{15:8} Then Joacim the high priest, and the ancients of the children of Israel that dwelt in Jerusalem, came to behold the good things that God had shewed to Israel, and to see Judith, and to salute her.

{15:9} And when they came unto her, they blessed her with one accord, and said unto her, Thou art the exaltation of Jerusalem, thou art the great glory of Israel, thou art the great rejoicing of our nation:

{15:10} Thou hast done all these things by thine hand: thou hast done much good to Israel, and God is pleased therewith: blessed be thou of the Almighty Lord for evermore. And all the people said, So be it.

{15:11} And the people spoiled the camp the space of thirty days: and they gave unto Judith Holofernes his tent, and all his plate, and beds, and vessels, and all his stuff: and she took it and laid it on her mule; and made ready her carts, and laid them thereon.

{15:12} Then all the women of Israel ran together to see her, and blessed her, and made a dance among them for her: and she took branches
in her hand, and gave also to the women that were with her.

{15:13} And they put a garland of olive upon her and her maid that was with her, and she went before all the people in the dance, leading all the women: and all the men of Israel followed in their armour with garlands, and with songs in their mouths.

{16:1} Then Judith began to sing this thanksgiving in all Israel, and all the people sang after her this song of praise.

{16:2} And Judith said, begin unto my God with timbrels, sing unto my Lord with cymbals: tune unto him a new psalm: exalt him, and call upon his name.

{16:3} For God breaketh the battles: for among the camps in the midst of the people he hath delivered me out of the hands of them that persecuted me.

{16:4} Assur came out of the mountains from the north, he came with ten thousands of his army, the multitude whereof stopped the torrents, and their horsemen have covered the hills.

{16:5} He bragged that he would burn up my borders, and kill my young men with the sword, and dash the sucking children against the ground, and make mine infants as a prey, and my virgins as a spoil.

{16:6} But the Almighty Lord hath disappointed them by the hand of a woman.

{16:7} For the mighty one did not fall by the young men, neither did the sons of the Titans smite him, nor high giants set upon him: but Judith the daughter of Merari weakened him with the beauty of her countenance.

{16:8} For she put off the garment of her widowhood for the exaltation of those that were oppressed in Israel, and anointed her face with ointment, and bound her hair in a tire, and took a linen garment to deceive him.

{16:9} Her sandals ravished his eyes, her beauty took his mind prisoner, and the fauchion passed through his neck.

{16:10} The Persians quaked at her boldness, and the Medes were daunted at her hardiness.

{16:11} Then my afflicted shouted for joy, and my weak ones cried aloud; but they were astonished: these lifted up their voices, but they were overthrown.

{16:12} The sons of the damsels have pierced them through, and wounded them as fugatives' children: they perished by the battle of the Lord.

{16:13} I will sing unto the Lord a new song: O Lord, thou art great and glorious, wonderful in strength, and invincible.

{16:14} Let all creatures serve thee: for thou spakest, and they were made, thou didst send forth thy spirit, and it created them, and there is none that can resist thy voice.

{16:15} For the mountains shall be moved from their foundations with the waters, the rocks shall melt as wax at thy presence: yet thou art merciful to them that fear thee.

{16:16} For all sacrifice is too little for a sweet savour unto thee, and all the fat is not sufficient for thy burnt offering: but he that feareth the Lord is great at all times.

{16:17} Woe to the nations that rise up against my kindred! the Lord Almighty will take vengeance of them in the day of judgment, in putting fire and worms in their flesh; and they shall feel them, and weep for ever.

{16:18} Now as soon as they entered into Jerusalem, they worshipped the Lord; and as soon as the people were purified, they offered their burnt offerings, and their free offerings, and their gifts.

{16:19} Judith also dedicated all the stuff of Holofernes, which the people had given her, and gave the canopy, which she had taken out of his bedchamber, for a gift unto the Lord.

{16:20} So the people continued feasting in Jerusalem before the sanctuary for the space of three months and Judith remained with them.

{16:21} After this time everyone returned to his own inheritance, and Judith went to Bethulia, and remained in her own possession, and was in her time honourable in all the country.

{16:22} And many desired her, but none knew her all the days of her life, after that Manasses her husband was dead, and was gathered to his people.

{16:23} But she increased more and more in honour, and waxed old in her husband's house, being an hundred and five years old, and made her maid free; so she died in Bethulia: and they buried her in the cave of her husband Manasses.

{16:24} And the house of Israel lamented her seven days: and before she died, she did distribute her goods to all them that were nearest of kindred to Manasses her husband, and to them that were the nearest of her kindred.

{16:25} And there was none that made the children of Israel any more afraid in the days of Judith, nor a long time after her death.

The Prayer of Manasseh

{1:1} O Lord, Almighty God of our fathers, Abraham, Isaac, and Jacob, and of their righteous seed; {1:2} who hast made heaven and earth, with all the ornament thereof; {1:3} who hast bound the sea by the word of thy commandment; who hast shut up the deep, and sealed it by thy terrible and glorious name; {1:4} whom all men fear, and tremble before thy power; for the majesty of thy glory cannot be borne, and thine angry threatening toward sinners is importable: {1:5} but thy merciful promise is unmeasurable and unsearchable; {1:6} for thou art the most high Lord, of great compassion, longsuffering, very merciful, and repentest of the evils of men. Thou, O Lord, according to thy great goodness hast promised repentance and forgiveness to them that have sinned against thee: and of thine infinite mercies hast appointed repentance unto sinners, that they may be saved. {1:7} Thou therefore, O Lord, that art the God of the just, hast not appointed repentance to the just, as to Abraham, and Isaac, and Jacob, which have not sinned against thee; but thou hast appointed repentance unto me that am a sinner: {1:8} for I have sinned above the number of the sands of the sea. My transgressions, O Lord, are multiplied: my transgressions are multiplied, and I am not worthy to behold and see the height of heaven for the multitude of mine iniquities. {1:9} I am bowed down with many iron bands, that I cannot lift up mine head, neither have any release: for I have provoked thy wrath, and done evil before thee: I did not thy will, neither kept I thy commandments: I have set up abominations, and have multiplied offences. {1:10} Now therefore I bow the knee of mine heart, beseeching thee of grace. {1:11} I have sinned, O Lord, I have sinned, and I acknowledge mine iniquities: {1:12} wherefore, I humbly beseech thee, forgive me, O Lord, forgive me, and destroy me not with mine iniquites. Be not angry with me forever, by reserving evil for me; neither condemn me to the lower parts of the earth. For thou art the God, even the God of them that repent; {1:13} and in me thou wilt shew all thy goodness: for thou wilt save me, that am unworthy, according to thy great mercy. {1:14} Therefore I will praise thee for ever all the days of my life: for all the powers of the heavens do praise thee, and thine is the glory for ever and ever. Amen.

The Song of Solomon

{1:1} The song of songs, which [is] Solomon's. {1:2} Let him kiss me with the kisses of his mouth: for thy love [is] better than wine. {1:3} Because of the savour of thy good ointments thy name [is as] ointment poured forth, therefore do the virgins love thee. {1:4} Draw me, we will run after thee: the king hath brought me into his chambers: we will be glad and rejoice in thee, we will remember thy love more than wine: the upright love thee. {1:5} I [am] black, but comely, O ye daughters of Jerusalem, as the tents of Kedar, as the curtains of Solomon. {1:6} Look not upon me, because I [am] black, because the sun hath looked upon me: my mother's children were angry with me; they made me the keeper of the vineyards; [but] mine own vineyard have I not kept. {1:7} Tell me, O thou whom my soul loveth, where thou feedest, where thou makest [thy flock] to rest at noon: for why should I be as one that turneth aside by the flocks of thy companions?

{1:8} If thou know not, O thou fairest among women, go thy way forth by the footsteps of the flock, and feed thy kids beside the shepherds' tents. {1:9} I have compared thee, O my love, to a company of horses in Pharaoh's chariots. {1:10} Thy cheeks are comely with rows [of jewels,] thy neck with chains [of gold.]{1:11} We will make thee borders of gold with studs of silver.

{1:12} While the king [sitteth] at his table, my spikenard sendeth forth the smell thereof. {1:13} A bundle of myrrh [is] my wellbeloved unto me; he shall lie all night betwixt my breasts. {1:14} My beloved [is] unto me [as] a cluster of camphire in the vineyards of En-gedi. {1:15} Behold, thou [art] fair, my love; behold, thou [art] fair; thou [hast] doves' eyes. {1:16} Behold, thou [art] fair, my beloved, yea, pleasant: also our bed [is] green. {1:17} The beams of our house [are] cedar, [and] our rafters of fir.

{2:1} I [am] the rose of Sharon, [and] the lily of the valleys. {2:2} As the lily among thorns, so [is] my love among the daughters. {2:3} As the apple tree among the trees of the wood, so [is] my beloved among the sons. I sat down under his shadow with great delight, and his fruit [was] sweet to my taste. {2:4} He brought me to the banqueting house, and his banner over me [was] love. {2:5} Stay me with flagons, comfort me with apples: for I [am] sick of love. {2:6} His left hand [is] under my head, and his right hand doth embrace me. {2:7} I charge you, O ye daughters of Jerusalem, by the roes, and by the hinds of the field, that ye stir not up, nor awake [my] love, till he please.

{2:8} The voice of my beloved! behold, he cometh leaping upon the mountains, skipping upon the hills. {2:9} My beloved is like a roe or a young hart: behold, he standeth behind our wall, he looketh forth at the windows, shewing himself through the lattice. {2:10} My beloved spake, and said unto me, Rise up, my love, my fair one, and come away. {2:11} For, lo, the winter is past, the rain is over [and] gone; {2:12}

The flowers appear on the earth; the time of the singing [of birds] is come, and the voice of the turtle is heard in our land; {2:13} The fig tree putteth forth her green figs, and the vines [with] the tender grape give a [good] smell. Arise, my love, my fair one, and come away.

{2:14} O my dove, [that art] in the clefts of the rock, in the secret [places] of the stairs, let me see thy countenance, let me hear thy voice; for sweet [is] thy voice, and thy countenance [is] comely. {2:15} Take us the foxes, the little foxes, that spoil the vines: for our vines [have] tender grapes.

{2:16} My beloved [is] mine, and I [am] his: he feedeth among the lilies. {2:17} Until the day break, and the shadows flee away, turn, my beloved, and be thou like a roe or a young hart upon the mountains of Bether.

{3:1} By night on my bed I sought him whom my soul loveth: I sought him, but I found him not. {3:2} I will rise now, and go about the city in the streets, and in the broad ways I will seek him whom my soul loveth: I sought him, but I found him not. {3:3} The watchmen that go about the city found me: [to whom I said,] Saw ye him whom my soul loveth? {3:4} [It was] but a little that I passed from them, but I found him whom my soul loveth: I held him, and would not let him go, until I had brought him into my mother's house, and into the chamber of her that conceived me. {3:5} I charge you, O ye daughters of Jerusalem, by the roes, and by the hinds of the field, that ye stir not up, nor awake [my] love, till he please.

{3:6} Who [is] this that cometh out of the wilderness like pillars of smoke, perfumed with myrrh and frankincense, with all powders of the merchant? {3:7} Behold his bed, which [is] Solomon's; threescore valiant men [are] about it, of the valiant of Israel. {3:8} They all hold swords, [being] expert in war: every man [hath] his sword upon his thigh because of fear in the night. {3:9} King Solomon made himself a chariot of the wood of Lebanon. {3:10} He made the pillars thereof [of] silver, the bottom thereof [of] gold, the covering of it [of] purple, the midst thereof being paved [with] love, for the daughters of Jerusalem. {3:11} Go forth, O ye daughters of Zion, and behold king Solomon with the crown wherewith his mother crowned him in the day of his espousals, and in the day of the gladness of his heart.

{4:1} Behold, thou [art] fair, my love; behold, thou [art] fair; thou [hast] doves' eyes within thy locks: thy hair [is] as a flock of goats, that appear from mount Gilead. {4:2} Thy teeth [are] like a flock [of sheep that are even] shorn, which came up from the washing; whereof every one bear twins, and none [is] barren among them. {4:3} Thy lips [are] like a thread of scarlet, and thy speech [is] comely: thy temples [are] like a piece of a pomegranate within thy locks. {4:4} Thy neck [is] like the tower of David builded for an armoury, whereon there hang a thousand bucklers, all shields of mighty men. {4:5} Thy two breasts [are] like two young roes that are twins, which feed among the lilies. {4:6} Until the day break, and the shadows flee away, I will get me to the mountain of myrrh, and to the hill of frankincense. {4:7} Thou [art] all fair, my love; [there is] no spot in thee.

{4:8} Come with me from Lebanon, [my] spouse, with me from Lebanon: look from the top of Amana, from the top of Shenir and Hermon, from the lions' dens, from the mountains of the leopards. {4:9} Thou hast ravished my heart, my sister, [my] spouse; thou hast ravished my heart with one of thine eyes, with one chain of thy neck. {4:10} How fair is thy love, my sister, [my] spouse! how much better is thy love than wine! and the smell of thine ointments than all spices! {4:11} Thy lips, O [my] spouse, drop [as] the honeycomb: honey and milk [are] under thy tongue; and the smell of thy garments [is] like the smell of Lebanon. {4:12} A garden inclosed [is] my sister, [my] spouse; a spring shut up, a fountain sealed. {4:13} Thy plants [are] an orchard of pomegranates, with pleasant fruits; camphire, with spikenard, {4:14} Spikenard and saffron; calamus and cinnamon, with all trees of frankincense; myrrh and aloes, with all the chief spices: {4:15} A fountain of gardens, a well of living waters, and streams from Lebanon.

{4:16} Awake, O north wind; and come, thou south; blow upon my garden, [that] the spices thereof may flow out. Let my beloved come into his garden, and eat his pleasant fruits.

{5:1} I am come into my garden, my sister, [my] spouse: I have gathered my myrrh with my spice; I have eaten my honeycomb with my honey; I have drunk my wine with my milk: eat, O friends; drink, yea, drink abundantly, O beloved.

{5:2} I sleep, but my heart waketh: [it is] the voice of my beloved that knocketh, [saying,] Open to me, my sister, my love, my dove, my undefiled: for my head is filled with dew, [and] my locks with the drops of the night. {5:3} I have put off my coat; how shall I put it on? I have washed my feet; how shall I defile them? {5:4} My beloved put in his hand by the hole [of the door,] and my bowels were moved for him. {5:5} I rose up to open to my beloved; and my hands dropped [with] myrrh, and my fingers [with] sweet smelling myrrh, upon the handles of the lock. {5:6} I opened to my beloved; but my beloved had withdrawn himself, [and] was gone: my soul failed when he spake: I sought him, but I could not find him; I called him, but he gave me no answer. {5:7} The watchmen that went about the city found me, they smote me, they wounded me; the keepers of the walls took away my veil from me. {5:8} I charge you, O daughters of Jerusalem, if ye find my beloved, that ye tell him, that I [am] sick of love.

{5:9} What [is] thy beloved more than [another] beloved, O thou fairest among women? what [is] thy beloved more than [another] beloved, that thou dost so charge us? {5:10} My beloved [is] white and ruddy, the chiefest among ten thousand. {5:11} His head [is as] the most fine gold, his locks [are] bushy, [and] black as a raven. {5:12} His eyes [are] as [the eyes] of doves by the rivers of waters, washed with milk, [and] fitly set. {5:13} His cheeks [are] as a bed of spices, [as] sweet flowers: his lips [like] lilies, dropping sweet smelling myrrh. {5:14} His hands [are as] gold rings set with the beryl: his belly [is as] bright ivory overlaid [with] sapphires. {5:15} His legs [are as] pillars of marble, set upon sockets of fine gold: his countenance [is] as Lebanon, excellent as the cedars. {5:16} His mouth [is] most sweet: yea, he [is] altogether lovely. This [is] my beloved, and this [is] my friend, O daughters of Jerusalem.

{6:1} Whither is thy beloved gone, O thou fairest among women? whither is thy beloved turned aside? that we may seek him with thee. {6:2} My beloved is gone down into his garden, to the beds of spices, to feed in the gardens, and to gather lilies. {6:3} I [am] my beloved's, and my beloved [is] mine: he feedeth among the lilies.

{6:4} Thou [art] beautiful, O my love, as Tirzah, comely as Jerusalem, terrible as [an army] with banners. {6:5} Turn away thine eyes from me, for they have overcome me: thy hair [is] as a flock of goats that appear from Gilead. {6:6} Thy teeth [are] as a flock of sheep which go up from the washing, whereof everyone beareth twins, and [there is] not one barren among them. {6:7} As a piece of a pomegranate [are] thy temples within thy locks. {6:8} There are threescore queens, and fourscore concubines, and virgins without number. {6:9} My dove, my undefiled is [but] one; she [is] the [only] one of her mother, she [is] the choice [one] of her that bare her. The daughters saw her, and blessed her; [yea,] the queens and the concubines, and they praised her.

{6:10} Who [is] she [that] looketh forth as the morning, fair as the moon, clear as the sun, [and] terrible as [an army] with banners? {6:11} I went down into the garden of nuts to see the fruits of the valley, [and] to see whether the vine flourished, [and] the pomegranates budded. {6:12} Or ever I was aware, my soul made me [like] the chariots of Amminadib. {6:13} Return, return, O Shulamite; return, return, that we may look upon thee. What will ye see in the Shulamite? As it were the company of two armies.

{7:1} How beautiful are thy feet with shoes, O prince's daughter! the joints of thy thighs [are] like jewels, the work of the hands of a cunning workman. {7:2} Thy navel [is like] a round goblet, [which] wanteth not liquor: thy belly [is like] an heap of wheat set about with lilies. {7:3} Thy two breasts [are] like two young roes [that are] twins. {7:4} Thy neck [is] as a tower of ivory; thine eyes [like] the fishpools in Heshbon, by the gate of Bath-rabbim: thy nose [is] as the tower of Lebanon which looketh toward Damascus. {7:5} Thine head upon thee [is] like Carmel, and the hair of thine head like purple; the king [is] held in the galleries. {7:0} How fair and how pleasant art thou, O love, for delights! {7:7} This thy stature is like to a palm tree, and thy breasts to clusters [of grapes.]{7:8} I said, I will go up to the palm tree, I will take hold of the boughs thereof: now also thy breasts shall be as clusters of the vine, and the smell of thy nose like apples; {7:9} And the roof of thy mouth like the best wine for my beloved, that goeth [down] sweetly, causing the lips of those that are asleep to speak.

{7:10} I [am] my beloved's, and his desire [is] toward me. {7:11} Come, my beloved, let us go forth into the field; let us lodge in the villages. {7:12} Let us get up early to the vineyards; let us see if the vine flourish, [whether] the tender grape appear, [and] the pomegranates bud forth: there will I give thee my loves. {7:13} The mandrakes give a smell, and at our gates [are] all manner of pleasant [fruits,] new and old, [which] I have laid up for thee, O my beloved.

{8:1} O that thou [wert] as my brother, that sucked the breasts of my mother! [when] I should find thee without, I would kiss thee; yea, I should not be despised. {8:2} I would lead thee, [and] bring thee into my mother's house, [who] would instruct me: I would cause thee to drink of spiced wine of the juice of my pomegranate. {8:3} His left hand [should be] under my head, and his right hand should embrace me. {8:4} I charge you, O daughters of Jerusalem, that ye stir not up, nor awake [my] love, until he please. {8:5} Who [is] this that cometh up from the wilderness, leaning upon her beloved? I raised thee up under the apple tree: there thy mother brought thee forth: there she brought thee forth

[that] bare thee.

{8:6} Set me as a seal upon thine heart, as a seal upon thine arm: for love [is] strong as death; jealousy [is] cruel as the grave: the coals thereof [are] coals of fire, [which hath a] most vehement flame. {8:7} Many waters cannot quench love, neither can the floods drown it: if [a] man would give all the substance of his house for love, it would utterly be contemned.

{8:8} We have a little sister, and she hath no breasts: what shall we do for our sister in the day when she shall be spoken for? {8:9} If she [be] a wall, we will build upon her a palace of silver: and if she [be] a door, we will inclose her with boards of cedar. {8:10} I [am] a wall, and my breasts like towers: then was I in his eyes as one that found favour. {8:11} Solomon had a vineyard at Baal-hamon; he let out the vineyard unto keepers; everyone for the fruit thereof was to bring a thousand [pieces] of silver. {8:12} My vineyard, which [is] mine, [is] before me: thou, O Solomon, [must have] a thousand, and those that keep the fruit thereof two hundred. {8:13} Thou that dwellest in the gardens, the companions hearken to thy voice: cause me to hear [it.]

{8:14} Make haste, my beloved, and be thou like to a roe or to a young hart upon the mountains of spices.

The History of Susanna

Set apart from the beginning of Daniel, because it is not in the Hebrew, as neither the Narration of Bel and the Dragon.

{1:1} There dwelt a man in Babylon, called Joacim:

{1:2} And he took a wife, whose name was Susanna, the daughter of Chelcias, a very fair woman, and one that feared the Lord.

{1:3} Her parents also were righteous, and taught their daughter according to the law of Moses.

{1:4} Now Joacim was a great rich man, and had a fair garden joining unto his house: and to him resorted the Jews; because he was more honourable than all others.

{1:5} The same year were appointed two of the ancients of the people to be judges, such as the Lord spake of, that wickedness came from Babylon from ancient judges, who seemed to govern the people.

{1:6} These kept much at Joacim's house: and all that had any suits in law came unto them.

{1:7} Now when the people departed away at noon, Susanna went into her husband's garden to walk.

{1:8} And the two elders saw her going in every day, and walking; so that their lust was inflamed toward her.

{1:9} And they perverted their own mind, and turned away their eyes, that they might not look unto heaven, nor remember just judgments.

{1:10} And albeit they both were wounded with her love, yet durst not one shew another his grief.

{1:11} For they were ashamed to declare their lust, that they desired to have to do with her.

{1:12} Yet they watched diligently from day to day to see her.

{1:13} And the one said to the other, Let us now go home: for it is dinner time.

{1:14} So when they were gone out, they parted the one from the other, and turning back again they came to the same place; and after that they had asked one another the cause, they acknowledged their lust: then appointed they a time both together, when they might find her alone.

{1:15} And it fell out, as they watched a fit time, she went in as before with two maids only, and she was desirous to wash herself in the garden: for it was hot.

{1:16} And there was no body there save the two elders, that had hid themselves, and watched her.

{1:17} Then she said to her maids, Bring me oil and washing balls, and shut the garden doors, that I may wash me.

{1:18} And they did as she bade them, and shut the garden doors, and went out themselves at privy doors to fetch the things that she had commanded them: but they saw not the elders, because they were hid.

{1:19} Now when the maids were gone forth, the two elders rose up, and ran unto her, saying,

{1:20} Behold, the garden doors are shut, that no man can see us, and we are in love with thee; therefore consent unto us, and lie with us.

{1:21} If thou wilt not, we will bear witness against thee, that a young man was with thee: and therefore thou didst send away thy maids from thee.

{1:22} Then Susanna sighed, and said, I am straitened on every side: for if I do this thing, it is death unto me: and if I do it not I cannot escape your hands.

{1:23} It is better for me to fall into your hands, and not do it, than to sin in the sight of the Lord.

{1:24} With that Susanna cried with a loud voice: and the two elders cried out against her.

{1:25} Then ran the one, and opened the garden door.

{1:26} So when the servants of the house heard the cry in the garden, they rushed in at the privy door, to see what was done unto her.

{1:27} But when the elders had declared their matter, the servants were greatly ashamed: for there was never such a report made of Susanna.

{1:28} And it came to pass the next day, when the people were assembled to her husband Joacim, the two elders came also full of mischievous imagination against Susanna to put her to death;

{1:29} And said before the people, Send for Susanna, the daughter of

Chelcias, Joacim's wife. And so they sent.

{1:30} So she came with her father and mother, her children, and all her kindred.

{1:31} Now Susanna was a very delicate woman, and beauteous to behold.

{1:32} And these wicked men commanded to uncover her face, (for she was covered) that they might be filled with her beauty.

{1:33} Therefore her friends and all that saw her wept.

{1:34} Then the two elders stood up in the midst of the people, and laid their hands upon her head.

{1:35} And she weeping looked up toward heaven: for her heart trusted in the Lord.

{1:36} And the elders said, As we walked in the garden alone, this woman came in with two maids, and shut the garden doors, and sent the maids away.

{1:37} Then a young man, who there was hid, came unto her, and lay with her.

{1:38} Then we that stood in a corner of the garden, seeing this wickedness, ran unto them.

{1:39} And when we saw them together, the man we could not hold: for he was stronger than we, and opened the door, and leaped out.

{1:40} But having taken this woman, we asked who the young man was, but she would not tell us: these things do we testify.

{1:41} Then the assembly believed them as those that were the elders and judges of the people: so they condemned her to death.

{1:42} Then Susanna cried out with a loud voice, and said, O everlasting God, that knowest the secrets, and knowest all things before they be:

{1:43} Thou knowest that they have borne false witness against me, and, behold, I must die; whereas I never did such things as these men have maliciously invented against me.

{1:44} And the Lord heard her voice.

{1:45} Therefore when she was led to be put to death, the Lord raised up the holy spirit of a young youth whose name was Daniel:

{1:46} Who cried with a loud voice, I am clear from the blood of this woman.

{1:47} Then all the people turned them toward him, and said, What mean these words that thou hast spoken?

{1:48} So he standing in the midst of them said, Are ye such fools, ye sons of Israel, that without examination or knowledge of the truth ye have condemned a daughter of Israel?

{1:49} Return again to the place of judgment: for they have borne false witness against her.

{1:50} Wherefore all the people turned again in haste, and the elders said unto him, Come, sit down among us, and shew it us, seeing God hath given thee the honour of an elder.

{1:51} Then said Daniel unto them, Put these two aside one far from another, and I will examine them.

{1:52} So when they were put asunder one from another, he called one of them, and said unto him, O thou that art waxen old in wickedness, now thy sins which thou hast committed aforetime are come to light.

{1:53} For thou hast pronounced false judgment and hast condemned the innocent and hast let the guilty go free; albeit the Lord saith, The innocent and righteous shalt thou not slay.

{1:54} Now then, if thou hast seen her, tell me, Under what tree sawest thou them companying together? Who answered, Under a mastick tree.

{1:55} And Daniel said, very well; thou hast lied against thine own head; for even now the angel of God hath received the sentence of God to cut thee in two.

{1:56} So he put him aside, and commanded to bring the other, and said unto him, O thou seed of Chanaan, and not of Juda, beauty hath deceived thee, and lust hath perverted thine heart.

{1:57} Thus have ye dealt with the daughters of Israel, and they for fear companied with you: but the daughter of Juda would not abide your wickedness.

{1:58} Now therefore tell me, under what tree didst thou take them companying together? Who answered, under an holm tree.

{1:59} Then said Daniel unto him, well; thou hast also lied against thine own head: for the angel of God waiteth with the sword to cut thee in two, that he may destroy you.

{1:60} With that all the assembly cried out with a loud voice, and praised God, who saveth them that trust in him.

{1:61} And they arose against the two elders, for Daniel had convicted them of false witness by their own mouth:

{1:62} And according to the law of Moses they did unto them in such sort as they maliciously intended to do to their neighbour: and they put them to death. Thus the innocent blood was saved the same day.

{1:63} Therefore Chelcias and his wife praised God for their daughter Susanna, with Joacim her husband, and all the kindred, because there was no dishonesty found in her.

{1:64} From that day forth was Daniel had in great reputation in the sight of the people.

The Book of Tobit

{1:1} The book of the words of Tobit, son of Tobiel, the son of Ananiel, the son of Aduel, the son of Gabael, of the seed of Asael, of the tribe of Nephthali;

{1:2} Who in the time of Enemessar king of the Assyrians was led captive out of Thisbe, which is at the right hand of that city, which is called properly Nephthali in Galilee above Aser.

{1:3} I Tobit have walked all the days of my life in the ways of truth and justice, and I did many almsdeeds to my brethren, and my nation, who came with me to Nineve, into the land of the Assyrians.

{1:4} And when I was in mine own country, in the land of Israel being but young, all the tribe of Nephthali my father fell from the house of Jerusalem, which was chosen out of all the tribes of Israel, that all the tribes should sacrifice there, where the temple of the habitation of the most High was consecrated and built for all ages.

{1:5} Now all the tribes which together revolted, and the house of my father Nephthali, sacrificed unto the heifer Baal.

{1:6} But I alone went often to Jerusalem at the feasts, as it was ordained unto all the people of Israel by an everlasting decree, having the firstfruits and tenths of increase, with that which was first shorn; and them gave I at the altar to the priests the children of Aaron.

{1:7} The first tenth part of all increase I gave to the sons of Aaron, who ministered at Jerusalem: another tenth part I sold away, and went, and spent it every year at Jerusalem:

{1:8} And the third I gave unto them to whom it was meet, as Debora my father's mother had commanded me, because I was left an orphan by my father.

{1:9} Furthermore, when I was come to the age of a man, I married Anna of mine own kindred, and of her I begat Tobias.

{1:10} And when we were carried away captives to Nineve, all my brethren and those that were of my kindred did eat of the bread of the Gentiles.

{1:11} But I kept myself from eating;

{1:12} Because I remembered God with all my heart.

{1:13} And the most High gave me grace and favour before Enemessar, so that I was his purveyor.

{1:14} And I went into Media, and left in trust with Gabael, the brother of Gabrias, at Rages a city of Media ten talents of silver.

{1:15} Now when Enemessar was dead, Sennacherib his son reigned in his stead; whose estate was troubled, that I could not go into Media.

{1:16} And in the time of Enemessar I gave many alms to my brethren, and gave my bread to the hungry,

{1:17} And my clothes to the naked: and if I saw any of my nation dead, or cast about the walls of Nineve, I buried him.

{1:18} And if the king Sennacherib had slain any, when he was come, and fled from Judea, I buried them privily; for in his wrath he killed many; but the bodies were not found, when they were sought for of the king.

{1:19} And when one of the Ninevites went and complained of me to the king, that I buried them, and hid myself; understanding that I was sought for to be put to death, I withdrew myself for fear.

{1:20} Then all my goods were forcibly taken away, neither was there any thing left me, beside my wife Anna and my son Tobias.

{1:21} And there passed not five and fifty days, before two of his sons killed him, and they fled into the mountains of Ararath; and Sarchedonus his son reigned in his stead; who appointed over his father's accounts, and over all his affairs, Achiacharus my brother Anael's son.

{1:22} And Achiacharus intreating for me, I returned to Nineve. Now Achiacharus was cupbearer, and keeper of the signet, and steward, and overseer of the accounts: and Sarchedonus appointed him next unto him: and he was my brother's son.

{2:1} Now when I was come home again, and my wife Anna was restored unto me, with my son Tobias, in the feast of Pentecost, which is the holy feast of the seven weeks, there was a good dinner prepared me, in the which I sat down to eat.

{2:2} And when I saw abundance of meat, I said to my son, Go and bring what poor man soever thou shalt find out of our brethren, who is mindful of the Lord; and, lo, I tarry for thee.

{2:3} But he came again, and said, Father, one of our nation is strangled, and is cast out in the marketplace.

{2:4} Then before I had tasted of any meat, I started up, and took him up into a room until the going down of the sun.

{2:5} Then I returned, and washed myself, and ate my meat in heaviness,

{2:6} Remembering that prophecy of Amos, as he said, Your feasts shall be turned into mourning, and all your mirth into lamentation.

{2:7} Therefore I wept: and after the going down of the sun I went and made a grave, and buried him.

{2:8} But my neighbours mocked me, and said, This man is not yet afraid to be put to death for this matter: who fled away; and yet, lo, he burieth the dead again.

{2:9} The same night also I returned from the burial, and slept by the wall of my courtyard, being polluted and my face was uncovered:

{2:10} And I knew not that there were sparrows in the wall, and mine eyes being open, the sparrows muted warm dung into mine eyes, and a whiteness came in mine eyes: and I went to the physicians, but they helped me not: moreover Achiacharus did nourish me, until I went into Elymais.

{2:11} And my wife Anna did take women's works to do.

{2:12} And when she had sent them home to the owners, they paid her wages, and gave her also besides a kid.

{2:13} And when it was in my house, and began to cry, I said unto her, From whence is this kid? is it not stolen? render it to the owners; for it is not lawful to eat any thing that is stolen.

{2:14} But she replied upon me, It was given for a gift more than the wages. Howbeit I did not believe her, but bade her render it to the owners: and I was abashed at her. But she replied upon me, Where are thine alms and thy righteous deeds? behold, thou and all thy works are known.

{3:1} Then I being grieved did weep, and in my sorrow prayed, saying,

{3:2} O Lord, thou art just, and all thy works and all thy ways are mercy and truth, and thou judgest truly and justly for ever.

{3:3} Remember me, and look on me, punish me not for my sins and ignorances, and the sins of my fathers, who have sinned before thee:

{3:4} For they obeyed not thy commandments: wherefore thou hast delivered us for a spoil, and unto captivity, and unto death, and for a proverb of reproach to all the nations among whom we are dispersed.

{3:5} And now thy judgments are many and true: deal with me according to my sins and my fathers': because we have not kept thy commandments, neither have walked in truth before thee.

{3:6} Now therefore deal with me as seemeth best unto thee, and command my spirit to be taken from me, that I may be dissolved, and become earth: for it is profitable for me to die rather than to live, because I have heard false reproaches, and have much sorrow: command therefore that I may now be delivered out of this distress, and go into the everlasting place: turn not thy face away from me.

{3:7} It came to pass the same day, that in Ecbatane a city of Media Sara the daughter of Raguel was also reproached by her father's maids;

{3:8} Because that she had been married to seven husbands, whom Asmodeus the evil spirit had killed, before they had lain with her. Dost thou not know, said they, that thou hast strangled thine husbands? thou hast had already seven husbands, neither wast thou named after any of them.

{3:9} Wherefore dost thou beat us for them? if they be dead, go thy ways after them, let us never see of thee either son or daughter.

{3:10} When she heard these things, she was very sorrowful, so that she thought to have strangled herself; and she said, I am the only daughter of my father, and if I do this, it shall be a reproach unto him, and I shall bring his old age with sorrow unto the grave.

{3:11} Then she prayed toward the window, and said, Blessed art thou, O Lord my God, and thine holy and glorious name is blessed and honourable for ever: let all thy works praise thee for ever.

{3:12} And now, O Lord, I set mine eyes and my face toward thee,

{3:13} And say, take me out of the earth, that I may hear no more the reproach.

{3:14} Thou knowest, Lord, that I am pure from all sin with man,

{3:15} And that I never polluted my name, nor the name of my father, in the land of my captivity: I am the only daughter of my father, neither hath he any child to be his heir, neither any near kinsman, nor any son of his alive, to whom I may keep myself for a wife: my seven husbands are already dead; and why should I live? but if it please not thee that I should die, command some regard to be had of me, and pity taken of me, that I hear no more reproach.

{3:16} So the prayers of them both were heard before the majesty of the great God.

{3:17} And Raphael was sent to heal them both, that is, to scale away the whiteness of Tobit's eyes, and to give Sara the daughter of Raguel for a wife to Tobias the son of Tobit; and to bind Asmodeus the evil spirit; because she belonged to Tobias by right of inheritance. The selfsame time came Tobit home, and entered into his house, and Sara the daughter of Raguel came down from her upper chamber.

{4:1} In that day Tobit remembered the money which he had committed to Gabael in Rages of Media,

{4:2} And said with himself, I have wished for death; wherefore do I not call for my son Tobias that I may signify to him of the money before I die?

{4:3} And when he had called him, he said, My son, when I am dead, bury me; and despise not thy mother, but honour her all the days of thy life, and do that which shall please her, and grieve her not.

{4:4} Remember, my son, that she saw many dangers for thee, when thou wast in her womb: and when she is dead, bury her by me in one grave.

{4:5} My son, be mindful of the Lord our God all thy days, and let not thy will be set to sin, or to transgress his commandments: do uprightly all thy life long, and follow not the ways of unrighteousness.

{4:6} For if thou deal truly, thy doings shall prosperously succeed to thee, and to all them that live justly.

{4:7} Give alms of thy substance; and when thou givest alms, let not thine eye be envious, neither turn thy face from any poor, and the face of God shall not be turned away from thee.

{4:8} If thou hast abundance give alms accordingly: if thou have but a little, be not afraid to give according to that little:

{4:9} For thou layest up a good treasure for thyself against the day of necessity.

{4:10} Because that alms do deliver from death, and suffereth not to come into darkness.

{4:11} For alms is a good gift unto all that give it in the sight of the most High.

{4:12} Beware of all whoredom, my son, and chiefly take a wife of the seed of thy fathers, and take not a strange woman to wife, which is not of thy father's tribe: for we are the children of the prophets, Noe, Abraham, Isaac, and Jacob: remember, my son, that our fathers from the beginning, even that they all married wives of their own kindred, and were blessed in their children, and their seed shall inherit the land.

{4:13} Now therefore, my son, love thy brethren, and despise not in thy heart thy brethren, the sons and daughters of thy people, in not taking a wife of them: for in pride is destruction and much trouble, and in lewdness is decay and great want: for lewdness is the mother of famine.

{4:14} Let not the wages of any man, which hath wrought for thee, tarry with thee, but give him it out of hand: for if thou serve God, he will also repay thee: be circumspect my son, in all things thou doest, and be wise in all thy conversation.

{4:15} Do that to no man which thou hatest: drink not wine to make thee drunken: neither let drunkenness go with thee in thy journey.

{4:16} Give of thy bread to the hungry, and of thy garments to them that are naked; and according to thine abundance give alms: and let not thine eye be envious, when thou givest alms.

{4:17} Pour out thy bread on the burial of the just, but give nothing to the wicked.

{4:18} Ask counsel of all that are wise, and despise not any counsel that is profitable.

{4:19} Bless the Lord thy God alway, and desire of him that thy ways may be directed, and that all thy paths and counsels may prosper: for every nation hath not counsel; but the Lord himself giveth all good things, and he humbleth whom he will, as he will; now therefore, my son, remember my commandments, neither let them be put out of thy mind.

{4:20} And now I signify this to they that I committed ten talents to Gabael the son of Gabrias at Rages in Media.

{4:21} And fear not, my son, that we are made poor: for thou hast much wealth, if thou fear God, and depart from all sin, and do that which is pleasing in his sight.

{5:1} Tobias then answered and said, Father, I will do all things which thou hast commanded me:

{5:2} But how can I receive the money, seeing I know him not?

{5:3} Then he gave him the handwriting, and said unto him, Seek thee a man which may go with thee, whiles I yet live, and I will give him wages: and go and receive the money.

{5:4} Therefore when he went to seek a man, he found Raphael that was an angel.

{5:5} But he knew not; and he said unto him, Canst thou go with me to Rages? and knowest thou those places well?

{5:6} To whom the angel said, I will go with thee, and I know the way well: for I have lodged with our brother Gabael.

{5:7} Then Tobias said unto him, Tarry for me, till I tell my father.

{5:8} Then he said unto him, Go and tarry not. So he went in and said to his father, Behold, I have found one which will go with me. Then he said, call him unto me, that I may know of what tribe he is, and whether he be a trusty man to go with thee.

{5:9} So he called him, and he came in, and they saluted one another.

{5:10} Then Tobit said unto him, Brother, shew me of what tribe and family thou art.

{5:11} To whom he said, Dost thou seek for a tribe or family, or an hired man to go with thy son? Then Tobit said unto him, I would know, brother, thy kindred and name.

{5:12} Then he said, I am Azarias, the son of Ananias the great, and of thy brethren.

{5:13} Then Tobit said, thou art welcome, brother; be not now angry with me, because I have enquired to know thy tribe and thy family; for thou art my brother, of an honest and good stock: for I know Ananias and Jonathas, sons of that great Samaias, as we went together to Jerusalem to worship, and offered the firstborn, and the tenths of the fruits; and they were not seduced with the error of our brethren: my brother, thou art of a good stock.

{5:14} But tell me, what wages shall I give thee? wilt thou a drachm a day, and things necessary, as to mine own son?

{5:15} Yea, moreover, if ye return safe, I will add something to thy wages.

{5:16} So they were well pleased. Then said he to Tobias, Prepare thyself for the journey, and God send you a good journey. And when his son had prepared all things for the journey, his father said, Go thou with this man, and God, which dwelleth in heaven, prosper your journey, and the angel of God keep you company. So they went forth both, and the young man's dog with them.

{5:17} But Anna his mother wept, and said to Tobit, Why hast thou sent away our son? is he not the staff of our hand, in going in and out before us?

{5:18} Be not greedy to add money to money: but let it be as refuse in respect of our child.

{5:19} For that which the Lord hath given us to live with doth suffice us.

{5:20} Then said Tobit to her, Take no care, my sister; he shall return in safety, and thine eyes shall see him.

{5:21} For the good angel will keep him company, and his journey shall be prosperous, and he shall return safe.

{5:22} Then she made an end of weeping.

{6:1} And as they went on their journey, they came in the evening to the river Tigris, and they lodged there.

{6:2} And when the young man went down to wash himself, a fish leaped out of the river, and would have devoured him.

{6:3} Then the angel said unto him, Take the fish. And the young man laid hold of the fish, and drew it to land.

{6:4} To whom the angel said, Open the fish, and take the heart and the liver and the gall, and put them up safely.

{6:5} So the young man did as the angel commanded him; and when they had roasted the fish, they did eat it: then they both went on their way, till they drew near to Ecbatane.

{6:6} Then the young man said to the angel, Brother Azarias, to what use is the heart and the liver and the gal of the fish?

{6:7} And he said unto him, Touching the heart and the liver, if a devil or an evil spirit trouble any, we must make a smoke thereof before the man or the woman, and the party shall be no more vexed.

{6:8} As for the gall, it is good to anoint a man that hath whiteness in his eyes, and he shall be healed.

{6:9} And when they were come near to Rages,

{6:10} The angel said to the young man, Brother, today we shall lodge with Raguel, who is thy cousin; he also hath one only daughter, named Sara; I will speak for her, that she may be given thee for a wife.

{6:11} For to thee doth the right of her appertain, seeing thou only art of her kindred.

{6:12} And the maid is fair and wise: now therefore hear me, and I will speak to her father; and when we return from Rages we will celebrate the marriage: for I know that Raguel cannot marry her to another according to the law of Moses, but he shall be guilty of death, because the right of inheritance doth rather appertain to thee than to any other.

{6:13} Then the young man answered the angel, I have heard, brother Azarias that this maid hath been given to seven men, who all died in the marriage chamber.

{6:14} And now I am the only son of my father, and I am afraid, lest if I go in unto her, I die, as the other before: for a wicked spirit loveth her, which hurteth no body, but those which come unto her; wherefore I also fear lest I die, and bring my father's and my mother's life because of me to the grave with sorrow: for they have no other son to bury them.

{6:15} Then the angel said unto him, Dost thou not remember the precepts which thy father gave thee, that thou shouldest marry a wife of thine own kindred? wherefore hear me, O my brother; for she shall be given thee to wife; and make thou no reckoning of the evil spirit; for this same night shall she be given thee in marriage.

{6:16} And when thou shalt come into the marriage chamber, thou shalt take the ashes of perfume, and shalt lay upon them some of the heart and liver of the fish, and shalt make a smoke with it:

{6:17} And the devil shall smell it, and flee away, and never come again any more: but when thou shalt come to her, rise up both of you, and pray to God which is merciful, who will have pity on you, and save you: fear not, for she is appointed unto thee from the beginning; and thou shalt preserve her, and she shall go with thee. Moreover I suppose that she shall bear thee children. Now when Tobias had heard these things, he loved her, and his heart was effectually joined to her.

{7:1} And when they were come to Ecbatane, they came to the house of Raguel, and Sara met them: and after they had saluted one another, she brought them into the house.

{7:2} Then said Raguel to Edna his wife, how like is this young man to Tobit my cousin!

{7:3} And Raguel asked them, from whence are ye, brethren? To whom they said, we are of the sons of Nephthalim, which are captives in Nineve.

{7:4} Then he said to them, do ye know Tobit our kinsman? And they said, we know him. Then said he, Is he in good health?

{7:5} And they said, He is both alive, and in good health: and Tobias said, He is my father.

{7:6} Then Raguel leaped up, and kissed him, and wept,

{7:7} And blessed him, and said unto him, Thou art the son of an honest and good man. But when he had heard that Tobit was blind, he was sorrowful, and wept.

{7:8} And likewise Edna his wife and Sara his daughter wept. Moreover they entertained them cheerfully; and after that they had killed a ram of the flock, they set store of meat on the table. Then said Tobias to Raphael, Brother Azarias, speak of those things of which thou didst talk in the way, and let this business be dispatched.

{7:9} So he communicated the matter with Raguel: and Raguel said to Tobias, Eat and drink, and make merry:

{7:10} For it is meet that thou shouldest marry my daughter: nevertheless I will declare unto thee the truth.

{7:11} I have given my daughter in marriage to seven men, who died that night they came in unto her: nevertheless for the present be merry. But Tobias said, I will eat nothing here, till we agree and swear one to another.

{7:12} Raguel said, then take her from henceforth according to the manner, for thou art her cousin, and she is thine, and the merciful God give you good success in all things.

{7:13} Then he called his daughter Sara, and she came to her father, and he took her by the hand, and gave her to be wife to Tobias, saying, Behold, take her after the law of Moses, and lead her away to thy father. And he blessed them;

{7:14} And called Edna his wife, and took paper, and did write an instrument of covenants, and sealed it.

{7:15} Then they began to eat.

{7:16} After Raguel called his wife Edna, and said unto her, Sister, prepare another chamber, and bring her in thither.

{7:17} Which when she had done as he had bidden her, she brought her thither: and she wept, and she received the tears of her daughter, and said unto her,

{7:18} Be of good comfort, my daughter; the Lord of heaven and earth give thee joy for this thy sorrow: be of good comfort, my daughter.

{8:1} And when they had supped, they brought Tobias in unto her.

{8:2} And as he went, he remembered the words of Raphael, and took the ashes of the perfumes, and put the heart and the liver of the fish thereupon, and made a smoke therewith.

{8:3} The which smell when the evil spirit had smelled, he fled into the utmost parts of Egypt, and the angel bound him.

{8:4} And after that they were both shut in together, Tobias rose out of the bed, and said, Sister, arise, and let us pray that God would have pity on us.

{8:5} Then began Tobias to say, Blessed art thou, O God of our fathers, and blessed is thy holy and glorious name for ever; let the heavens bless thee, and all thy creatures.

{8:6} Thou madest Adam, and gavest him Eve his wife for an helper and stay: of them came mankind: thou hast said, It is not good that man should be alone; let us make unto him an aid like unto himself.

{8:7} And now, O Lord, I take not this my sister for lust but uprightly: therefore mercifully ordain that we may become aged together.

{8:8} And she said with him, Amen.

{8:9} So they slept both that night. And Raguel arose, and went and made a grave,

{8:10} Saying, I fear lest he also be dead.

{8:11} But when Raguel was come into his house,

{8:12} He said unto his wife Edna. Send one of the maids, and let her see whether he be alive: if he be not, that we may bury him, and no man know it.

{8:13} So the maid opened the door, and went in, and found them both asleep,

{8:14} And came forth, and told them that he was alive.

{8:15} Then Raguel praised God, and said, O God, thou art worthy to be praised with all pure and holy praise; therefore let thy saints praise thee with all thy creatures; and let all thine angels and thine elect praise thee for ever.

{8:16} Thou art to be praised, for thou hast made me joyful; and that is not come to me which I suspected; but thou hast dealt with us according to thy great mercy.

{8:17} Thou art to be praised because thou hast had mercy of two that were the only begotten children of their fathers: grant them mercy, O Lord, and finish their life in health with joy and mercy.

{8:18} Then Raguel bade his servants to fill the grave.

{8:19} And he kept the wedding feast fourteen days.

{8:20} For before the days of the marriage were finished, Raguel had said unto him by an oath, that he should not depart till the fourteen days of the marriage were expired;

{8:21} And then he should take the half of his goods, and go in safety to his father; and should have the rest when I and my wife be dead.

{9:1} Then Tobias called Raphael, and said unto him,

{9:2} Brother Azarias, take with thee a servant, and two camels, and go to Rages of Media to Gabael, and bring me the money, and bring him to the wedding.

{9:3} For Raguel hath sworn that I shall not depart.

{9:4} But my father counteth the days; and if I tarry long, he will be very sorry.

{9:5} So Raphael went out, and lodged with Gabael, and gave him the handwriting: who brought forth bags which were sealed up, and gave them to him.

{9:6} And early in the morning they went forth both together, and came to the wedding: and Tobias blessed his wife.

{10:1} Now Tobit his father counted every day: and when the days of the journey were expired, and they came not,

{10:2} Then Tobit said, are they detained? or is Gabael dead, and there is no man to give him the money?

{10:3} Therefore he was very sorry.

{10:4} Then his wife said unto him, my son is dead, seeing he stayeth long; and she began to wail him, and said,

{10:5} Now I care for nothing, my son, since I have let thee go, the light of mine eyes.

{10:6} To whom Tobit said, hold thy peace, take no care, for he is safe.

{10:7} But she said, hold thy peace, and deceive me not; my son is dead. And she went out every day into the way which they went, and did eat no meat on the daytime, and ceased not whole nights to bewail her son Tobias, until the fourteen days of the wedding were expired, which Raguel had sworn that he should spend there. Then Tobias said to Raguel, Let me go, for my father and my mother look no more to see me.

{10:8} But his father in law said unto him, tarry with me, and I will send to thy father, and they shall declare unto him how things go with thee.

{10:9} But Tobias said, no; but let me go to my father.

{10:10} Then Raguel arose, and gave him Sara his wife, and half his goods, servants, and cattle, and money:

{10:11} And he blessed them, and sent them away, saying, The God of heaven give you a prosperous journey, my children.

{10:12} And he said to his daughter, Honour thy father and thy mother in law, which are now thy parents, that I may hear good report of thee. And he kissed her. Edna also said to Tobias, The Lord of heaven restore thee, my dear brother, and grant that I may see thy children of my daughter Sara before I die, that I may rejoice before the Lord: behold, I commit my daughter unto thee of special trust; where are do not entreat her evil.

{11:1} After these things Tobias went his way, praising God that he had given him a prosperous journey, and blessed Raguel and Edna his wife, and went on his way till they drew near unto Nineve.

{11:2} Then Raphael said to Tobias, Thou knowest, brother, how thou didst leave thy father:

{11:3} Let us haste before thy wife, and prepare the house.

{11:4} And take in thine hand the gall of the fish. So they went their way, and the dog went after them.

{11:5} Now Anna sat looking about toward the way for her son.

{11:6} And when she espied him coming, she said to his father, Behold, thy son cometh, and the man that went with him.

{11:7} Then said Raphael, I know, Tobias, that thy father will open his eyes.

{11:8} Therefore anoint thou his eyes with the gall, and being pricked therewith, he shall rub, and the whiteness shall fall away, and he shall see thee.

{11:9} Then Anna ran forth, and fell upon the neck of her son, and said unto him, Seeing I have seen thee, my son, from henceforth I am content to die. And they wept both.

{11:10} Tobit also went forth toward the door, and stumbled: but his son ran unto him,

{11:11} And took hold of his father: and he strake of the gall on his fathers' eyes, saying, Be of good hope, my father.

{11:12} And when his eyes began to smart, he rubbed them;

{11:13} And the whiteness pilled away from the corners of his eyes: and when he saw his son, he fell upon his neck.

{11:14} And he wept, and said, blessed art thou, O God, and blessed is thy name for ever; and blessed are all thine holy angels:

{11:15} For thou hast scourged, and hast taken pity on me: for, behold, I see my son Tobias. And his son went in rejoicing, and told his father the great things that had happened to him in Media.

{11:16} Then Tobit went out to meet his daughter in law at the gate of Nineve, rejoicing and praising God: and they which saw him go marvelled, because he had received his sight.

{11:17} But Tobias gave thanks before them, because God had mercy on him. And when he came near to Sara his daughter in law, he blessed her, saying, Thou art welcome, daughter: God be blessed, which hath brought thee unto us, and blessed be thy father and thy mother. And there was joy among all his brethren which were at Nineve.

{11:18} And Achiacharus, and Nasbas his brother's son, came:

{11:19} And Tobias' wedding was kept seven days with great joy.

{12:1} Then Tobit called his son Tobias, and said unto him, My son, see that the man have his wages, which went with thee, and thou must give him more.

{12:2} And Tobias said unto him, O father, it is no harm to me to give him half of those things which I have brought:

{12:3} For he hath brought me again to thee in safety, and made whole my wife, and brought me the money, and likewise healed thee.

{12:4} Then the old man said, It is due unto him.

{12:5} So he called the angel, and he said unto him, Take half of all that ye have brought and go away in safety.

{12:6} Then he took them both apart, and said unto them, Bless God, praise him, and magnify him, and praise him for the things which he hath done unto you in the sight of all that live. It is good to praise God, and exalt his name, and honourably to shew forth the works of God; therefore be not slack to praise him.

{12:7} It is good to keep close the secret of a king, but it is honourable to reveal the works of God. Do that which is good, and no evil shall touch you.

{12:8} Prayer is good with fasting and alms and righteousness. A little with righteousness is better than much with unrighteousness. It is better to give alms than to lay up gold:

{12:9} For alms doth deliver from death, and shall purge away all sin. Those that exercise alms and righteousness shall be filled with life:

{12:10} But they that sin are enemies to their own life

{12:11} Surely I will keep close nothing from you. For I said, It was good to keep close the secret of a king, but that it was honourable to reveal the works of God.

{12:12} Now therefore, when thou didst pray, and Sara thy daughter in law, I did bring the remembrance of your prayers before the Holy One: and when thou didst bury the dead, I was with thee likewise.

{12:13} And when thou didst not delay to rise up, and leave thy dinner, to go and cover the dead, thy good deed was not hid from me: but I was with thee.

{12:14} And now God hath sent me to heal thee and Sara thy daughter in law.

{12:15} I am Raphael, one of the seven holy angels, which present the prayers of the saints, and which go in and out before the glory of the Holy One.

{12:16} Then they were both troubled, and fell upon their faces: for they feared.

{12:17} But he said unto them, Fear not, for it shall go well with you; praise God therefore.

{12:18} For not of any favour of mine, but by the will of our God I came; wherefore praise him for ever.

{12:19} All these days I did appear unto you; but I did neither eat nor drink, but ye did see a vision.

{12:20} Now therefore give God thanks: for I go up to him that sent me; but write all things which are done in a book.

{12:21} And when they arose, they saw him no more.

{12:22} Then they confessed the great and wonderful works of God, and how the angel of the Lord had appeared unto them.

{13:1} Then Tobit wrote a prayer of rejoicing, and said, Blessed be God that liveth for ever, and blessed be his kingdom.

{13:2} For he doth scourge, and hath mercy: he leadeth down to hell, and bringeth up again: neither is there any that can avoid his hand.

{13:3} Confess him before the Gentiles, ye children of Israel: for he hath scattered us among them.

{13:4} There declare his greatness, and extol him before all the living: for he is our Lord, and he is the God our Father for ever.

{13:5} And he will scourge us for our iniquities, and will have mercy again, and will gather us out of all nations, among whom he hath scattered us.

{13:6} If ye turn to him with your whole heart, and with your whole mind, and deal uprightly before him, then will he turn unto you, and will not hide his face from you. Therefore see what he will do with you, and confess him with your whole mouth, and praise the Lord of might, and extol the everlasting King. In the land of my captivity do I praise him, and declare his might and majesty to a sinful nation. O ye sinners, turn and do justice before him: who can tell if he will accept you, and have mercy on you?

{13:7} I will extol my God, and my soul shall praise the King of heaven, and shall rejoice in his greatness.

{13:8} Let all men speak, and let all praise him for his righteousness.

{13:9} O Jerusalem, the holy city, he will scourge thee for thy children's works, and will have mercy again on the sons of the righteous.

{13:10} Give praise to the Lord, for he is good: and praise the everlasting King, that his tabernacle may be builded in thee again with joy, and let him make joyful there in thee those that are captives, and love in thee for ever those that are miserable.

{13:11} Many nations shall come from far to the name of the Lord God with gifts in their hands, even gifts to the King of heaven; all generations shall praise thee with great joy.

{13:12} Cursed are all they which hate thee, and blessed shall all be which love thee for ever.

{13:13} Rejoice and be glad for the children of the just: for they shall be gathered together, and shall bless the Lord of the just.

{13:14} O blessed are they which love thee, for they shall rejoice in thy peace: blessed are they which have been sorrowful for all thy scourges; for they shall rejoice for thee, when they have seen all thy glory, and shall be glad for ever.

{13:15} Let my soul bless God the great King.

{13:16} For Jerusalem shall be built up with sapphires and emeralds, and precious stone: thy walls and towers and battlements with pure gold.

{13:17} And the streets of Jerusalem shall be paved with beryl and carbuncle and stones of Ophir.

{13:18} And all her streets shall say, Alleluia; and they shall praise him, saying, blessed be God, which hath extolled it for ever.

{14:1} So Tobit made an end of praising God.

{14:2} And he was eight and fifty years old when he lost his sight, which was restored to him after eight years: and he gave alms, and he increased in the fear of the Lord God, and praised him.

{14:3} And when he was very aged he called his son, and the sons of his son, and said to him, my son, take thy children; for, behold, I am aged, and am ready to depart out of this life.

{14:4} Go into Media my son, for I surely believe those things which Jonas the prophet spake of Nineve, that it shall be overthrown; and that for a time peace shall rather be in Media; and that our brethren shall lie scattered in the earth from that good land: and Jerusalem shall be desolate, and the house of God in it shall be burned, and shall be desolate for a time;

{14:5} And that again God will have mercy on them, and bring them again into the land, where they shall build a temple, but not like to the first, until the time of that age be fulfilled; and afterward they shall return from all places of their captivity, and build up Jerusalem gloriously, and the house of God shall be built in it for ever with a glorious building, as the prophets have spoken thereof.

{14:6} And all nations shall turn, and fear the Lord God truly, and shall bury their idols.

{14:7} So shall all nations praise the Lord, and his people shall confess God, and the Lord shall exalt his people; and all those which love the Lord God in truth and justice shall rejoice, shewing mercy to our brethren.

{14:8} And now, my son, depart out of Nineve, because that those things which the prophet Jonas spake shall surely come to pass.

{14:9} But keep thou the law and the commandments, and shew thyself merciful and just, that it may go well with thee.

{14:10} And bury me decently, and thy mother with me; but tarry no longer at Nineve. Remember, my son, how Aman handled Achiacharus that brought him up, how out of light he brought him into darkness, and how he rewarded him again: yet Achiacharus was saved, but the other had his reward: for he went down into darkness. Manasses gave alms, and escaped
the snares of death which they had set for him: but Aman fell into the snare, and perished.

{14:11} Wherefore now, my son, consider what alms doeth, and how righteousness doth deliver. When he had said these things, he gave up the ghost in the bed, being an hundred and eight and fifty years old; and he buried him honourably.

{14:12} And when Anna his mother was dead, he buried her with his father. But Tobias departed with his wife and children to Ecbatane to Raguel his father in law,

{14:13} Where he became old with honour, and he buried his father and mother in law honourably, and he inherited their substance, and his father Tobit's.

{14:14} And he died at Ecbatane in Media, being an hundred and seven and twenty years old.

{14:15} But before he died he heard of the destruction of Nineve, which was taken by Nabuchodonosor and Assuerus: and before his death he

rejoiced over Nineve.

The Book of Wisdom or The Wisdom of Solomon

{1:1} Love righteousness, ye that be judges of the earth: think of the Lord with a good (heart,) and in simplicity of heart seek him.

{1:2} For he will be found of them that tempt him not; and sheweth himself unto such as do not distrust him.

{1:3} For froward thoughts separate from God: and his power, when it is tried, reproveth the unwise.

{1:4} For into a malicious soul wisdom shall not enter; nor dwell in the body that is subject unto sin.

{1:5} For the holy spirit of discipline will flee deceit, and remove from thoughts that are without understanding, and will not abide when unrighteousness cometh in.

{1:6} For wisdom is a loving spirit; and will not acquit a blasphemer of his words: for God is witness of his reins, and a true beholder of his heart, and a hearer of his tongue.

{1:7} For the Spirit of the Lord filleth the world: and that which containeth all things hath knowledge of the voice.

{1:8} Therefore he that speaketh unrighteous things cannot be hid: neither shall vengeance, when it punisheth, pass by him.

{1:9} For inquisition shall be made into the counsels of the ungodly: and the sound of his words shall come unto the Lord for the manifestation of his wicked deeds.

{1:10} For the ear of jealousy heareth all things: and the noise of murmurings is not hid.

{1:11} Therefore beware of murmuring, which is unprofitable; and refrain your tongue from backbiting: for there is no word so secret, that shall go for nought: and the mouth that belieth slayeth the soul.

{1:12} Seek not death in the error of your life: and pull not upon yourselves destruction with the works of your hands.

{1:13} For God made not death: neither hath he pleasure in the destruction of the living.

{1:14} For he created all things, that they might have their being: and the generations of the world were healthful; and there is no poison of destruction in them, nor the kingdom of death upon the earth:

{1:15} (For righteousness is immortal:)

{1:16} But ungodly men with their works and words called it to them: for when they thought to have it their friend, they consumed to nought, and made a covenant with it, because they are worthy to take part with it.

{2:1} For the ungodly said, reasoning with themselves, but not aright, Our life is short and tedious, and in the death of a man there is no remedy: neither was there any man known to have returned from the grave.

{2:2} For we are born at all adventure: and we shall be hereafter as though we had never been: for the breath in our nostrils is as smoke, and a little spark in the moving of our heart:

{2:3} Which being extinguished, our body shall be turned into ashes, and our spirit shall vanish as the soft air,

{2:4} And our name shall be forgotten in time, and no man shall have our works in remembrance, and our life shall pass away as the trace of a cloud, and shall be dispersed as a mist, that is driven away with the beams of the sun, and overcome with the heat thereof.

{2:5} For our time is a very shadow that passeth away; and after our end there is no returning: for it is fast sealed, so that no man cometh again.

{2:6} Come on therefore, let us enjoy the good things that are present: and let us speedily use the creatures like as in youth.

{2:7} Let us fill ourselves with costly wine and ointments: and let no flower of the spring pass by us:

{2:8} Let us crown ourselves with rosebuds, before they be withered:

{2:9} Let none of us go without his part of our voluptuousness: let us leave tokens of our joyfulness in every place: for this is our portion, and our lot is this.

{2:10} Let us oppress the poor righteous man, let us not spare the widow, nor reverence the ancient gray hairs of the aged.

{2:11} Let our strength be the law of justice: for that which is feeble is found to be nothing worth.

{2:12} Therefore let us lie in wait for the righteous; because he is not for our turn, and he is clean contrary to our doings: he upbraideth us with our offending the law, and objecteth to our infamy the transgressings of our education.

{2:13} He professeth to have the knowledge of God: and he calleth himself the child of the Lord.

{2:14} He was made to reprove our thoughts.

{2:15} He is grievous unto us even to behold: for his life is not like other men's, his ways are of another fashion.

{2:16} We are esteemed of him as counterfeits: he abstaineth from our ways as from filthiness: he pronounceth the end of the just to be blessed, and maketh his boast that God is his father.

{2:17} Let us see if his words be true: and let us prove what shall happen in the end of him.

{2:18} For if the just man be the son of God, he will help him, and deliver him from the hand of his enemies.

{2:19} Let us examine him with despitefulness and torture, that we may know his meekness, and prove his patience.

{2:20} Let us condemn him with a shameful death: for by his own saying he shall be respected.

{2:21} Such things they did imagine, and were deceived: for their own wickedness hath blinded them.

{2:22} As for the mysteries of God, they kn ew them not: neither hoped they for the wages of righteousness, nor discerned a reward for blameless souls.

{2:23} For God created man to be immortal, and made him to be an image of his own eternity.

{2:24} Nevertheless through envy of the devil came death into the world: and they that do hold of his side do find it.

{3:1} But the souls of the righteous are in the hand of God, and there shall no torment touch them.

{3:2} In the sight of the unwise they seemed to die: and their departure is taken for misery,

{3:3} And their going from us to be utter destruction: but they are in peace.

{3:4} For though they be punished in the sight of men, yet is their hope full of immortality.

{3:5} And having been a little chastised, they shall be greatly rewarded: for God proved them, and found them worthy for himself.

{3:6} As gold in the furnace hath he tried them, and received them as a burnt offering.

{3:7} And in the time of their visitation they shall shine, and run to and fro like sparks among the stubble.

{3:8} They shall judge the nations, and have dominion over the people, and their Lord shall reign for ever.

{3:9} They that put their trust in him shall understand the truth: and such as be faithful in love shall abide with him: for grace and mercy is to his saints, and he hath care for his elect.

{3:10} But the ungodly shall be punished according to their own imaginations, which have neglected the righteous, and forsaken the Lord.

{3:11} For whoso despiseth wisdom and nurture, he is miserable, and their hope is vain, their labours unfruitful, and their works unprofitable:

{3.12} Their wives are foolish, and their children wicked:

{3:13} Their offspring is cursed. Wherefore blessed is the barren that is undefiled, which hath not known the sinful bed: she shall have fruit in the visitation of souls.

{3:14} And blessed is the eunuch, which with his hands hath wrought no iniquity, nor imagined wicked things against God: for unto him shall be given the special gift of faith, and an inheritance in the temple of the Lord more acceptable to his mind.

{3:15} For glorious is the fruit of good labours: and the root of wisdom shall never fall away.

{3:16} As for the children of adulterers, they shall not come to their perfection, and the seed of an unrighteous bed shall be rooted out.

{3:17} For though they live long, yet shall they be nothing regarded: and their last age shall be without honour.

{3:18} Or, if they die quickly, they have no hope, neither comfort in the day of trial.

{3:19} For horrible is the end of the unrighteous generation.

{4:1} Better it is to have no children, and to have virtue: for the memorial thereof is immortal: because it is known with God, and with men.

{4:2} When it is present, men take example at it; and when it is gone, they desire it: it weareth a crown, and triumpheth for ever, having gotten the victory, striving for undefiled rewards.

{4:3} But the multiplying brood of the ungodly shall not thrive, nor take deep rooting from bastard slips, nor lay any fast foundation.

{4:4} For though they flourish in branches for a time; yet standing not last, they shall be shaken with the wind, and through the force of winds they shall be rooted out.

{4:5} The imperfect branches shall be broken off, their fruit unprofitable, not ripe to eat, yea, meet for nothing.

{4:6} For children begotten of unlawful beds are witnesses of wickedness against their parents in their trial.

{4:7} But though the righteous be prevented with death, yet shall he be in rest.

{4:8} For honourable age is not that which standeth in length of time, nor that is measured by number of years.

{4:9} But wisdom is the gray hair unto men, and an unspotted life is old age.

{4:10} He pleased God, and was beloved of him: so that living among sinners he was translated.

{4:11} Yea speedily was he taken away, lest that wickedness should alter his understanding, or deceit beguile his soul.

{4:12} For the bewitching of naughtiness doth obscure things that are honest; and the wandering of concupiscence doth undermine the simple mind.

{4:13} He, being made perfect in a short time, fulfilled a long time:

{4:14} For his soul pleased the Lord: therefore hasted he to take him away from among the wicked.

{4:15} This the people saw, and understood it not, neither laid they up this in their minds, That his grace and mercy is with his saints, and that he hath respect unto his chosen.

{4:16} Thus the righteous that is dead shall condemn the ungodly which are living; and youth that is soon perfected the many years and old age of the unrighteous.

{4:17} For they shall see the end of the wise, and shall not understand what God in his counsel hath decreed of him, and to what end the Lord hath set him in safety.

{4:18} They shall see him, and despise him; but God shall laugh them to scorn: and they shall hereafter be a vile carcase, and a reproach among the dead for evermore.

{4:19} For he shall rend them, and cast them down headlong, that they shall be speechless; and he shall shake them from the foundation; and they shall be utterly laid waste, and be in sorrow; and their memorial shall perish.

{4:20} And when they cast up the accounts of their sins, they shall come with fear: and their own iniquities shall convince them to their face.

{5:1} Then shall the righteous man stand in great boldness before the face of such as have afflicted him, and made no account of his labours.

{5:2} When they see it, they shall be troubled with terrible fear, and shall be amazed at the strangeness of his salvation, so far beyond all that they looked for.

{5:3} And they repenting and groaning for anguish of spirit shall say within themselves, This was he, whom we had sometimes in derision, and a proverb of reproach:

{5:4} We fools accounted his life madness, and his end to be without honour:

{5:5} How is he numbered among the children of God, and his lot is among the saints!

{5:6} Therefore have we erred from the way of truth, and the light of righteousness hath not shined unto us, and the sun of righteousness rose not upon us.

{5:7} We wearied ourselves in the way of wickedness and destruction: yea, we have gone through deserts, where there lay no way: but as for the way of the Lord, we have not known it.

{5:8} What hath pride profited us? or what good hath riches with our vaunting brought us?

{5:9} All those things are passed away like a shadow, and as a post that hasted by;

{5:10} And as a ship that passeth over the waves of the water, which when it is gone by, the trace thereof cannot be found, neither the pathway of the keel in the waves;

{5:11} Or as when a bird hath flown through the air, there is no token of her way to be found, but the light air being beaten with the stroke of her wings and parted with the violent noise and motion of them, is passed through, and therein afterwards no sign where she went is to be found;

{5:12} Or like as when an arrow is shot at a mark, it parteth the air, which immediately cometh together again, so that a man cannot know where it went through:

{5:13} Even so we in like manner, as soon as we were born, began to draw to our end, and had no sign of virtue to shew; but were consumed in our own wickedness.

{5:14} For the hope of the Godly is like dust that is blown away with the wind; like a thin froth that is driven away with the storm; like as the smoke which is dispersed here and there with a tempest, and passeth away as the remembrance of a guest that tarrieth but a day.

{5:15} But the righteous live for evermore; their reward also is with the Lord, and the care of them is with the most High.

{5:16} Therefore shall they receive a glorious kingdom, and a beautiful crown from the Lord's hand: for with his right hand shall he cover them, and with his arm shall he protect them.

{5:17} He shall take to him his jealousy for complete armour, and make the creature his weapon for the revenge of his enemies.

{5:18} He shall put on righteousness as a breastplate, and true judgment instead of an helmet.

{5:19} He shall take holiness for an invincible shield.

{5:20} His severe wrath shall he sharpen for a sword, and the world shall fight with him against the unwise.

{5:21} Then shall the right aiming thunderbolts go abroad; and from the clouds, as from a well drawn bow, shall they fly to the mark.

{5:22} And hailstones full of wrath shall be cast as out of a stone bow, and the water of the sea shall rage against them, and the floods shall cruelly drown them.

{5:23} Yea, a mighty wind shall stand up against them, and like a storm shall blow them away: thus iniquity shall lay waste the whole earth, and ill dealing shall overthrow the thrones of the mighty.

{6:1} Hear therefore, O ye kings, and understand; learn, ye that be judges of the ends of the earth.

{6:2} Give ear, ye that rule the people, and glory in the multitude of nations.

{6:3} For power is given you of the Lord, and sovereignty from the Highest, who shall try your works, and search out your counsels.

{6:4} Because, being ministers of his kingdom, ye have not judged aright, nor kept the law, nor walked after the counsel of God;

{6:5} Horribly and speedily shall he come upon you: for a sharp judgment shall be to them that be in high places.

{6:6} For mercy will soon pardon the meanest: but mighty men shall be mightily tormented.

{6:7} For he which is Lord over all shall fear no man's person, neither shall he stand in awe of any man's greatness: for he hath made the small and great, and careth for all alike.

{6:8} But a sore trial shall come upon the mighty.

{6:9} Unto you therefore, O kings, do I speak, that ye may learn wisdom, and not fall away.

{6:10} For they that keep holiness holily shall be judged holy: and they that have learned such things shall find what to answer.

{6:11} Wherefore set your affection upon my words; desire them, and ye shall be instructed.

{6:12} Wisdom is glorious, and never fadeth away: yea, she is easily seen of them that love her, and found of such as seek her.

{6:13} She preventeth them that desire her, in making herself first known unto them.

{6:14} Whoso seeketh her early shall have no great travail: for he shall find her sitting at his doors.

{6:15} To think therefore upon her is perfection of wisdom: and whoso watcheth for her shall quickly be without care.

{6:16} For she goeth about seeking such as are worthy of her, sheweth herself favourably unto them in the ways, and meeteth them in every thought.

{6:17} For the very true beginning of her is the desire of discipline; and the care of discipline is love;

{6:18} And love is the keeping of her laws; and the giving heed unto her laws is the assurance of incorruption;

{6:19} And incorruption maketh us near unto God:

{6:20} Therefore the desire of wisdom bringeth to a kingdom.

{6:21} If your delight be then in thrones and sceptres, O ye kings of the people, honour wisdom, that ye may reign for evermore.

{6:22} As for wisdom, what she is, and how she came up, I will tell you, and will not hide mysteries from you: but will seek her out from the beginning of her nativity, and bring the knowledge of her into light, and will not pass over the truth.

{6:23} Neither will I go with consuming envy; for such a man shall have no fellowship with wisdom.

{6:24} But the multitude of the wise is the welfare of the world: and a wise king is the upholding of the people.

{6:25} Receive therefore instruction through my words, and it shall do you good.

{7:1} I myself also am a mortal man, like to all, and the offspring of him that was first made of the earth,

{7:2} And in my mother's womb was fashioned to be flesh in the time of ten months, being compacted in blood, of the seed of man, and the pleasure that came with sleep.

{7:3} And when I was born, I drew in the common air, and fell upon the earth, which is of like nature, and the first voice which I uttered was crying, as all others do.

{7:4} I was nursed in swaddling clothes, and that with cares.

{7:5} For there is no king that had any other beginning of birth.

{7:6} For all men have one entrance into life, and the like going out.

{7:7} Wherefore I prayed, and understanding was given me: I called upon God, and the spirit of wisdom came to me.

{7:8} I preferred her before sceptres and thrones, and esteemed riches nothing in comparison of her.

{7:9} Neither compared I unto her any precious stone, because all gold in respect of her is as a little sand, and silver shall be counted as clay before her.

{7:10} I loved her above health and beauty, and chose to have her instead of light: for the light that cometh from her never goeth out.

{7:11} All good things together came to me with her, and innumerable riches in her hands.

{7:12} And I rejoiced in them all, because wisdom goeth before them: and I knew not that she was the mother of them.

{7:13} I learned diligently, and do communicate her liberally: I do not hide her riches.

{7:14} For she is a treasure unto men that never faileth: which they that use become the friends of God, being commended for the gifts that come from learning.

{7:15} God hath granted me to speak as I would, and to conceive as is meet for the things that are given me: because it is he that leadeth unto wisdom, and directeth the wise.

{7:16} For in his hand are both we and our words; all wisdom also, and knowledge of workmanship.

{7:17} For he hath given me certain knowledge of the things that are, namely, to know how the world was made, and the operation of the elements:

{7:18} The beginning, ending, and midst of the times: the alterations of the turning of the sun, and the change of seasons:

{7:19} The circuits of years, and the positions of stars:

{7:20} The natures of living creatures, and the furies of wild beasts: the violence of winds, and the reasonings of men: the diversities of plants and the virtues of roots:

{7:21} And all such things as are either secret or manifest, them I know.

{7:22} For wisdom, which is the worker of all things, taught me: for in her is an understanding spirit holy, one only, manifold, subtil, lively, clear, undefiled, plain, not subject to hurt, loving the thing that is good quick, which cannot be letted, ready to do good,

{7:23} Kind to man, steadfast, sure, free from care, having all power, overseeing all things, and going through all understanding, pure, and most subtil, spirits.

{7:24} For wisdom is more moving than any motion: she passeth and goeth through all things by reason of her pureness.

{7:25} For she is the breath of the power of God, and a pure influence flowing from the glory of the Almighty: therefore can no defiled thing fall into her.

{7:26} For she is the brightness of the everlasting light, the unspotted mirror of the power of God, and the image of his goodness.

{7:27} And being but one, she can do all things: and remaining in herself, she maketh all things new: and in all ages entering into holy souls, she maketh them friends of God, and prophets.

{7:28} For God loveth none but him that dwelleth with wisdom.

{7:29} For she is more beautiful than the sun, and above all the order of stars: being compared with the light, she is found before it.

{7:30} For after this cometh night: but vice shall not prevail against wisdom.

{8:1} Wisdom reacheth from one end to another mightily: and sweetly doth she order all things.

{8:2} I loved her, and sought her out from my youth, I desired to make her my spouse, and I was a lover of her beauty.

{8:3} In that she is conversant with God, she magnifieth her nobility: yea, the Lord of all things himself loved her.

{8:4} For she is privy to the mysteries of the knowledge of God, and a lover of his works.

{8:5} If riches be a possession to be desired in this life; what is richer than wisdom, that worketh all things?

{8:6} And if prudence work; who of all that are is a more cunning workman than she?

{8:7} And if a man love righteousness her labours are virtues: for she teacheth temperance and prudence, justice and fortitude: which are such things, as en can have nothing more profitable in their life.

{8:8} If a man desire much experience, she knoweth things of old, and conjectureth aright what is to come: she knoweth the subtilties of speeches, and can expound dark sentences: she foreseeth signs and wonders, and the events of seasons and times.

{8:9} Therefore I purposed to take her to me to live with me, knowing that she would be a counsellor of good things, and a comfort in cares and grief.

{8:10} For her sake I shall have estimation among the multitude, and honour with the elders, though I be young.

{8:11} I shall be found of a quick conceit in judgment, and shall be admired in the sight of great men.

{8:12} When I hold my tongue, they shall bide my leisure, and when I speak, they shall give good ear unto me: if I talk much, they shall lay their hands upon their mouth.

{8:13} Moreover by the means of her I shall obtain immortality, and leave behind me an everlasting memorial to them that come after me.

{8:14} I shall set the people in order, and the nations shall be subject unto me.

{8:15} Horrible tyrants shall be afraid, when they do but hear of me; I shall be found good among the multitude, and valiant in war.

{8:16} After I am come into mine house, I will repose myself with her: for her conversation hath no bitterness; and to live with her hath no sorrow, but mirth and joy.

{8:17} Now when I considered these things in myself, and pondered them in my heart, how that to be allied unto wisdom is immortality;

{8:18} And great pleasure it is to have her friendship; and in the works of her hands are infinite riches; and in the exercise of conference with her, prudence; and in talking with her, a good report; I went about seeking how to take her to me.

{8:19} For I was a witty child, and had a good spirit.

{8:20} Yea rather, being good, I came into a body undefiled.

{8:21} Nevertheless, when I perceived that I could not otherwise obtain her, except God gave her me; and that was a point of wisdom also to know whose gift she was; I prayed unto the Lord, and besought him, and with my whole heart I said,

{9:1} O God of my fathers, and Lord of mercy, who hast made all things with thy word,

{9:2} And ordained man through thy wisdom, that he should have dominion over the creatures which thou hast made,

{9:3} And order the world according to equity and righteousness, and execute judgment with an upright heart:

{9:4} Give me wisdom, that sitteth by thy throne; and reject me not from among thy children:

{9:5} For I thy servant and son of thine handmaid am a feeble person, and of a short time, and too young for the understanding of judgment and laws.

{9:6} For though a man be never so perfect among the children of men, yet if thy wisdom be not with him, he shall be nothing regarded.

{9:7} Thou hast chosen me to be a king of thy people, and a judge of thy sons and daughters:

{9:8} Thou hast commanded me to build a temple upon thy holy mount, and an altar in the city wherein thou dwellest, a resemblance of the holy tabernacle, which thou hast prepared from the beginning.

{9:9} And wisdom was with thee: which knoweth thy works, and was present when thou madest the world, and knew what was acceptable in thy sight, and right in thy commandments.

{9:10} O send her out of thy holy heavens, and from the throne of thy glory, that being present she may labour with me, that I may know what is pleasing unto thee.

{9:11} For she knoweth and understandeth all things, and she shall lead me soberly in my doings, and preserve me in her power.

{9:12} So shall my works be acceptable, and then shall I judge thy people righteously, and be worthy to sit in my father's seat.

{9:13} For what man is he that can know the counsel of God? or who can think what the will of the Lord is?

{9:14} For the thoughts of mortal men are miserable, and our devices are but uncertain.

{9:15} For the corruptible body presseth down the soul, and the earthy tabernacle weigheth down the mind that museth upon many things.

{9:16} And hardly do we guess aright at things that are upon earth, and with labour do we find the things that are before us: but the things that are in heaven who hath searched out?

{9:17} And thy counsel who hath known, except thou give wisdom, and send thy Holy Spirit from above?

{9:18} For so the ways of them which lived on the earth were reformed, and men were taught the things that are pleasing unto thee, and were saved through wisdom.

{10:1} She preserved the first formed father of the world, that was created alone, and brought him out of his fall,

{10:2} And gave him power to rule all things.

{10:3} But when the unrighteous went away from her in his anger, he perished also in the fury wherewith he murdered his brother.

{10:4} For whose cause the earth being drowned with the flood, wisdom again preserved it, and directed the course of the righteous in a piece of wood of small value.

{10:5} Moreover, the nations in their wicked conspiracy being confounded, she found out the righteous, and preserved him blameless unto God, and kept him strong against his tender compassion toward his son.

{10:6} When the ungodly perished, she delivered the righteous man, who fled from the fire which fell down upon the five cities.

{10:7} Of whose wickedness even to this day the waste land that smoketh is a testimony, and plants bearing fruit that never come to ripeness: and a standing pillar of salt is a monument of an unbelieving soul.

{10:8} For regarding not wisdom, they gat not only this hurt, that they knew not the things which were good; but also left behind them to the world a memorial of their foolishness: so that in the things wherein they offended they could not so much as be hid.

{10:9} But wisdom delivered from pain those that attended upon her.

{10:10} When the righteous fled from his brother's wrath she guided him in right paths, shewed him the kingdom of God, and gave him knowledge of holy things, made him rich in his travels, and multiplied the fruit of his labours.

{10:11} In the covetousness of such as oppressed him she stood by him, and made him rich.

{10:12} She defended him from his enemies, and kept him safe from those that lay in wait, and in a sore conflict she gave him the victory; that he might know that goodness is stronger than all.

{10:13} When the righteous was sold, she forsook him not, but delivered him from sin: she went down with him into the pit,

{10:14} And left him not in bonds, till she brought him the sceptre of the kingdom, and power against those that oppressed him: as for them that had accused him, she shewed them to be liars, and gave him perpetual glory.

{10:15} She delivered the righteous people and blameless seed from the nation that oppressed them.

{10:16} She entered into the soul of the servant of the Lord, and withstood dreadful kings in wonders and signs;

{10:17} Rendered to the righteous a reward of their labours, guided them in a marvellous way, and was unto them for a cover by day, and a light of stars in the night season;

{10:18} Brought them through the Red sea, and led them through much water:

{10:19} But she drowned their enemies, and cast them up out of the bottom of the deep.

{10:20} Therefore the righteous spoiled the ungodly, and praised thy holy name, O Lord, and magnified with one accord thine hand, that fought for them.

{10:21} For wisdom opened the mouth of the dumb, and made the tongues of them that cannot speak eloquent.

{11:1} She prospered their works in the hand of the holy prophet.

{11:2} They went through the wilderness that was not inhabited, and pitched tents in places where there lay no way.

{11:3} They stood against their enemies, and were avenged of their adversaries.

{11:4} When they were thirsty, they called upon thee, and water was given them out of the flinty rock, and their thirst was quenched out of the hard stone.

{11:5} For by what things their enemies were punished, by the same they in their need were benefited.

{11:6} For instead of a perpetual running river troubled with foul blood,

{11:7} For a manifest reproof of that commandment, whereby the infants were slain, thou gavest unto them abundance of water by a means which they hoped not for:

{11:8} Declaring by that thirst then how thou hadst punished their adversaries.

{11:9} For when they were tried albeit but in mercy chastised, they knew how the ungodly were judged in wrath and tormented, thirsting in another manner than the just.

{11:10} For these thou didst admonish and try, as a father: but the other, as a severe king, thou didst condemn and punish.

{11:11} Whether they were absent or present, they were vexed alike.

{11:12} For a double grief came upon them, and a groaning for the remembrance of things past.

{11:13} For when they heard by their own punishments the other to be benefited, they had some feeling of the Lord.

{11:14} For whom they respected with scorn, when he was long before thrown out at the casting forth of the infants, him in the end, when they saw what came to pass, they admired.

{11:15} But for the foolish devices of their wickedness, wherewith being deceived they worshipped serpents void of reason, and vile beasts, thou didst send a multitude of unreasonable beasts upon them for vengeance;

{11:16} That they might know, that wherewithal a man sinneth, by the same also shall he be punished.

{11:17} For thy Almighty hand, that made the world of matter without form, wanted not means to send among them a multitude of bears or fierce lions,

{11:18} Or unknown wild beasts, full of rage, newly created, breathing out either a fiery vapour, or filthy scents of scattered smoke, or shooting horrible sparkles out of their eyes:

{11:19} Whereof not only the harm might dispatch them at once, but also the terrible sight utterly destroy them.

{11:20} Yea, and without these might they have fallen down with one blast, being persecuted of vengeance, and scattered abroad through the breath of thy power: but thou hast ordered all things in measure and number and weight.

{11:21} For thou canst shew thy great strength at all times when thou wilt; and who may withstand the power of thine arm?

{11:22} For the whole world before thee is as a little grain of the balance, yea, as a drop of the morning dew that falleth down upon the earth.

{11:23} But thou hast mercy upon all; for thou canst do all things, and winkest at the sins of men, because they should amend.

{11:24} For thou lovest all the things that are, and abhorrest nothing which thou hast made: for never wouldest thou have made any thing, if thou hadst hated it.

{11:25} And how could any thing have endured, if it had not been thy will? or been preserved, if not called by thee?

{11:26} But thou sparest all: for they are thine, O Lord, thou lover of souls.

{12:1} For thine incorruptible Spirit is in all things.

{12:2} Therefore chastenest thou them by little and little that offend, and warnest them by putting them in remembrance wherein they have offended, that leaving their wickedness they may believe on thee,

O Lord.

{12:3} For it was thy will to destroy by the hands of our fathers both those old inhabitants of thy holy land,

{12:4} Whom thou hatedst for doing most odious works of witchcrafts, and wicked sacrifices;

{12:5} And also those merciless murderers of children, and devourers of man's flesh, and the feasts of blood,

{12:6} With their priests out of the midst of their idolatrous crew, and the parents, that killed with their own hands souls destitute of help:

{12:7} That the land, which thou esteemedst above all other, might receive a worthy colony of God's children.

{12:8} Nevertheless even those thou sparedst as men, and didst send wasps, forerunners of thine host, to destroy them by little and little.

{12:9} Not that thou wast unable to bring the ungodly under the hand of the righteous in battle, or to destroy them at once with cruel beasts, or with one rough word:

{12:10} But executing thy judgments upon them by little and little, thou gavest them place of repentance, not being ignorant that they were a naughty generation, and that their malice was bred in them, and that their cogitation would never be changed.

{12:11} For it was a cursed seed from the beginning; neither didst thou for fear of any man give them pardon for those things wherein they sinned.

{12:12} For who shall say, what hast thou done? or who shall withstand thy judgment? or who shall accuse thee for the nations that perish, whom thou made? or who shall come to stand against thee, to be revenged for the unrighteous men?

{12:13} For neither is there any God but thou that careth for all, to whom thou mightest shew that thy judgment is not unright.

{12:14} Neither shall king or tyrant be able to set his face against thee for any whom thou hast punished.

{12:15} Forsomuch then as thou art righteous thyself, thou orderest all things righteously: thinking it not agreeable with thy power to condemn him that hath not deserved to be punished.

{12:16} For thy power is the beginning of righteousness, and because thou art the Lord of all, it maketh thee to be gracious unto all.

{12:17} For when men will not believe that thou art of a full power, thou shewest thy strength, and among them that know it thou makest their boldness manifest.

{12:18} But thou, mastering thy power, judgest with equity, and orderest us with great favour: for thou mayest use power when thou wilt.

{12:19} But by such works hast thou taught thy people that the just man should be merciful, and hast made thy children to be of a good hope that thou givest repentance for sins.

{12:20} For if thou didst punish the enemies of thy children, and the condemned to death, with such deliberation, giving them time and place, whereby they might be delivered from their malice:

{12:21} With how great circumspection didst thou judge thine own sons, unto whose fathers thou hast sworn, and made covenants of good promises?

{12:22} Therefore, whereas thou dost chasten us, thou scourgest our enemies a thousand times more, to the intent that, when we judge, we should carefully think of thy goodness, and when we ourselves are judged, we should look for mercy.

{12:23} Wherefore, whereas men have lived dissolutely and unrighteously, thou hast tormented them with their own abominations.

{12:24} For they went astray very far in the ways of error, and held them for gods, which even among the beasts of their enemies were despised, being deceived, as children of no understanding.

{12:25} Therefore unto them, as to children without the use of reason, thou didst send a judgment to mock them.

{12:26} But they that would not be reformed by that correction, wherein he dallied with them, shall feel a judgment worthy of God.

{12:27} For, look, for what things they grudged, when they were punished, that is, for them whom they thought to be gods; [now] being punished in them, when they saw it, they acknowledged him to be the true God, whom before they denied to know: and therefore came extreme damnation upon them.

{13:1} Surely vain are all men by nature, who are ignorant of God, and could not out of the good things that are seen know him that is: neither by considering the works did they acknowledge the workmaster;

{13:2} But deemed either fire, or wind, or the swift air, or the circle of the stars, or the violent water, or the lights of heaven, to be the gods which govern the world.

{13:3} With whose beauty if they being delighted took them to be gods; let them know how much better the Lord of them is: for the first author of beauty hath created them.

{13:4} But if they were astonished at their power and virtue, let them understand by them, how much mightier he is that made them.

{13:5} For by the greatness and beauty of the creatures proportionably the maker of them is seen.

{13:6} But yet for this they are the less to be blamed: for they peradventure err, seeking God, and desirous to find him.

{13:7} For being conversant in his works they search him diligently, and believe their sight: because the things are beautiful that are seen.

{13:8} Howbeit neither are they to be pardoned.

{13:9} For if they were able to know so much, that they could aim at the world; how did they not sooner find out the Lord thereof?

{13:10} But miserable are they, and in dead things is their hope, who call them gods, which are the works of men's hands, gold and silver, to shew art in, and resemblances of beasts, or a stone good for nothing, the work of an ancient hand.

{13:11} Now a carpenter that felleth timber, after he hath sawn down a tree meet for the purpose, and taken off all the bark skilfully round about, and hath wrought it handsomely, and made a vessel thereof fit for the service of man's life;

{13:12} And after spending the refuse of his work to dress his meat, hath filled himself;

{13:13} And taking the very refuse among those which served to no use, being a crooked piece of wood, and full of knots, hath carved it diligently, when he had nothing else to do, and formed it by the skill of his understanding, and fashioned it to the image of a man;

{13:14} Or made it like some vile beast, laying it over with vermilion, and with paint colouring it red, and covering every spot therein;

{13:15} And when he had made a convenient room for it, set it in a wall, and made it fast with iron:

{13:16} For he provided for it that it might not fall, knowing that it was unable to help itself; for it is an image, and hath need of help:

{13:17} Then maketh he prayer for his goods, for his wife and children, and is not ashamed to speak to that which hath no life.

{13:18} For health he calleth upon that which is weak: for life prayeth to that which is dead; for aid humbly beseecheth that which hath least means to help: and for a good journey he asketh of that which cannot set a foot forward:

{13:19} And for gaining and getting, and for good success of his hands, asketh ability to do of him, that is most unable to do any thing.

{14:1} Again, one preparing himself to sail, and about to pass through the raging waves, calleth upon a piece of wood more rotten than the vessel that carrieth him.

{14:2} For verily desire of gain devised that, and the workman built it by his skill.

{14:3} But thy providence, O Father, governeth it: for thou hast made a way in the sea, and a safe path in the waves;

{14:4} Shewing that thou canst save from all danger: yea, though a man went to sea without art.

{14:5} Nevertheless thou wouldest not that the works of thy wisdom should be idle, and therefore do men commit their lives to a small piece of wood, and passing the rough sea in a weak vessel are saved.

{14:6} For in the old time also, when the proud giants perished, the hope of the world governed by thy hand escaped in a weak vessel, and left to all ages a seed of generation.

{14:7} For blessed is the wood whereby righteousness cometh.

{14:8} But that which is made with hands is cursed, as well it, as he that made it: he, because he made it; and it, because, being corruptible, it was called god.

{14:9} For the ungodly and his ungodliness are both alike hateful unto God.

{14:10} For that which is made shall be punished together with him that made it.

{14:11} Therefore even upon the idols of the Gentiles shall there be a visitation: because in the creature of God they are become an abomination, and stumblingblocks to the souls of men, and a snare to the feet of the unwise.

{14:12} For the devising of idols was the beginning of spiritual fornication, and the invention of them the corruption of life.

{14:13} For neither were they from the beginning, neither shall they be for ever.

{14:14} For by the vain glory of men they entered into the world, and therefore shall they come shortly to an end.

{14:15} For a father afflicted with untimely mourning, when he hath made an image of his child soon taken away, now honoured him as a god, which was then a dead man, and delivered to those that were under him ceremonies and sacrifices.

{14:16} Thus in process of time an ungodly custom grown strong was kept as a law, and graven images were worshipped by the commandments of
kings.

{14:17} Whom men could not honour in presence, because they dwelt far off, they took the counterfeit of his visage from far, and made an express image of a king whom they honoured, to the end that by this their forwardness they might flatter him that was absent, as if he were present.

{14:18} Also the singular diligence of the artificer did help to set forward the ignorant to more superstition.

{14:19} For he, peradventure willing to please one in authority, forced all his skill to make the resemblance of the best fashion.

{14:20} And so the multitude, allured by the grace of the work, took him now for a god, which a little before was but honoured.

{14:21} And this was an occasion to deceive the world: for men, serving either calamity or tyranny, did ascribe unto stones and stocks the incommunicable name.

{14:22} Moreover this was not enough for them, that they erred in the knowledge of God; but whereas they lived in the great war of ignorance, those so great plagues called they peace.

{14:23} For whilst they slew their children in sacrifices, or used secret ceremonies, or made revellings of strange rites;

{14:24} They kept neither lives nor marriages any longer undefiled: but either one slew another traiterously, or grieved him by adultery.

{14:25} So that there reigned in all men without exception blood, manslaughter, theft, and dissimulation, corruption, unfaithfulness, tumults, perjury,

{14:26} Disquieting of good men, forgetfulness of good turns, defiling of souls, changing of kind, disorder in marriages, adultery, and shameless uncleanness.

{14:27} For the worshipping of idols not to be named is the beginning, the cause, and the end, of all evil.

{14:28} For either they are mad when they be merry, or prophesy lies, or live unjustly, or else lightly forswear themselves.

{14:29} For insomuch as their trust is in idols, which have no life; though they swear falsely, yet they look not to be hurt.

{14:30} Howbeit for both causes shall they be justly punished: both because they thought not well of God, giving heed unto idols, and also unjustly swore in deceit, despising holiness.

{14:31} For it is not the power of them by whom they swear: but it is the just vengeance of sinners, that punisheth always the offence of the ungodly.

{15:1} But thou, O God, art gracious and true, longsuffering, and in mercy ordering all things,

{15:2} For if we sin, we are thine, knowing thy power: but we will not sin, knowing that we are counted thine.

{15:3} For to know thee is perfect righteousness: yea, to know thy power is the root of immortality.

{15:4} For neither did the mischievous invention of men deceive us, nor an image spotted with divers colours, the painter's fruitless labour;

{15:5} The sight whereof enticeth fools to lust after it, and so they desire the form of a dead image, that hath no breath.

{15:6} Both they that make them, they that desire them, and they that worship them, are lovers of evil things, and are worthy to have such things to trust upon.

{15:7} For the potter, tempering soft earth, fashioneth every vessel with much labour for our service: yea, of the same clay he maketh both the vessels that serve for clean uses, and likewise also all such as serve to the contrary: but what is the use of either sort, the potter himself is the judge.

{15:8} And employing his labours lewdly, he maketh a vain god of the same clay, even he which a little before was made of earth himself, and within a little while after returneth to the same, out when his life which was lent him shall be demanded.

{15:9} Notwithstanding his care is, not that he shall have much labour, nor that his life is short: but striveth to excel goldsmiths and silversmiths, and endeavoureth to do like the workers in brass, and counteth it his glory to make counterfeit things.

{15:10} His heart is ashes, his hope is more vile than earth, and his life of less value than clay:

{15:11} Forasmuch as he knew not his Maker, and him that inspired into him an active soul, and breathed in a living spirit.

{15:12} But they counted our life a pastime, and our time here a market for gain: for, say they, we must be getting every way, though it be by evil means.

{15:13} For this man, that of earthly matter maketh brittle vessels and graven images, knoweth himself to offend above all others.

{15:14} And all the enemies of thy people, that hold them in subjection, are most foolish, and are more miserable than very babes.

{15:15} For they counted all the idols of the heathen to be gods: which neither have the use of eyes to see, nor noses to draw breath, nor ears to hear, nor fingers of hands to handle; and as for their feet, they are slow to go.

{15:16} For man made them, and he that borrowed his own spirit fashioned them: but no man can make a god like unto himself.

{15:17} For being mortal, he worketh a dead thing with wicked hands: for he himself is better than the things which he worshippeth: whereas he lived once, but they never.

{15:18} Yea, they worshipped those beasts also that are most hateful: for being compared together, some are worse than others.

{15:19} Neither are they beautiful, so much as to be desired in respect of beasts: but they went without the praise of God and his blessing.

{16:1} Therefore by the like were they punished worthily, and by the multitude of beasts tormented.

{16:2} Instead of which punishment, dealing graciously with thine own people, thou preparedst for them meat of a strange taste, even quails to stir up their appetite:

{16:3} To the end that they, desiring food, might for the ugly sight of the beasts sent among them lothe even that, which they must needs desire; but these, suffering penury for a short space, might be made partakers of a strange taste.

{16:4} For it was requisite, that upon them exercising tyranny should come penury, which they could not avoid: but to these it should only be shewed how their enemies were tormented.

{16:5} For when the horrible fierceness of beasts came upon these, and they perished with the stings of crooked serpents, thy wrath endured not for ever:

{16:6} But they were troubled for a small season, that they might be admonished, having a sign of salvation, to put them in remembrance of the commandment of thy law.

{16:7} For he that turned himself toward it was not saved by the thing that he saw, but by thee, that art the Saviour of all.

{16:8} And in this thou madest thine enemies confess, that it is thou who deliverest from all evil:

{16:9} For them the bitings of grasshoppers and flies killed, neither was there found any remedy for their life: for they were worthy to be punished by such.

{16:10} But thy sons not the very teeth of venomous dragons overcame: for thy mercy was ever by them, and healed them.

{16:11} For they were pricked, that they should remember thy words; and were quickly saved, that not falling into deep forgetfulness, they might be continually mindful of thy goodness.

{16:12} For it was neither herb, nor mollifying plaister, that restored them to health: but thy word, O Lord, which healeth all things.

{16:13} For thou hast power of life and death: thou leadest to the gates of hell, and bringest up again.

{16:14} A man indeed killeth through his malice: and the spirit, when it is gone forth, returneth not; neither the soul received up cometh again.

{16:15} But it is not possible to escape thine hand.

{16:16} For the ungodly, that denied to know thee, were scourged by the strength of thine arm: with strange rains, hails, and showers, were they persecuted, that they could not avoid, and through fire were they consumed.

{16:17} For, which is most to be wondered at, the fire had more force in the water, that quencheth all things: for the world fighteth for the righteous.

{16:18} For sometime the flame was mitigated, that it might not burn up the beasts that were sent against the ungodly; but themselves might see and perceive that they were persecuted with the judgment of God.

{16:19} And at another time it burneth even in the midst of water above the power of fire, that it might destroy the fruits of an unjust land.

{16:20} Instead whereof thou feddest thine own people with angels' food, and didst send them from heaven bread prepared without their labour, able to content every man's delight, and agreeing to every taste.

{16:21} For thy sustenance declared thy sweetness unto thy children, and serving to the appetite of the eater, tempered itself to every man's liking.

{16:22} But snow and ice endured the fire, and melted not, that they might know that fire burning in the hail, and sparkling in the rain, did destroy the fruits of the enemies.

{16:23} But this again did even forget his own strength, that the righteous might be nourished.

{16:24} For the creature that serveth thee, who art the Maker increaseth his strength against the unrighteous for their punishment, and abateth his strength for the benefit of such as put their trust in thee.

{16:25} Therefore even then was it altered into all fashions, and was obedient to thy grace, that nourisheth all things, according to the desire of them that had need:

{16:26} That thy children, O Lord, whom thou lovest, might know, that it is not the growing of fruits that nourisheth man: but that it is thy word, which preserveth them that put their trust in thee.

{16:27} For that which was not destroyed of the fire, being warmed with a little sunbeam, soon melted away:

{16:28} That it might be known, that we must prevent the sun to give thee thanks, and at the dayspring pray unto thee.

{16:29} For the hope of the unthankful shall melt away as the winter's hoar frost, and shall run away as unprofitable water.

{17:1} For great are thy judgments, and cannot be expressed: therefore unnurtured souls have erred.

{17:2} For when unrighteous men thought to oppress the holy nation; they being shut up in their houses, the prisoners of darkness, and fettered with the bonds of a long night, lay [there] exiled from the eternal providence.

{17:3} For while they supposed to lie hid in their secret sins, they were scattered under a dark veil of forgetfulness, being horribly astonished, and troubled with [strange] apparitions.

{17:4} For neither might the corner that held them keep them from fear: but noises [as of waters] falling down sounded about them, and sad visions appeared unto them with heavy countenances.

{17:5} No power of the fire might give them light: neither could the bright flames of the stars endure to lighten that horrible night.

{17:6} Only there appeared unto them a fire kindled of itself, very dreadful: for being much terrified, they thought the things which they saw to be worse than the sight they saw not.

{17:7} As for the illusions of art magick, they were put down, and their vaunting in wisdom was reproved with disgrace.

{17:8} For they, that promised to drive away terrors and troubles from a sick soul, were sick themselves of fear, worthy to be laughed at.

{17:9} For though no terrible thing did fear them; yet being scared with beasts that passed by, and hissing of serpents,

{17:10} They died for fear, denying that they saw the air, which could of no side be avoided.

{17:11} For wickedness, condemned by her own witness, is very timorous, and being pressed with conscience, always forecasteth grievous things.

{17:12} For fear is nothing else but a betraying of the succours which reason offereth.

{17:13} And the expectation from within, being less, counteth the ignorance more than the cause which bringeth the torment.

{17:14} But they sleeping the same sleep that night, which was indeed intolerable, and which came upon them out of the bottoms of inevitable hell,

{17:15} Were partly vexed with monstrous apparitions, and partly fainted, their heart failing them: for a sudden fear, and not looked for, came upon them.

{17:16} So then whosoever there fell down was straitly kept, shut up in a prison without iron bars,

{17:17} For whether he were husbandman, or shepherd, or a labourer in the field, he was overtaken, and endured that necessity, which could not be avoided: for they were all bound with one chain of darkness.

{17:18} Whether it were a whistling wind, or a melodious noise of birds among the spreading branches, or a pleasing fall of water running violently,

{17:19} Or a terrible sound of stones cast down, or a running that could not be seen of skipping beasts, or a roaring voice of most savage wild beasts, or a rebounding echo from the hollow mountains; these things made them to swoon for fear.

{17:20} For the whole world shined with clear light, and none were hindered in their labour:

{17:21} Over them only was spread an heavy night, an image of that darkness which should afterward receive them: but yet were they unto themselves more grievous than the darkness.

{18:1} Nevertheless thy saints had a very great light, whose voice they hearing, and not seeing their shape, because they also had not suffered the same things, they counted them happy.

{18:2} But for that they did not hurt them now, of whom they had been wronged before, they thanked them, and besought them pardon for that they had been enemies.

{18:3} Instead whereof thou gavest them a burning pillar of fire, both to be a guide of the unknown journey, and an harmless sun to entertain them honourably.

{18:4} For they were worthy to be deprived of light and imprisoned in darkness, who had kept thy sons shut up, by whom the uncorrupt light of the law was to be given unto the world.

{18:5} And when they had determined to slay the babes of the saints, one child being cast forth, and saved, to reprove them, thou tookest away the multitude of their children, and destroyedst them altogether in a mighty water.

{18:6} Of that night were our fathers certified afore, that

assuredly knowing unto what oaths they had given credence, they might afterwards be of good cheer.

{18:7} So of thy people was accepted both the salvation of the righteous, and destruction of the enemies.

{18:8} For wherewith thou didst punish our adversaries, by the same thou didst glorify us, whom thou hadst called.

{18:9} For the righteous children of good men did sacrifice secretly, and with one consent made a holy law, that the saints should be like partakers of the same good and evil, the fathers now singing out the songs of praise.

{18:10} But on the other side there sounded an ill according cry of the enemies, and a lamentable noise was carried abroad for children that were bewailed.

{18:11} The master and the servant were punished after one manner; and like as the king, so suffered the common person.

{18:12} So they all together had innumerable dead with one kind of death; neither were the living sufficient to bury them: for in one moment the noblest offspring of them was destroyed.

{18:13} For whereas they would not believe any thing by reason of the enchantments; upon the destruction of the firstborn, they acknowledged this people to be the sons of God.

{18:14} For while all things were in quiet silence, and that night was in the midst of her swift course,

{18:15} Thine Almighty word leaped down from heaven out of thy royal throne, as a fierce man of war into the midst of a land of destruction,

{18:16} And brought thine unfeigned commandment as a sharp sword, and standing up filled all things with death; and it touched the heaven, but it stood upon the earth.

{18:17} Then suddenly visions of horrible dreams troubled them sore, and terrors came upon them unlooked for.

{18:18} And one thrown here, and another there, half dead, shewed the cause of his death.

{18:19} For the dreams that troubled them did foreshew this, lest they should perish, and not know why they were afflicted.

{18:20} Yea, the tasting of death touched the righteous also, and there was a destruction of the multitude in the wilderness: but the wrath endured not long.

{18:21} For then the blameless man made haste, and stood forth to defend them; and bringing the shield of his proper ministry, even prayer, and the propitiation of incense, set himself against the wrath, and so brought the calamity to an end, declaring that he was thy servant.

{18:22} So he overcame the destroyer, not with strength of body, nor force of arms, but with a word subdued him that punished, alleging the oaths and covenants made with the fathers.

{18:23} For when the dead were now fallen down by heaps one upon another, standing between, he stayed the wrath, and parted the way to the living.

{18:24} For in the long garment was the whole world, and in the four rows of the stones was the glory of the fathers graven, and thy Majesty upon the daidem of his head.

{18:25} Unto these the destroyer gave place, and was afraid of them: for it was enough that they only tasted of the wrath.

{19:1} As for the ungodly, wrath came upon them without mercy unto the end: for he knew before what they would do;

{19:2} How that having given them leave to depart, and sent them hastily away, they would repent and pursue them.

{19:3} For whilst they were yet mourning and making lamentation at the graves of the dead, they added another foolish device, and pursued them as fugitives, whom they had intreated to be gone.

{19:4} For the destiny, whereof they were worthy, drew them unto this end, and made them forget the things that had already happened, that they might fulfil the punishment which was wanting to their torments:

{19:5} And that thy people might pass a wonderful way: but they might find a strange death.

{19:6} For the whole creature in his proper kind was fashioned again anew, serving the peculiar commandments that were given unto them, that thy children might be kept without hurt:

{19:7} As namely, a cloud shadowing the camp; and where water stood before, dry land appeared; and out of the Red sea a way without impediment; and out of the violent stream a green field:

{19:8} Wherethrough all the people went that were defended with thy hand, seeing thy marvellous strange wonders.

{19:9} For they went at large like horses, and leaped like lambs, praising thee, O Lord, who hadst delivered them.

{19:10} For they were yet mindful of the things that were done while they sojourned in the strange land, how the ground brought forth flies instead of cattle, and how the river cast up a multitude of frogs instead of fishes.

{19:11} But afterwards they saw a new generation of fowls, when, being led with their appetite, they asked delicate meats.

{19:12} For quails came up unto them from the sea for their contentment.

{19:13} And punishments came upon the sinners not without former signs by the force of thunders: for they suffered justly according to their own wickedness, insomuch as they used a more hard and hateful behaviour toward strangers.

{19:14} For the Sodomites did not receive those, whom they knew not when they came: but these brought friends into bondage, that had well deserved of them.

{19:15} And not only so, but peradventure some respect shall be had of those, because they used strangers not friendly:

{19:16} But these very grievously afflicted them, whom they had received with feastings, and were already made partakers of the same laws with them.

{19:17} Therefore even with blindness were these stricken, as those were at the doors of the righteous man: when, being compassed about with horrible great darkness, every one sought the passage of his own doors.

{19:18} For the elements were changed in themselves by a kind of harmony, like as in a psaltery notes change the name of the tune, and yet are always sounds; which may well be perceived by the sight of the things that have been done.

{19:19} For earthly things were turned into watery, and the things, that before swam in the water, now went upon the ground.

{19:20} The fire had power in the water, forgetting his own virtue: and the water forgat his own quenching nature.

{19:21} On the other side, the flames wasted not the flesh of the corruptible living things, though they walked therein; neither melted they the icy kind of heavenly meat that was of nature apt to melt.

{19:22} For in all things, O Lord, thou didst magnify thy people, and glorify them, neither didst thou lightly regard them: but didst assist them in every time and place.

Made in the USA
Las Vegas, NV
24 April 2021